The New Book
of Pirate Songs

"Captain Roberts' Crew Carousing at Old Calabar River," a wood engraving from *The Pirates Own Book* by Charles Ellms (Boston, 1837), purporting to show cohorts of the infamous Welsh pirate Bartholomew Roberts (1682-1722) at leisure ashore in Nigeria (West Africa), circa 1721. The author claims that "Roberts and his crew were so fortunate as to capture several vessels and to render their liquor so plentiful, that it was esteemed a crime against Providence not to be continually drunk."

The New Book of Pirate Songs

Stuart M. Frank

Senior Curator, New Bedford Whaling Museum
Executive Director Emeritus, Kendall Whaling Museum

CAMSCO MUSIC
East Windsor, New Jersey
2011

The New Book of Pirate Songs

including materials that appeared in
The Book of Pirate Songs © 1998 by Stuart M. Frank

Published by CAMSCO Music
145 Hickory Corner Road, East Windsor, NJ 08520

ISBN 978-1-935243-92-2 (Paper)
ISBN 978-1-935243-93-9 (Cloth)

Grateful acknowledgement is made for permission to quote manuscripts and reprint images in the collections of the New Bedford Whaling Museum and the New Bedford Free Public Library; and to publishers for permission to quote from works in their copyright:

The Canadian Reprography Collective, Toronto, Ontario; and Goose Lane Editions, Fredericton, New Brunswick; for the words and music to "The Bold Pirate" and "The Demon of the Sea," in Edward D. Ives, *Folksongs of New Brunswick* (Fredericton: Goose Lane Editions; and Toronto: The Canadian Reprography Collective, 1989), pp. 151-153.

The Cayman Islands National Archive and Cayman Islands Free Press, George Town, Grand Cayman, for the "Pirate Song," sung by Captain Carl Bush, in *Our Island's Past*, Volume III: Traditional Songs from the Cayman Islands (1996), pp 10-11.

The Colonial Williamsburg Foundation, Williamsburg, Va., for the words and music to "Captain Thunder," in John Edwards, *A Williamsburg Songbook* (New York: Holt, Rinehart & Winston, 1964), pp. 55-58.

William Main Doerflinger, for "Bold Manning" and "The Female Warrior," in his *Songs of the Sailor and Lumberman* (New York: Macmillan, [1951] 1972), pp. 139-141 and 143-144.

Farrar, Straus & Giroux, Inc., New York, N.Y., for the words and music of "Bold Kidd, the Pirate," in Helen Hartness Flanders and Marguerite Olney, *Ballads Migrant in New England* (New York: Farrar, Straus & Young, 1953), pp. 16-17.

Harvard University Press, Cambridge, Mass., for the music to "Kelly the Pirate," in W. Roy Mackenzie, *Ballads and Sea Songs from Nova Scotia* (© 1928 by the President and Fellows of Harvard College), #81B, p. 400.

The Heirs of Fanny Eckstorm and Mary Winslow Smyth, for texts of "The Bold Pirate" and "Bold Manan the Pirate," in Fanny Eckstorm and Mary Winslow Smyth, *Minstrelsy of Maine* (1927), pages 254-256 and 259-264.

The National Museums of Canada, Ottawa, for the text of "Bold Daniel," in MacEdward Leach, *Folk Ballads and Songs of the Lower Labrador Coast* (Ottawa: National Museum of Canada, 1965), #57, pp. 154-155.

Routledge & Kegan Paul, Ltd., London, for the music to "Sam Hall," in Stan Hugill, *Shanties from the Seven Seas* (London: Routledge & Kegan Paul; New York: E.P. Dutton, [1961] 1966), p. 449.

Rutgers University Press, New Brunswick, N.J., for the music of "Russell's Farewell" and "Sound a Charge," in Claude M. Simpson, *The British Broadside Ballad and Its Music* (1966), pages 622 and 673.

The Times-Tribune Company, Altoona, Pa., for the text of "The Cruise in the Lowlands Low," in Henry W. Shoemaker, *Mountain Minstrelsy of Pennsylvania* (1931), pp. 132-133.

The University of Oklahoma Press, Norman, Okla., for the words and music of "Andrew Barton," in Ethel Moore and Chauncey O. Moore, *Ballads and Folk Songs of the Southwest* (1964), #48, pp. 115-116.

The University of Pennsylvania Press, Philadelphia, for the music to "The Green Willow Tree," in Helen Hartness Flanders, *Ancient Ballads Traditionally Sung in New England* (4 vols., 1960-65), Vol. IV, p. 195.

COVER ILLUSTRATION   by C.B. Leighton Lithographers (London), from the sheet music for *Le Franc Corsaire,* a so-called "Quadrille Maritime" composed for the piano by Camille Schubert [né Prillipp] (1810-1889), Opus 99;

"*At the dog watch, all hands came on deck, and stood round the weather side of the forecastle, or sat upon the windlass, and sung sea songs, and those ballads of pirates and highwaymen, which sailors delight in.*"

— Richard Henry Dana, Jr.
Two Years Before the Mast (1840)

Table of Contents

Introduction

At the dog watch, all hands came on deck, and stood round the weather side of the forecastle,
or sat upon the windlass, and sung sea songs, and those ballads of pirates and highwaymen,
which sailors delight in.   — Richard Henry Dana, Jr., *Two Years Before the Mast* (1840)

This is not a book about pirates so much as it is a book about *songs* about pirates. The two
are not the same. For the pirates of history — the likes of Henry Avery, Bartholomew Roberts,
"Calico Jack" Rackham, Mary Read, and Edward Teach, known as "Blackbeard" — were, many
of them, brutal, cruel, and insatiable in their lust for adventure and gold. They were outlaws,
feared and alienated by society. At best they were vague in their national allegiances, at worst
traitorous and murderous, only dimly aware of any higher purpose or nobility to which other men
aspire. Real pirates were, by design, a breed apart — vagabonds, iconoclasts, renegades. To
succeed, a pirate captain had simultaneously to be a seaman, soldier, marksman, swordsman,
administrator, and entrepreneur. Even so, oddly, few real pirates ever made it into ballads and
songs about pirates. Most pirates of song and ballad are imaginary or generic, they are almost
always overtly romanticized, and few of their deeds can compare with the actual evil and
brutality perpetrated by real pirates on the high seas.

Even so, a few words must be said about pirates, piracy, and pirate history. Much more will
be said in the introductions to the various chapters and in the headnotes for each song.

A Few Words about Pirates

From a scholarly point of view, pirate history has become a thorny issue. There is a lot of
malarkey afoot about pirates nowadays, not only mistaken "facts" about historical pirates that are
promoted by popular books, movies, and songs, but also a surfeit of socio-economic theory,
recently hatched, which celebrates the so-called democratic, anti-authoritarian, and egalitarian
virtues of pirate society — which were real — while overlooking or soft-peddling the violence,
brutality, and savage misanthropy of piracy as a livelihood and as a social malaise.

It is often pointed out that pirate captains were chosen or elected on the combined basis of
administrative and martial "merit" and could be summarily dismissed by general consensus; that
pirates customarily drew up written articles in which behavioral expectations were made explicit
and contractually binding; that they had a non-hierarchical social order according to which they
divided their plunder in equal or pro-rated shares; and that they had a highly developed system,
not unlike insurance policies, by which specific sums were paid to their wounded brethren to
compensate particular body parts lost or disabilities suffered in the line of duty. In recent years,
a few scholars have pointed to the entrepreneurial propensities and unconventional sociopolitical
protocols of life "on the account," and the anti-authoritarian basis upon which individual pirate
ships and shoreside pirate communities were managed, and have identified admirable rudiments
of democracy, egalitarianism, and free trade. This contains elements of truth but it is hardly the
point, any more than it is the point that Nero may have played the fiddle rather well.

One supposes that a loveless upbringing, boredom at school, and diminishing prospects could
produce a wayward hoodlum who, having gone to sea one step ahead of the magistrate, might
fall into evil company and be tempted to join a pirate crew; and in such a case his plight may be
deserving of sympathy. One can imagine the frustration and swelling anger of some independent-
minded young seaman, even if well brought up, adequately schooled, and initially well-inten-
tioned, if he were beset by the cruelty and brutality that sometimes walked the quarterdecks of
naval ships, privateers, and merchantmen — anger that, under extreme duress, might explode
uncontrollably into mutiny, and then, there being no going back, slide into piracy. And one can
only have pity for the abysmal luck, profound stupidity, or overweening arrogance of William

Kidd, who seems to have fallen into piracy unwittingly as an ill-starred function of bureaucratic politics, and, unable to extricate himself, swung at the gallows. But whatever noble motives revisionist scholars may embrace in celebrating the virtues of freedom, democracy, social justice, and equitable distribution of wealth, the fact remains that in the context of piracy these must be evaluated with care. Pirates were by definition thieves, traitors, and murderers, hardly convincing models of social equity and nobility of purpose. Whatever fine and noble aspirations may be ascribed to them (and it is difficult to identify any), whatever practical concessions they may have made to democracy and fair treatment in pursuit of viable governance, whatever romantic visions of them we may construe, pirates were no humanitarians cherishing fond hopes for the welfare and ennoblement of humanity. Rather, in the aggregate, any goodwill they may have had was extended only to their pirate brethren. Their very livelihood was premised upon violence and destruction, the forceful confiscation of others' property for their own aggrandizement, often depriving their victims of life and liberty by pillage, rape, and murder, sometimes merely for their own amusement. Even when it was merciful, respectful, and polite, pirate business was always conducted with unlawful force and the threat of humiliation and death. That it may also have been conducted without the impediments of imperialistic political philosophy and racial prejudice is secondary. Whatever the entrepreneurial predilections, egalitarian impulses, and democratic sympathies pirates may have exhibited — and the evidence is, at best, subjective — pirates were parasites and destroyers, sociopaths who reserved freedom of self-determination exclusively to themselves. It would be a pathetic travesty, indeed, were our concepts of freedom and democracy to be so distorted as to place the semblance of parochial social equity above the most fundamental of all democratic values, the respect for life and for human dignity.

By contrast, it is worth pointing out that David Cordingly, a distinguished British historian and art historian fully aware of the merits of these revisionist views, and an able contextualist in his own right, has not fallen prey to extremist myopia. His well-balanced, stylish, fastidiously researched treatises on piracy are paragons of clear-headed historical discourse, unencumbered by overweening theory and with no political axe to grind. For good or for ill, in compiling this anthology I have relied upon Cordingly to clarify unclarities and mediate among disparate inter pretations of fact, and I can recommend his books *Pirates: Fact and Fiction* (1992), *Under the Black Flag* (1995), and *Pirates: Terror on the High Seas from the Caribbean to the South China Sea* (1996) as the most reliably authoritative essays about pirates ever written in English.

A Few Words about the Songs and the Organization of this Anthology

There have been ballads in English about pirates for almost five hundred years — perhaps considerably longer, if "John Dory" [#1] be as old as it appears. Throughout that entire history, as a body the ballads have been equivocal or ambivalent. Only a handful excoriate pirates for their infamous cruelty and brutality. Some are cast as expiative confessions in the shadow of a waiting hangman, warning other young men about the pitfalls of a rover's life. Several tell of narrow escapes, or fierce sea-battles in which the pirates are vanquished and rectitude triumphs. Many, especially the ones written by professional tunesmiths and hack poets for the music-hall stage and songster press, romanticize, Robin Hood-like, the freebooters' adventurous life outside the law. Which is to say that neither the narrative content nor the moral character of pirate songs adopts any single point of view or achieves any kind of consensus about pirates; rather, they span almost the entire spectrum of possible interpretations.

Part of this is because of ignorance. We know of no single instance in which any ballad or song was written by an actual pirate, expressing the well-informed views of someone who lived the pirate life. In fact, many of the old ballads — the ones that arose prior to the mid 18th century and are anthologized in Part One—tend to fall into the heroic mode, where the question of piracy as we understand it today never arises. The characters in these songs are buccaneers in the

Elizabethan sense, and questions of transgressions of law or violations of morality when applied to them are largely questions of political affiliation and national point of view. Among these old ballads are also a few that narrate (or purport to narrate) the exploits of actual pirates, like John Ward and William Kidd; but these few are mostly speculative, and, with the exception of the very penitent "Captain Kidd" [#14] — which has little to say about actual piracy and much to say about salvation — they were never.much sung.

Broadside ballads from the late 18th to the mid 19th century—the ones in Part Two—are a bit more diverse. Whatever their origins, in the hands of actual seaman over the years some have taken on the nautical-technical sophistication and stalwart, salty atmosphere of authentic sea ballads. Part Three has a topical rather than chronological basis, being devoted to songs about women at sea engaged in piratical sea-battles: most of these women are first-class heroes who leapt from the pages of 19th-century broadsides into the minds and hearts of "the folk." Part Four is the corral for so-called Parlor Songs, which were essentially show-tunes and professional compositions intended for home consumption, produced between the 1830s and 1860s. These are mostly blithe, unrealistic, and overtly romantic, despite which — or perhaps because of which — a few of them were popular among sailors on shipboard. Part Five is a collection of songs (some of which appear never to have had tunes) harvested from the pages of printed songsters. Some of these are amoral confections, others are downright dull, and few exhibit any appreciable literary merit. However, all of them are part of the American cavalcade (with a fair portion borrowed from the British Isles); all of them were foisted on the public in the guise of authenticity. They appeared in such places as *The American Sailor's Songster, The Pirate's Songster,* and *The Buccaneer's Songster* — all of which were produced *for* sailors, rather than *by* sailors; or were sold under those titles to hoodwink the public into the delusion that the songs were actually sung by sailors, rather than created for them. And, finally, Part Six contains a few pieces that do not exactly fit the mission and compass of the anthology, but simply couldn't be left out.

A Few Words about Bibliography and the Ballads and Songs in this Anthology

The textual notes throughout refer to works by several ballad scholars who defined the genre and provided foundation taxonomic guidelines. These are monumental resources, indispensable to any responsible study of folk songs. At the end of the 19th century, Professor Francis James Child established the canon of *The English and Scottish Popular Ballads* (5 vols., 1883-98); and adhering to Child's canon, B.H. Bronson anthologized and analyzed literally thousands of surviving ballad melodies (*The Traditional Tunes of the Child Ballads,* 4 vols., 1959-72). Claude M. Simpson definitively presents a comprehensive spectrum of contemporaneous tunes, drawn from a variety of printed sources, notably including academic compositions and stage productions that were often the sources of materials recovered from oral tradition, but which are often neglected by folklorists (*The British Broadside Ballad and its Music,* 1966). G. Malcolm Laws produced *Native American Balladry* (1959) and *American Balladry from British Broadsides* (1964), establishing a classification system for latter-day ballads that entered or became fixed in tradition by virtue of texts printed in late 18th and 19th centuries.

Specifically regarding the songs and ballads actually sung by sailors on shipboard, there are several outstanding authoritative compilations. Frederick Pease Harlow's *Chanteying Aboard American Ships* (1962) is drawn from the author's lifelong career at sea, beginning in the 1870s. Captain W.B. Whall, a British master mariner, was at sea around the same time; his *Sea Songs and Shanties* was first published in 1910 and has been in print continuously ever since. Joanna Colcord, daughter of an American sea captain, accompanied her family to sea in the last part of the 19th century; her *Roll and Go* (1924), revised and expanded as *Songs of the American Sailor-men* (1938), is the finest and most carefully annotated of the firsthand anthologies. Stan Hugill, reputedly the last British chanteyman, put together the monumental compilation *Shanties from the Seven Seas* (1961). Among latter-day anthologies, William Main Doerflinger's *Songs of the Sailor and Lumberman* (1972), expanded from *Shantymen and Shantyboys* (1951), is based upon American and Canadian sources; Roy Palmer's *Oxford Book of Sea Songs* (1986) is quintessentially British; both are distinguished by fine scholarship and responsible commentary. My own *Jolly Sailors Bold: Ballads and Songs of the American Sailor* (2010) is a broad-based anthology of authentic texts excavated from sailors' shipboard manuscripts, reunited with their original tunes, in most cases being the earliest versions of the ballads and songs ever recovered from tradition. Also noteworthy are the compilation of *Naval Songs* (1889) by Rear-Admiral Stephen B. Luce, founder of the United States Naval War College in Newport, R.I.; Frederick Pease Harlow's autobiographical narrative, *The Making of a Sailor* (1928), in which chanteys and songs of various kinds appear in their original shipboard contexts; and Stan Hugill's *Shanties and Sailors' Songs* (1969), an eccentric but highly informative sailor's-eye-view of the genre. Pirate songs in these anthologies are few, despite Richard Henry Dana, Jr.'s claim in *Two Years Before the Mast* (1840) that pirate songs were great favorites at sea.

The ballads and songs anthologized here are drawn from a wide variety of sources, including field collections of folk songs, original sheet music, published anthologies, and sailors' shipboard manuscripts. For the most part, they are quoted directly, with only minimal attempts to correct irregular spelling, punctuation, and syntax (specific sources are listed on pages 147-152). Texts and tunes vary substantially among the multiplicity of sources consulted; occasionally, faithfully quoting the printed texts and tunes resulted in minor inconsistencies which I have not attempted to rectify. Musical notation presents its own special problems, principal among them that the count — the number of beats in a measure — was found to be in error in some of the printed sources quoted. Wherever possible, such metrical anomalies have been corrected.

The endeavor has been to include as many songs about pirates from the Age of Sail as could be found, including authentic folksongs that circulated with or without the assistance of the popular press, as well as songs created for popular consumption in a commercial marketplace. Historical and bibliographical head notes are provided to enhance contextual understanding of individual pieces and the various genres; textual variants have been included where it seemed appropriate and worthwhile; music is provided where the tune or tunes are known; and chords for accompaniment on guitar, banjo, piano, organ, or accordion are suggested. While historical appropriateness and faithfulness to the original genres are factors to be considered in adapting the songs and devising arrangements, there is nothing inherently sacred and inviolate about the accompaniments here. Singers are encouraged to transpose the songs into whatever keys may be singable in their own ranges, and to experiment with whatever alternative accompaniments may suit their individual singing and playing styles. Serious pianists and accompanists are encouraged to seek out the sheet music arrangements and other formal settings that are cited in the text or listed among the "Sources" (pages 147ff): many of them are available online. The objective is to enjoy the songs — many of which are clever, some of which are quite beautiful, and which in the aggregtae constitute a long tradition that spans six centuries—without going overboard extolling the virtues of piracy itself.

Preface to the Second Edition

Since *The Book of Pirate Songs* was first published in 1998, the collections and publications of the Kendall Whaling Museum have been incorporated into the New Bedford Whaling Museum; and, happily, successful sales and favorable reviews of *The Book of Pirate Songs* now enable publication of this expanded edition, providing an opportunity to include songs and illustrations that were omitted from the original volume.

A few words should be said about the contents. One of the reviewers of the original edition, while favorably disposed to the anthology as a whole, expressed disappointment that it did not encompass pirate songs from the 20th century. Indeed, there are 20th-century pirate songs that might be worth including on purely aesthetic grounds, and perhaps others that, like the old ballads in this volume, are authentically rooted in oral tradition, or which, analogously to the broadside ballads, parlor songs, and music-hall pieces here, were produced by such mainstream commercial sources as Tin Pan Alley, Hollywood, or the popular stage; or which have some other kind of redeeming social or historical relevance. These are valid notions but are beside the point. The original anthology was conceived as an historical collection addressing the heritage of pirate-related songs in English that were current in the Age of Sail, and was never intended as a catch-all for anything and everything ever sung about pirates. More significantly, as people familiar with maritime history, nautical music, and historical shipboard songs will appreciate, the sharp division between the Age of Sail and what followed in the Age of Steam is a distinction that is neither arbitrary nor meaningless. Of course, sail and steam were to a degree chronologically contemporaneous, overlapping in their technological advances and commercial applications during the latter two-thirds of the 19th century and the first quarter of the 20th, as steam gradually encroached upon and finally supplanted sail. However, in standpoint of the working sailor, with regard to the specific tasks and occupational hazards of his day-to-day activities on shipboard, his quality of life at sea, the stability or instability of his employment, and his stunted unionization movement ashore, sail and steam differed markedly.

The transition to steam made a dramatic difference that was obvious not only to the sailors themselves and to shoreside organizations that attempted to alleviate their debased and degraded condition, but also to critics, commentators, analysts, novelists, playwrights, and social theorists, from Joseph Conrad, John Masefield, and Eugene O'Neill to Andrew Feruseth, Elmo P. Hohman, and James C. Healey. The distinction is between Melville's Billy Budd, say, and O'Neill's Hairy Ape. Conrad's narratives (for example, "Youth" and "Narcissus"), Masefield's poetry (across the boards), and O'Neill's dialogue (note Driscoll and Yank in *The Moon of the Caribbees* and *The Hairy Ape*) bring this vividly and palpably to life. There still are pirates today, of course, evil-doers on the High Seas as terrible and bloodthirsty and voracious as any who sailed in the days of Blackbeard and Bartholomew Roberts. But they have not inspired a ballad literature and they inhabit a distinct and separate ethos.

Many modern songs about pirates have been retrospective confections about centuries past and (largely because vernacular song is no longer a primary means of communal expression) have not confronted the issue of contemporaneous piracy. Current types of pirates in the 20th and 21st centuries are of a decidedly different stamp than their Age of Sail forebears, with speed-boats and automatic weapons but with none of the aspect of romance that attached to the colorful pillagers of yore. The classic encounter of agonizingly slow-sailing, wind-powered vessels that come into sight hours before closing quarters, was replaced in the 20th century by blitzkrieg swiftness. The classic pirate's methodology was intimidation combined with comparative speed and a reputation for ruthless brutality, backed by heavy firepower. In the 20th century it became stealth, speed, and bombast. Classic pirates, whether they crossed the broad oceans or skulked along shore, were inveterate sailors, often skilled navigators, sometimes even self-proclaimed patriots; and, rightly or wrongly, their exploits captured the popular imagination and resulted in musical and pictorial art. And most of the poetic imagining was done in their own time, when the piracy depicted was a clear-and-present danger or recent reality. Not so the latter-day variety. Such songs and pictures of pirates as emerged in the Age of Steam have been retrospective, even nostalgic. The Hollywood confections made for the movies, a few college songs that express the robust energy of campus theatricals and football rivalries, and television productions intended to promote entertainments or sell products, are separate classes worthy of note in their own right and of evaluation on their own merits and shortfalls. One could hope that a skilled Americanist or trained sociologist will take them up in studies focused upon notions about pirates that have arisen since the Age of Sail, and perhaps a music critic or two will undertake to appraise their aesthetic value. But there are no songs about modern pirates that sailors and landsmen sing in fear or admiration. In short, while the 20th- and 21st-century stuff surely merits attention in a variety of contexts, most of what was produced by way of pirate songs in the 20th century, whatever their aesthetic merits and popular cultural sway, are not suitable for scrutiny in the historical contexts with which this anthology is concerned.

Accordingly, *The Book of Pirate Songs* was intentionally limited to the Age of Sail, which for maritime historians, museum curators, sailing enthusiasts, devotees of authentic pirate lore, and fans of old sea songs requires little explanation or justification. The idea was, and remains, to present only songs and texts in the English language that were contemporaneous with the life and times of sailors among whom the classic pirates, buccaneers, and corsairs were a reality, presenting palpable danger — despite that many of the songs themselves minimize the brutality, maximize the romance, and trivialize the whole notion of piracy on the High Seas. This *"New" Book of Pirate Songs* conforms to this original plan and merely adds additional pieces, additional contexts, and some recently discovered musical settings to the original inventory — songs from England, Scotland, Ireland, and North America: a handful of authentic broadside ballads, twelve "composed" songs that were manufactured for the parlor, music hall, and stage, and a handful of miscellaneous pieces, all of which, like the ballads and songs in the original edition, reflect elements of the popular culture from which they sprung. A few were produced by songwriters and composers who were reasonably notable and influential in their time. Most, however, are generic and were never on the lips of all English-singing peoples. Of the new additions, only four —"Captain Coulston," "Hicks the Pirate," "The *Brooklyn*," and "Liverpool Play"—can lay claim, in varying degrees, to authentic folk origins. There are two newly-found original melodies for texts that were excavated from songsters for the first edition but for which no tunes could be located at that time. The other newcomers are taken from sheet music that eluded detection for the first go-round, largely because they were never sufficiently popular to be anthologized in their own time. It is hoped that the resulting ensemble is not only more complete but also a better rounded representation of musical pirate lore in the Age of Sail, both for study and for singing.

Acknowledgements

In preparing this anthology I am indebted to the generosity of a number of people who, over the past two decades, made helpful suggestions, provided citations, facilitated access to collections, granted permission for quotations and illustrations, imparted insights into particular ballads and songs, produced photographs, assisted with proofreading and indexing, and generally provided encouragement: Herman L. Belmar, W. Jeffrey Bolster, Ellen R. Cohn, the late William Main Doerflinger, Michael P. Dyer, Dr. Paul Fees, Steve Gardham, William Gilkerson, Joseph Hickerson, Henry Hornblower III, the late Stan Hugill, Andrew Jacobson, Jay Kaufman, Louisa Killen, David Kleiman, the late Robert A. Kotta, Michael Lapides, Edward J. Lefkowicz, the late Alan Lomax, Sandy Marrone, Katie Mello, Laura Pereira, the late Buck Ramsey, Donald E. Ridley, Richard M. Swiderski, Lillian Turner, Robert J. Walser, Jeff Warner, Michel Zilberstein, the gracious Volunteers at the New Bedford Whaling Museum Research Library, and the helpful staffs of the American Antiquarian Society in Worcester, the Music Department at the Boston Public Library, the John Hay Library of Brown University, the New Bedford Free Public Library, the Sharon [Mass.] Public Library, and the Wheaton College Library [Norton, Mass.].

For assistance with locating current holders of copyright, and for permission to quote copyrighted folkloric materials in the original edition, I am indebted to the Canadian Reprography Collective (Toronto), the Cayman Islands National Archive and Cayman Islands Free Press (George Town, Grand Cayman), The Colonial Williamsburg Foundation (Williamsburg, Va.), the late William Main Doerflinger, E.P. Dutton & Co. (New York), Farrar, Straus & Giroux (New York), Goose Lane Editions (Fredericton, N.B.), the Harvard University Press (Cambridge, Mass.), the Houghton Mifflin Company (Boston and New York), the Kendall Whaling Museum (Sharon, Mass.), the National Museums of Canada (Ottawa), the New Bedford Whaling Museum, Routledge & Kegan Paul, Ltd. (London), the Rutgers University Press (New Brunswick, N.J.), the Times Tribune Company (Altoona, Pa.), the University of Oklahoma Press (Norman), and the University of Pennsylvania Press (Philadelphia).

I am especially grateful to Gare B. Reid, Ellen R. Cohn, Steve Gardham, and Mary Malloy for proofreading various stages of the manuscript, though any remaining errors are my own, and for a host of invaluable suggestions and improvements; and to Catherine Reynolds for proofreading and indispensable assistance building the index.

I am of course thrilled that Dick Greenhaus and CAMSCO Music agreed to publish and distribute this edition, and I thank him and his associates for their patience in producing this book as well as my *Jolly Sailors Bold: Ballads and Songs of the American Sailor*.

For much else, I am indebted to my wife and partner, Mary Malloy, who reviewed the music and proofread much of the text, and who has the best pirate laugh I know.

The New Book
of Pirate Songs

Blackletter ballad cut representing a Renaissance-era London street-ballad singer and seller,
reproduced as an illustration in John Payne Collier, ed., *Book of the Roxburghe Ballads* (London, 1847),
page xxix, where the source, original context, and publishing history are not identified.

Part One: The Old Ballads

The introduction of movable type in Europe in late 15th century precipitated one of the most profound upheavals in human history. Over the next several generations print revolutionized the production and dissemination of information and opinion, ultimately democratizing accessibility and laying the groundwork for the kind of informed electorate on which democracy is said to depend. With the resulting increase in literacy, gradually what had hitherto been communicated only through speech or through song became viable in print; and printed media began to erode and supplant the spoken word and the old bardic narrative traditions that had largely sustained European civilization for twenty centuries. Devoted at first to materials of a religious character, print increasingly accommodated the creation and distribution of the secular and the political. In Tudor England, while the churches and taverns remained centers of community life, more and more were printed media becoming the pipeline feeding the marketplace of ideas; more and more were news and opinion being produced and circulated as printed proclamations, pamphlets, broadsides, and, eventually, newspapers and magazines.

Among the new features on this changing landscape were ballads and songs — many of them harvested from centuries-old traditions of singing and recitation, some few dating back as far as early medieval times, and many others that were timely, topical, and up to date, reflecting current events even as they unfolded. As the Homeric epics had been recorded, codified, and stabilized centuries earlier by the not-so-simple act of writing them down in Greek, so too, now, some of the older ballads, songs, and poems, alongside the ones of later and contemporaneous vintage, were committed to permanent language and circulated cheaply in print — perhaps occasioning a larger audience and wider recognition for all of them, but at least preserving narrative materials that might otherwise have fallen from favor and become extinct.

The heritage of early ballads from the epoch spanning the 16th century through much of the 18th — roughly coinciding with the American colonial era — was appreciated in some quarters almost from the first. The most prominent early enthusiast was Samuel Pepys (1633-1703), the famous diarist and British naval administrator: his eminent collection is one of several now housed in great libraries in Great Britain and America. With this glorious resource at hand, serious scholarly interest took firm hold in the 19th century, culminating in Francis James Child of Harvard University, whose lifework was comprehensively to collect and organize ballads in a compendium entitled *The English and Scottish Popular Ballads* (published in five volumes during 1883-98). Child's canon has been regarded with nearly universal approbation on both sides of the Atlantic.

The criteria that Child adopted, while not exactly controversial, have occasioned criticism for taking too little account of what "the folk" may actually have sung (as opposed to what may have been printed), for including materials that were not real folk ballads according to one definition or another, and for excluding particular ballads that should have had an excellent claim. For more than a century Child's opus has provided a viable inventory by virtue of which scholars, singers, and casual readers can get a handle on the literature and deal with it intelligently; and for more than a century it has been a touchstone, providing a basic of authentic old ballads in English against which to measure the dissemination of ballads in "oral tradition" (that is, of ballads that were actually sung and were found still to be in active circulation when, beginning at the end of the 19th century, collectors actually took to "recovering" them from singers "in the field").

However, certain shortcomings and flaws in the Child canon are particularly significant here, as Child is occasionally misleading or mistaken about nautical content and does not adequately reveal the true character of some of the pirate ballads which, temporally and topically, come well within the scope of his great opus. For example, Child's analysis of "Sir Andrew Barton" [#2] is purely from the English perspective and his scholarly discussion completely sidesteps the coeval Scottish point of view, which truly discloses the political origins of the ballad in the larger context of European international affairs. Comparison of the English and Scottish perspectives reveals a great deal about ballads and about propaganda as well as about piracy.

To his detriment, Child is also too prone to place the literary and stylistic qualities of ballads above their musical, historical, and contextual significance. In the case of "Sir Andrew Barton" [#2] and "Henry Martin" [#3], for example, he definitively identifies them as genetically related, the latter ballad being descended directly from the former; but he fails to separate them as having become truly distinct, which, in historical terms, they are unequivocally: "Sir Andrew Barton" is about actual, historical kings and popes playing out international political objectives on the high seas, but in the "Henry Martin" form it becomes the story of a pirate, plain and simple, out to make money, without explicit political overtones. Whatever its ancestry, "Henry Martin" has become something substantively distinct from "Sir Andrew Barton," a difference that the Child taxonomy fails to recognize. Likewise with "The *George Aloe* and the *Sweepstake*" [#5]: in its original form it is about a famous Elizabethan buccaneer, but reincarnated as "High Barbary" [#6], the form cherished and preserved through the Stuart and Hanoverian periods, it is impelled by an appreciation of the emerging vitality of the Royal Navy as sentinel of Britain's mercantile prowess. A similar, but less pronounced distinction can be drawn between "Sir Walter Raleigh Sailing in the Lowlands" [#7] and "The *Bold Trinity*" [#8].

Another case in point is "Captain Ward" [#9] and its sequel, "Dansekar the Dutchman" [#10], which were published together in 1609 while the corsairs Ward and Dansekar were still active in the Mediterranean. Child mentions these ballads but does not include them. But he does include a later, apocryphal ballad called "Captain Ward and the *Rainbow*" (Child #287), which, while it is in most respects a better ballad and probably should have been included too, it should not have eclipsed the two earlier "Captain Ward" ballads. As contemporaneous compositions, "Captain Ward" and "Dansekar" share a certain historical authority and were widely circulated in their day. Similarly, apparently owing to its scarcity in print, Child omitted entirely one of the most widely disseminated English pirate ballads of all, "Captain Kidd" [#14], notwithstanding that it was first published in immediate conjunction with Kidd's execution in 1701 and has enjoyed persistent popularity in tradition ever since. There are younger, less important ballads of lesser quality in the Child canon, some of which were never sung at all or are only known in a single manifestation; "Captain Kidd" should be there, too.

Such relatively minor omissions and shortcomings should not detract from the tremendous residual value of the Child anthology or its often insightful historical annotations. Were he presented all the facts, Professor Child well might have wished to make the appropriate revisions. The point is that during the century-and-more since the publication of *The English and Scottish Popular Ballads,* certain omissions and shortcomings have become evident, suggesting that Child's opus is neither sacred writ nor entirely flawless: there is room to enlarge upon his insights without violating the spirit of his work.*

Illustration: Woodcut representing shipbuilding, a stock piece used to illustrate Renaissance-era blackletter ballads; reproduced in John Payne Collier, ed., *A Book of the Roxburghe Ballads* (London, 1847), page 79, where it accompanies a ballad entitled "The Widow of Watling Street" (London, c1597). It actually seems better suited to "John Dory" [#1].

* An example is the parallel canon of later "broadside ballads" compiled by G. Malcolm Laws in *American Balladry from British Broadsides* and *Native American Balladry.* The fact is that during the period following the epoch addressed by Child — that is, an era roughly coeval with the Industrial Revolution and the first eight or nine decades of American Independence — the methods of production and means of dissemination of ballads (new ones as well as old ones) were in many ways analogous to those of the earlier period. In the 19th century, these latter-day ballads were very much in circulation, very much a part of the shared heritage of ballads that inspired Child. Like Child's, Laws' taxonomy, though not exhaustive, is comprehensive, providing a viable regime for the study of these later materials. Accordingly, Laws provides the rubric for later sections here on "Broadside Ballads" and songs of "Women in Buccaneer's Clothing."

JOHN DORY
(Child #284)

"John Dory" is one of the earliest surviving sea ballads in English and seems to retain the form and syntax of a ballad much older still, perhaps as early as Chaucer's era. C.H. Firth reports that it is "mentioned" in 1575; the poet Richard Carew called it "old" in 1602; and the first recorded printing was in Thomas Ravenscroft's *Deuteromelia* in 1609. "It refers to no known historical event, but is perhaps a traditional account of some incident in the Hundred Years' War" (Firth, 341). Carew speaks of it in his *Survey of Cornwall* (1602): "The prowess of one Nicholas, son to a widow near Foy, is descanted upon in an *old three-man's song,* namely, how he fought bravely at sea, with one John Dory (a Genoway [Genoese], as I conjecture), set forth by John, the French King, and after much blood shed on both sides, took and slew him." Chappell adds, "King John of France died a prisoner in England in 1364," in the reign of Edward I. The oar-powered galley mentioned in stanza 5 also suggests an early vintage. According to Simpson, "The account of John Dory's entering the service of King John II of France and of his being captured at sea by one Nicholas of Cornwall must have had wide currency during the 17th century, for frequent allusions treat it as a familiar or even a hackneyed subject.... For all its popularity, there is no record of 'John Dory' or any of its parodies on extant broadsides." That it involves piracy is not entirely clear, but Masefield groups it among songs and poems about pirates and smugglers.

1   As it fell on a holy-day, and upon a holy tide-a;
     John Dory bought him an ambling nag, to Paris for to ride-a

2   And when John Dory to Paris was come, a little before the gate-a,
     John Dory was fitted, the porter was witted, to let him in thereat-a.

3   The first man that John Dory did meet, was good King John of France-a;
     John Dory could well of his courtesie, but fell down in a trance-a.

4   "A pardon, a pardon, my liege and my king, for my merie men and for me-a;
     And all the churles in merie England, Ile bring them all bound to thee-a."

5   And Nicholl was then a Cornish man, a little beside Bohide-a.
     And he made forth a good blacke barke, with fiftie good oares on a side-a.

6   "Run up, my boy, unto the maine-top, and looke what thou canst spie-a."
     "Who ho! who ho! a goodly ship I do see, I trow it be John Dory-a."

7   They hoist their sailes, both top and top, the messeine and all was tride-a;
     And every man stood to his lot, whatever should betide-a.

8   The roaring cannons then were plide, and dub-a-dub went the drumme-a.
     The braying trumpets lowd they cride to courage both all and some-a.

9   The grapling hooks were brought at length, the browne bill and the sword-a;
     John Dory at length, for all his strength, was clapt fast under board-a.

SIR ANDREW BARTON
A True Relation of the life and death of
Sir Andrew Barton, a Pyrate and Rover on the Seas.

(Child #167)

Based on actual historical events spanning the last part of the 15th century and first part of the 16th, "Sir Andrew Barton" may be the earliest surviving pirate ballad in English; it is certainly the earliest scenario of swashbuckling freebooters on the high seas to be narrated in an English ballad. According to Bronson (III:133), it was very popular in the 16th century and remained so well into the 18th. On the other hand, as the earliest known broadsides of "Sir Andrew Barton" were not printed until circa 1648-80, several other pirate ballads may predate it in print. And while it has not had the subsequent staying-power among mariners and shore folk that other pirate ballads have enjoyed — even the original air may be lost — "Andrew Barton" is a hoary cornerstone of the sea-rover repertoire, the direct ancestor of "Henry Martin" [#3 below].

In Tudor times and for centuries after, there was a formal distinction between true *piracy on the high seas* — the pelagic preying upon seagoing ships of any nationality for pure adventure and pecuniary gain — and *privateering,* which has many times been called merely a legalized form of piracy. Privateering was premised upon so-called Letters of Marque, licenses issued by the crown or Parliament authorizing specified privately-owned vessels to harass and plunder hostile shipping. Privateering was widely regarded as a necessary adjunct to naval operations in wartime, as navies themselves were not yet sufficiently developed to inflict the kind of damage on merchant shipping and enemy supply-lines that privateers seemed so capable and enthusiastic about inflicting. The prime incentives, of course, were fun and profit. Licensed privateers were not subject to the whims and dictates of the Admiralty, thus could operate virtually without restriction. The proceeds of plunder were wholly or largely retained by the captors as booty, though in some circumstances there was a formula for division with government authority, a practice increasingly adopted in later centuries. Naturally enough, as candidates for sea-roving adventure were not necessarily the most genteel and cooperative of Crown subjects, errors and excesses were many: in the Tudor and Stuart eras at least, the distinction between piracy and letter-of-marque privateering was not so finely drawn. Buccaneers characteristically adopted liberal interpretations of their licenses, often navigating rather freely among the legal niceties. The net effect is epitomized in "Sir Andrew Barton" in the English merchant's reluctance to send ships and cargo to sea, lest they be plundered: "Sir Andrew Barton makes us quail" (stanza 4).

The historical basis for the narrative casts doubt upon the English claim of piracy. Were the Scottish interpretation consulted, it would seem more to do with papal machinations and the balance of power in Europe. In 1476 a "richly loaded" Scottish ship commanded by Andrew Barton's father was taken by a Portuguese squadron under questionable circumstances, and the Scottish king issued letters-of-reprisal authorizing the Bartons to plunder Portuguese shipping. Thirty years later, Andrew and his two brothers — all three of them "men of note in the naval history of Scotland"— were still seeking redress. The usual excesses occurred, in which Andrew "took the Englishmen's goods" under pretext of their being Portuguese; and this is the source of his fearsome reputation as "a pirate of the sea." The English story is that despite protests from England and Portugal, James IV of Scotland reissued Barton's letters-of-reprisal in 1506; thus, in 1511, the Earl of Surrey and his sons, sailing as privateers under authority granted by the young King Henry VIII, went after Andrew and vanquished him at sea (Child III:334-338). The Scottish story, in the words of Scots historian Andrew Lang, is that "in 1507 the pope failed to draw James into the league formed to check French aggression in Italy... [thus] the Holy League of 1511 against France found James committed to the cause of the old French alliance" (*Enc. Brit.,* 11th ed., 24:442). Far from being a pirate, Sir Andrew Barton was the legitimate admiral of King James; he died of wounds sustained in a patriotic engagement arising from Scotland's de facto alliance with France against England and the Holy League.

The air specified in the original broadsides of "Sir Andrew Barton" is "Come follow my love," which Bronson (III:133) identifies with "The Fair Flower of Northumberland." Orthodox traditional renditions of "Fair Flower" printed by Motherwell and Greig are lovely jig tunes, quite Scottish in flavor, well suited to the love-song lyrics of the ballad for which the air takes its name (Child #9) as well as to the pastoral imagery, regal stature, and lyrical qualities of "Sir Andrew Barton." The differences between the two forms of the tune are subtle but substantial, and the performer will want to choose carefully between them. Bronson gives a variety of other tunes culled from tradition. For practicality's sake actual performance may require abbreviation of the text: many of the 66 stanzas can be cut without doing serious damage to the story if care be taken not to compromise the balanced redundancy that typifies ballads of this vintage.

TUNE A: "The Flower of Northumberland," from Motherwell, *Minstrelsy, Ancient and Modern,* 1827, #2. To accommodate the lyrics the melody is slightly adjusted by the addition of the first measure and slurs.

TUNE B: "The Fair Flower of Northumberland," per Greig, *Last Leaves of Traditional Ballads and Ballad Airs,* 1925, p. 9. Transposed from A Major. To accommodate the lyrics the melody is slightly adjusted by the addition of a first measure and slurs.

1   When Flora, with her flagrant flowers,
        Bedekt the earth so trim and gay,
    And Neptune, with his dainty showers,
        Came to present the month of May,

2   King Henry would a-hunting ride;
        Over the river of Thames past he,
    Unto a mountain-top also
        Did walk, some pleasure for to see.

3   Where forty merchants he espy'd,
        With fifty sail, come towards him,
    Who then no sooner were arriv'd,
        But on their knees did thus complain.

4   "An't please Your Grace, we cannot sail
        To France no voyage, to be sure,
    But Sir Andrew Barton makes us quail,
        And robs us of our merchant-ware."

5   Vext was the king, and turned him,
        Said to the lords of high degree,
    "Have I ne'r a lord within my realm
        Dare fetch that traitor unto me?"

6   To him repli'd Lord Charles Howard:
        "I will, my liege, with heart and hand:
    If it please you grant me leave, he said,
        I will perform what you command."

7 To him then spake King Henry:
    "I fear, my lord, you are too young."
  "No whit at all, my liege," quoth he;
    "I hope to prove in valour strong.

8 "The Scottish knight I vow to seek,
    In what place soever he be,
  And bring a shore, with all his might,
    Or into Scotland he shall carry me."

9 "A hundred men," the king then said,
    "Out of my realm shall chosen be,
  Besides saylors and ship-boys
    To guide a great ship on the sea.

10 "Bow-men and gunners of good skill
    Shall for this service chosen be,
  And they at thy command and will
    In all affairs shall wait on thee."

11 Lord Howard called a gunner then
    Who was the best in all the realm;
  His age was threescore years and ten,
    And Peter Simon was his name.

12 "Now Peter," said he, "we're bound to sea
    To fetch a traitor with good speed,
  And over a hundred gunners good,
    I've chosen thee to be the head."

13 "My liege," says he, "if ye have chosen me
    O'er a hundred men to be the head,
  Upon my mast I hang'd shall be,
    If I miss twelve score
        on a shilling's breadth."

14 My lord call'd then a bow-man rare,
    Whose hands and acts had gained fame,
  A gentleman born in Yorkshire,
    And William Horsly was his name.

15 "Horsly," quoth he, "I must to sea,
    To seek a traitor, with great speed;
  Of a hundred bow-men brave," quoth he,
    "I have chosen thee to be the head."

16. "If you, my lord, have chosen me
    Of a hundred men to be the head,
  Upon the main-mast I'll hanged be,
    If twelve-score I miss one shilling's
       breadth."

17 Lord Howard then, of courage bold,
    Went to the sea with pleasant cheer,
  Not curb'd with winters piercing cold,
    Though it was the stormy time of year.

18 Not long had he been the sea,
    No more in days but only three,
  Till one Henry Hunt he there espied,
    A merchant of Newcastle was he.

19 To him Lord Howard call'd out amain,
    And strictly charged him to stand;
  Demanding then from whence he came,
    And whence he did intend to land.

20. The merchant then made answer soon,
    With heavy heart and careful mind,
  "My lord, my ship it doth belong
    Unto Newcastle upon Tyne."

21 "Canst thou shew me," the lord did say,
    "As thou didst sail by day and night,
  A Scottish rover on the sea,
    His name is Andrew Barton, Knight?"

22 The merchant sigh'd and said, "Alas!
    Full over well I do him know;
  God keep you from his tyranny,
    For I was his prisoner but yesterday.

23 "As I, my lord, did pass from France,
    A Bordeaux voyage to take so far,
  I met with Sir Andrew Barton thence,
    Who robb'd me of my merchant-ware.

24 "And muckle debts, God knows, I owe,
    If every man would crave his own;
  And I am bound to London now,
    Of our gracious king to beg a boon."

25 "Will you go with me,"
        said Howard then,
    "And once that villain let me see,
  For every penny he's from thee ta'en,
    I'll double the same with shillings three."

26 "Now, God forbid," the merchant said;
    "I fear your aim that you will miss;
  God keep you from his tyranny,
    For little you know what man he is.

27 "He is brass within and steel without,
    His ship most huge and mighty strong,
With eighteen pieces strong and stout,
    He carrieth on each side along.

28 "And he has beams for his top-castle,
    Which is also being huge and high,
That neither English nor Portuguese
    Can pass Sir Andrew Barton by."

29 "Bad news thou tells," then said the lord,
    "To welcome strangers to the sea;
But, as I said, I'll brig him aboard,
    Or into Scotland he shall carry me."

30 The merchant said, "If you will do so,
    Take counsel, then I pray withal:
Let no man to his top-castle go,
    Nor strive to let his beam down fall.

31 Lend me seven pieces of ordnance, then
    Of each side of my ship," quoth he,
"And to-morrow, my lord,
        twixt six and seven,
    Again I will your Honour see.

32. "A glass I'll set that may be seen
    Whether you sail by day or night;
And to-morrow, be sure, before seven,
    You shall see Sir Andrew Barton,
        knight."

33 The merchant set my lord a glass,
    So well apparent in his sight
That on the morrow, as his promise was,
    He saw Sir Andrew Barton, knight.

34 The lord then swore a mighty oath,
    "Now by the heavens that be of might,
By faith, believe me, and by troth,
    I think hc is a worthy knight.

35 "Fetch me my lyon out of hand,
    Set up our rose and streamers high;
Set up withal a willow-wand,
    That merchant-like we may pass by."

36 Thus bravely did Lord Howard pass,
    And did on anchor rise so high;
No top-sail at last did he upcast,
    But like a foe did him defile.

37 Sir Andrew Barton seeing him
    Thus scornfully to pass by,
As though he cared not a pin,
    For him and all his company,

38 Then called he his men amain,
    "Fetch back yon peddlar now,"
        quoth he,
"And against this way he comes again
    I'll teach him well his courtesie."

39 A piece of ordnance soon was shot
    By this proud pirate fiercely then
Into Lord Howard's middle deck,
    Which cruel shot killed fourteen men.

40 My lord called then on Peter Simon:
    "Look now thy word do stand in stead,
For thou shalt be hanged on main-mast
    If thou miss twelve score a shilling's
        breadth."

41 Then Peter Simon gave a shot,
    Which did Sir Andrew muckle scare,
For it came so holy at his deck,
    Kill'd fifteen of his men of war.

42 "Alas!" then said the pyrate stout,
    "I am in danger now, I see;
This is some lord, I greatly doubt,
    That is set on to conquer me."

43 Then Henry Hunt, with rigor hot,
    Came bravely on the other side,
Who likewise shot in at his deck,
    And kill'd fifty of his men beside.

44 Then, "Out, alas!" Sir Andrew cri'd,
    "What may a man now think or say!
Yon merchant thief that pierceth me,
    He was my prisoner yesterday."

45 Sir Andrew call'd on Gordon then,
    And bade him to the top-castle go,
And bid his beams he should let fall,
    For he greatly fear'd an overthrow.

46 The lord call'd Horsly now in haste:
    "Look that thy word stand now in stead,
For thou shalt be hanged on main-mast
    If thou miss twelve score one
        shilling's breadth."

47   Then up the mast-tree swarved he,
       This stout and mighty Gordon;
    But Horsly, he most happily
       Shot him under the collar-bone.

48   Sir Andrew call'd his nephew then,
       Said, "Sisters sons I have no more;
    Three hundred pounds I'll give to thee,
       If thou wilt to top-castle go."

49   Then stoutly he began to climb,
       From off the mast scorn'd to depart;
    But Horsly soon prevented him,
       And deadly pierced him to the heart.

50   His men being slain, then up amain
       Did this proud pyrate climb with speed,
    Armour of proof he had put on,
       And did not dint of arrow dread.

51   "Come hither, Horsly," said the lord,
       "See thine arrow aim aright;
    Great means to thee I will afford,
       And if you speed, I'll make you a
         knight."

52   Sir Andrew did climb up the tree,
       With right good will and all his main;
    Then upon the breast hit Horsly he,
       Till the arrow did return again.

53   But Horsly spied a private place,
       With perfect eye and secret art;
    His arrow swiftly flew apace,
       And smote Sir Andrew to the heart.

54   "Fight on, fight on, my merry men all,
       A little I am hurt, yet not slain;
    I'll but lie down and bleed a while,
       And come and fight with you again.

55   "And do not," he said, "fear English
         rogues,
       And of your foes stand not in awe,
    But stand fast by St. Andrew's cross,
       Until you hear my whistle blow."

56   But they never heard his whistle blow,
       Which made them sore afraid;
    Then Horsly said, "My lord, aboard,
       For Sir Andrew Barton's dead."

57   Thus boarded they this gallant ship,
       With right good will and all their main,
    Eighteen score Scots alive in it,
       Besides as many more were slain.

58   The lord went where Sir Andrew lay,
       And quickly thence cut off his head;
    "I should forsake England many a day,
       If thou wert alive as thou art dead."

59   Thus from the wars Lord Howard came,
       With muckle joy and triumphing;
    The pyrate's head he brought along
       For to present unto our king:

60   Who briefly then to him did say,
       Before he knew well what was done,
    "Where is the knight and pyrate gay?
       That I myself may give the doom."

61   "You may thank God," then said the lord,
       "And four men in the ship," quoth he,
    "That we are safely come ashore,
       Sith you had never such an enemy:

62   "There's Henry Hunt, and Peter Simon,
       William Horsly, and Peter's son:
    Therefore reward them for their pains,
       For they did service at thy turn."

63   The king he said to Henry Hunt,
       "In lue of what he hath from thee ta'en,
    I give to thee a noble a day,
       Sir Andrew's whistle and his chain.

64   "To Peter Simon a crown a day,
       And a half-crown a day to Peter's son,
    And that was for a shot so gay,
       Which bravely brought Sir Andrew
         down.

65   "Horsly, I will make thee a knight,
       And in Yorkshire thou shalt dwell:
    Lord Howard shall Earl Bury height,
       For this title he deserveth well.

66   "Six shillings to our English men,
       Who in this fight did stoutly stand,
    And twelve pence a day unto the Scots,
       Till they come to my brother king's
         high land

HENRY MARTIN
[Henry Martyn; Salt Sea; The Three Brothers]
(Child #250)

The descendant of "Sir Andrew Barton" [#2], "Henry Martin" is a well known and widely distributed English ballad that has an extensive history in oral tradition and print. Professor Child quips that it "must have sprung from the ashes of 'Andrew Barton,' of which name Henry Martyn would be no extraordinary corruption" (Child IV:393). Bronson respectfully argues for an even closer relationship: "The life history of ['Sir Andrew Barton'] cannot justly be separated from that of its avatar, 'Henry Martyn' (No. 250). The present division [between the two ballads] is made only out of deference to Child's example and for the sake of consistency of method" (III:133). This is valid only up to a point. The ancient forms of "Sir Andrew Barton" are normally quite detailed, feature recurrent Homeric epithets and echoing phrases, and are staffed with a cast of specific characters, some of them actual historical personages — not the least of whom is King Henry himself. On the other hand, "Henry Martin" is a simpler yarn of common piracy: the king and court, the noble lords, and the champion archers and gunners are all absent; likewise the Homeric epithets and much of the bardic redundancy; likewise any partisan politics between England and Scotland. "Sir Andrew Barton" explicitly transpires on the international stage, with the fates of empires weighing in the balance. By contrast, "Henry Martin" is a straightforward yarn about a self-interested pirate out to make money "on the account."

The "Henry Martin" form has been collected throughout the British Isles and North America; it is thus unaccountably rare on shipboard, with only a few seamen's transcriptions recovered. The reason for this may be that the ballad was not picked up by the 19th-century ballad and songster printers, who seem to have provided seamen a surprisingly large proportion of their shipboard repertoire. Sailor William Keith's text, written into his shipboard journal on Yankee merchant and whaling voyages in the 1860s, appears not to have been unduly influenced by printed broadsides and is likely the degenerated product of oral transmission; it may even have been transcribed directly from singing. A distinguishing feature is that it is strangely, naively Americanized in a few minor ways, beginning with the very first line. The ballad customarily opens with some form of the line, "There were three brothers in merry Scotland." But here the line is, "In Scotland city there lived three brothers," which seems to lose track of the song's place of origin—as though the actual name of "Scotland's city" couldn't be remembered; or as though referring, say, to a city named Scotland. In any case, the notion here is rather more distant from any clear idea of Scotland than might be the case in British texts. Not surprisingly, in the sailor's text there is also a better quotient of authentic nautical lingo than is sometimes found in versions from the hinterlands. Over the course of three centuries various melodies have been joined to the lyrics, but the one recovered by Cecil J. Sharp in Somerset (England) around 1909 resembles others collected in North America and appears to be indigenous to the ballad.

There were three broth-ers in mer-ry Scot-land, In mer-ry Scot-land there were three, And they did cast

lots which of them should go, should go, should go,   And turn rob-ber all on the salt sea.

"HENRY MARTIN." Composite text based on Cecil Sharp, *One Hundred English Folksongs*, #1.

1. There were three brothers in merry Scotland,
   In merry Scotland there were three,
   And they did cast lots which of them should go,
       should go, should go,
   And turn robber all on the salt sea.

2. The lot it fell upon Henry Martin,
   The youngest of all the three,
   That he should turn robber all on the salt sea,
       the salt sea, the salt sea,
   For to maintain his two brothers and he.

3. They were not a-sailing but a long winter's night
   And part of a short winter's day,
   When Henry espied a stout lofty ship,
       lofty ship, lofty ship,
   Come a-bearing down on them straightway

4. "Hello, hello," cries Henry Martin,
   "What makes you sail so nigh?"
   "We're a rich merchant ship bound for fair London town,
       London town, London town;
   Will you please for to let us pass by?"

5. "Oh no, oh no," cries Henry Martin,
   "That thing it never can be,
   For I have turned robber all on the salt sea,
       the salt sea, the salt sea,
   For to maintain my two brothers and me.

6. "So lower your topsail and bow down your mizzen,
   Bow yourselves under my lee,
   Or else I shall give you a fast flowing ball,
       flowing ball, flowing ball,
   And cast your dear bodies all in the salt sea."

7. So broadside and broadside and at it they went
   For fully two hours or three,
   Until Henry Martin he gave the death shot,
       the death shot, the death shot,
   And cast their dear bodies all in the salt sea.

8. Bad news, bad news to old England came,
   Bad news to fair London town:
   There's been a rich vessel and she's cast away,
       cast away, cast away;
   And all of her merry men drowned.

B

"SALT SEA": Journal of William H. Keith, whaling schooner *William Martin* of Boston, merchant schooners *Edith May* of Wellfleet, *Cora Nash* of Boston, etc., circa 1865-72 [Kendall Collection, New Bedford Whaling Museum]. With a few adjustments to text and tune, these lyrics are also compatible with the air for "Andrew Bardeen" [#4].

1. In Scotland city there lived three brothers,
    Three brothers of late, brothers three.
    And they did cast lots to see which of them
    Should go robbing on the salt sea.
    Chorus: Salt sea. And they did cast &c. &c.

2. The lot it fell to Henry Martin,
    The youngest of these brothers three,
    That he should go robbing all on the salt sea
    To maintain his two brothers and he.
    Cho.—   And he (*Repeat last two lines*)

3. They sailed all night until the morning
    Until the morning sailed he
    Then they espied a tall lofty ship
    Come sailing down under their lee.
    Cho.—:   Their lee. (*Repeat last two lines*)

4. Who's there, who's there cries Henry Martin
    Who's there comes sailing so nigh.
    T'is a rich merchant ship to London she's bound
    If you please you may let her pass by.
    Cho.—   Pass by. &c. &c.

5. Back your main topsail and heave your ship to
    Come drift down under my lee,
    And I will take from you your rich flowing gold,
    and your bodies I'll sink in the sea.
    Cho.—   Salt sea &c. &c.

6. I'll not back my main topsail nor heave my ship to
    Nor come down under your lee.
    But we will save from you our rich flowing gold
    And our bodies we'll save from the sea.
    Cho.—   Salt sea &c. &c.

7. Broadsides, broadsides they gave to each other
    Broadsides they gave two or three.
    When Henry Martin gave them their death wound
    And their bodies he sank in the sea.
    Cho.—   Salt sea &c. &c.

8. Bad news bad news go tell to old England
    Bad news I tell unto thee.
    For a rich merchant ship has been robbed, set adrift
    And her mariners sunk in the sea
    Cho.—   Salt sea &c. &c. (*Finis*)

ANDREW BARDEEN

This remarkable ballad, recovered from oral tradition in Oklahoma, is the most explicit of a small family of "Henry Martin" variants that preserve crucial elements of the original 16th-century story of "Sir Andrew Barton" [#2] which are extinct in "Henry Martin" [#3]; these are seamlessly interwoven with remnants of "Captain Ward and the *Rainbow*" [#11]. "Andrew Bardeen" is, of course, a closer rendition of the original name "Andrew Barton" than "Henry Martin"; so, too, the names Andrew Bardean, Andrew Bartin, Andrew Bretan, and other American variants. Beyond simple nomenclature, the Oklahoma ballad preserves the two-part narrative structure of "Andrew Barton" (an ancient bardic format also found in the *Iliad-Odyssey* and *Beowulf* epics); the catch phrase "not a pin"; and a vestige of a metaphor rendered in "Sir Andrew Barton" as "brass within and steel without," but which in "Andrew Bardeen" becomes "brass on the outside … and steel within," almost as it is in "Captain Ward and the *Rainbow*." From *"Rainbow"* also comes the pirate's boast, "Go tell the King of England, / Go tell him thus for me, / If he reigns king of all the land / I will reign king of the sea." More significantly, "Andrew Bardeen" uniquely retains a shadow of the original conflict between England and Scotland, crucial in "Sir Andrew Barton" but absent in "Henry Martin," and it features the English king as an actual character — though, clouded by subsequent history, the more familiar moniker of a later monarch is substituted: Henry VIII becomes King George, and the English commander, Lord Charles Howard, becomes Charles Stewart, an odd name indeed for a captain on the English side. Such transformations of names, including royal names, are common (Sir Walter Scott says of the ballad "King Henrie": "A modernized copy has been published, under the title of 'Courteous King Jamie'" [1810, III:64]). Added to the greater familiarity of King George, American texts may have been influenced by the fame of Commodore Charles Stewart who, as master of the USS *Constitution,* took two British ships in a single action, as related in the ballad "The Noble Charles Stewart" (McCarty 1842, II:181). Nevertheless, the final outcome of "Andrew Bardeen" is more "Henry Martin" than "Sir Andrew Barton," for here the Scottish pirate wins — twice. Unfortunately, the tune, faithfully transcribed by Moore & Moore as received from a singer in Oklahoma [Tune A], is flawed; thus, to paraphrase Maud Karpeles, a tune "corrected for singing" is also provided [B].

TUNE A - "Andrew Bardeen" (Oklahoma), as reported in Moore & Moore, *Ballads and Folk Songs of the Southwest,* 1964.

There were three broth-ers in old Scot-land, Three lov-ing broth-ers were they, They cast lots to see Which

one of the three, Should go sail-ing all o'er the salt sea, To main - tain his two broth-ers and he.

TUNE B - "Andrew Bardeen": composite, transposed to the key of A minor and regularized for singing. For the text to fit the melody requires some adjustments of meter in most stanzas, and repetition of the last line in each of the stanzas except the first.

There were three broth - ers in old Scot-land, Three lov-ing broth-ers were they, They cast lots to see

Which one of the three, Should go sail-ing all o'er the salt sea, To main - tain his two broth-ers and he.

1

There were three brothers in old Scotland,
Three loving brothers were they.
They cast lots to see which one of the three
Should go sailing all o'er the salt sea
To maintain his two brothers and he.

2

It fell to the youngest, called Andrew Bardeen,
He being the youngest of the three,
That he should go sailing all o'er the salt sea
To maintain his two brothers and he,

3

They had not been sailing
       but weeks two or three
Till a vessel they did espy;
A vessel was sailing far off and far on;
At length it came sailing close by.

4

"What vessel, what vessel?"
       cried Andrew Bardeen,
"What vessel and where are you bound?"
"We are the rich merchant from old Scotland,
And will you please let us pass by?"

5

"Oh no, oh no," cried Andrew Bardeen,
"Oh no, and that can never be;
But your ship and your cargo, I'll take away
And your merry crew drown in the sea."

6

Sad news, sad news went home to the king,
Sad news with a woeful sound,
That a rich merchant's vessel had been
       taken away
And all his merry crew drowned.

7

"Go build me a vessel,"
       cried Captain Charles Stewart,
Go build it strong and secure,
That Andrew Bardeen can not take away.
My life no longer shall endure.

8

They had not been sailing
       but weeks two or four,
Till a vessel they did espy;
A vessel was sailing far off and on;
At length it came sailing close by.

9

What vessel, what vessel?"
       cried Captain Charles Stewart;
"What vessel and where are you bound?"
"We are the robbers from old Scotland,
And will you please let us pass by?"

10

"Oh no, oh no," cried Captain Charles Stewart,
"Oh no, and that can never be;
But your ship and your cargo, I'll take away
And your merry crew drown in the sea."

11

"Come on, come on," cried Andrew Bardeen,
"I value you not one pin;
For if you can show brass on the outside,
Why we are good steel within."

12

All at once then the battle began,
And cannons loud did roar.
They had not bee fighting an hour and a half,
Till Captain Charles Stewart gave o'er.

13

"Go home, go home," cried Andrew Bardeen,
"And tell King George for me
If he can reign king over all dry land,
I can reign king o'er the sea."

5
THE *GEORGE ALOE* AND THE *SWEEPSTAKE*
The Sailor's onely Delight, Shewing the brave Fight between the
George-Aloe, the *Sweepstake,* and certain Frenchmen at Sea

(Child #285)

A portion of "The Sailor's Only Delight" appears in *The Noble Kinsman,* a play published in 1634 that was at one time spuriously attributed to William Shakespeare and John Fletcher. Firth suggests that the ballad may have an historical basis in the issuance of official letters-of-marque for an English privateer named *Sweepstakes* in 1596; and Child mentions an air called "The Saylor's Joy" that was registered in 1595 but is now evidently extinct, to which "The *George Aloe* and the *Sweepstake*" is said originally to have been sung. The ballad was probably first printed around that same time, roughly achieving its full dimensions by 1611, when an expanded version of it was registered and published. "High Barbary" ("The Coasts of Barbary") [#6] is the incarnation in which the ballad was known to sailors in the 19th century. Neither Child nor Bronson distinguishes the two as separate ballads, though they are textually quite different and "George Aloe" hardly qualifies as a proper "pirate" ballad at all (of the broadside texts consulted, only a single line in the specimen quoted by Child, "We be French *rebels, a roving* on the sea," suggests that this may be an encounter with pirate freebooters, rather than with a conventional foreign armed merchantman, naval vessel, or legitimately licensed privateer).

Bronson (IV:306) reports that there is no musical record of either form of the ballad earlier than the 20th century. However, this is not strictly accurate, as it fails to take into account the nautical literature. "High Barbary" was printed with the standard text and tune in 1883, in an anonymous collection of *Naval Songs* published in New York; also in the various editions of the *Naval Songs* anthology edited by Admiral S.B. Luce (1889 etc.); and in Captain W.B. Whall's *Sea Songs and Chanteys*, which, while it was not published until 1910, arguably reflects the state of sea music as Whall knew it circa 1870. However, as Bronson himself points out, of the fifteen tunes he gives for the ballad, fourteen — including the one called "The *George Aloe* and the *Sweepstake*" — are merely variant forms of the same melody (the one presented in *Naval Songs* and by Luce and Whall); and only one, entitled "The Coasts of Barbary," collected in 1894 "from the singing of a tramp in North Devon [England]," is sufficiently different possibly to represent another, perhaps older strain of melodic tradition.

The George Al-oe and the Sweep - stake, too, With hey, with hoe, for and a non-ny no,

O, they were mer-chant-men, and bound for the Safee, And a - longst the Coast of Bar - bar - y.

1
The George Aloe, and the Sweepstake, too,
With hey, with hoe, for and a nony no,
O, they were Merchant men, and bound for Safee,
And alongst the Coast of Barbary

2

The George Aloe to anchor came
And the jolly Swepstake kept upon her way

3

They had not sailed leagues two or three,
But they met with a French
        Man of War upon the sea.

4

All hail, all hail, you lusty Gallants,
Of whence is your fair ship,
        and whither are you bound?

5

O we are English merchantmen,
      sailing for Safee,
And we be French rebels, a roving on the sea.

6

Amaine, amaine, you gallant Englishman,
Come you French swabs,
        and strike down your sail.

7

They laid us aboard on the starboard side,
And they overthrew us into the sea so wide.

8

When tidings to the George Aloe came,
That the jolly Sweepstake
        by a Frenchman was ta'en,

9

To top! To top, thou little ship-boy!
And see if this French
        Man of War thou canst descry.

10

A sail, a sail, under our lee,
Yea, and another under her bow.

11

Weigh anchor, Weigh anchor,
     O jolly boat-swain,
We will take this Frenchman, if we can.

12

We had not sailed leagues two or three,
But we met the French
        Man of War upon the sea.

13

All hail, all hail, you lusty Gallants,
Of whence is your fair ship,
        and whither are you bound?

14

O, we are a merchant-man
      and bound for Safee,
Aye, we are French-men, roving upon the sea.

15

Amaine, Amaine, you English dogs!
Come about, you French rogues,
        and strike down your sails.

16

The first good shot that the George Aloe shot,
He made the Frenchman's hearts sore afraid.

17

The second shot the George Aloe shot,
He struck their main-mast over the board.

18

Have mercy, have mercy,
      you brave English men,
O what have you done with our Bretheren?
     As they sailed in Barbarie?

19

We laid them aboard on the starboard side,
And we threw them into the sea so wide.

20

Such mercy as you have shewed unto them,
Then the like mercy shall you have again.

21

We laid them aboard on the larboard side,
And we threw them into the sea so wide.

22

Lord, how it grieves our hearts full Sore,
To see the drown'd Frenchmen
      swim along the shore.

23

Now gallant seamen all, adieu,
   With hey, with hoe, for and a nony no;
This is the last newes that I can write to you.
   To England's coast from Barbarie.

HIGH BARBARY
[The Coasts of Barbary; The Salcombe Seaman's Flaunt to the Proud Pirate]
(Laws #K-33)

"High Barbary" is the 18th- and 19th-century manifestation of the Elizabethan ballad of circa 1596 entitled, "The Sailor's Onely Delight, Shewing the brave Fight between the George-Aloe, the Sweepstake, and certain Frenchmen at Sea" (Child #285) [#5]. As noted above, Bronson conforms to the Child canon in classifying "The *George-Aloe* and the *Sweepstake*" and "High Barbary" as variants of the same ballad, parent and offspring. Yet there are good textual reasons to regard "High Barbary" as more than merely a shortened or degraded version of the older ballad. Not only is "High Barbary" the byproduct of a separate and much later generation of broadside balladry, it is the only incarnation whereof there is evidence of it having been sung at sea in the 19th century — quite commonly, in fact — and its reduction has been so complete that it retains nothing of the Anglo-French privateering aspect of the precursor. Hence, it has lost the political overtones and gained a heightened sense of freebooting piracy. Moreover, in the older ballad the aggressors are put ashore; or, more precisely, they are thrown overboard and allowed to try to swim ashore, but it is not clear whether they survive (Firth's text has them *"swim* along the shore"; Child's says merely, *"float* along the shore"). In any case, their vessel is presumably taken as a prize. By contrast, in "High Barbary" the ships fire "broadside-to-broadside" in a fight to the finish, and the pirate ship is sunk. Unlike the parent ballad, in "High Barbary" out-and-out piracy is quite explicit, and in most manifestations piracy is specifically differentiated from licensed privateering (see stanza 3 in Text B, stanza 5 in the others).

"High Barbary" has been sung in naval wardrooms at least since Nelson's time. Probably thanks to its hearty double refrain, it was also occasionally used before the mast as a chantey. Among deepwater sailors the tune has been stable and the narrative consistent with the hallmark theme: two "lofty" or "noble" ships sail from England (their names differ in the many variants extant) and vanquish a Barbary corsair in a blaze of cannon fire. The whalemen's manuscripts of the 1860s [Texts B and C] are manifestations of the ballad situated chronologically about mid-way between Herman Melville's mention of it in *Omoo* (1847) and pioneering efforts to collect folk songs from oral tradition around the turn of the 20th century.

A.

"High Barbary," from R-Adm. S.B. Luce, *Naval Songs* [1889], pp. 76f. Unlike the parent ballad ("The *George Aloe* and the *Sweepstake*"), out-and-out piracy is here quite explicit and in stanza 5 is specifically differentiated from licensed privateering.

1   There were two lofty ships from Old England came,
     Blow high! blow low! and so sailed we;
   One was the Prince Rupert, and the other Prince of Wales,
     Cruising down along the coast of the High Barbaree

2   "Aloft! aloft!" our jolly bos'n cries,
   "Look ahead, look astern, look a-weather and alee."

3   "There's none upon the stern, there's none upon the lee,
   But there's a lofty ship to windward, she is sailing fast and free."

4   "Oh! hail her, oh! hail her," our gallant captain cried,
   "Are you a man-of-war or a privateer?" said he.

5.   "Oh! I am no man-of-war—no privateer," said she,
   But I am a salt-sea Pirate, a-looking o'r my fee!"

6   "If you are a jolly pirate, I'd have you come this way!
   Bring out your quarter-guns, boys; we'll show these pirates play."

7   'Twas broadside to broadside a long time they lay,
   Until the Prince Rupert shot the Pirate's masts away.

8   "Oh, quarter! oh, quarter!" these pirates did cry,
   But the quarters that we gave them—we sunk them in the sea.

B.

Text from Holmes C. Fisher, written in the journal of George Wilbur Piper of Concord, New Hampshire, aboard the whaleship *Europa* of Edgartown, Martha's Vineyard, 1868-70; signed "Your friend & Shipmate / Holmes C. Fisher. Edgartown, Mass." If anything, this whalemen's text is the more dramatic, as it seems to appreciate that in ship parlance, "broadside-to-broadside" *can* mean merely "side by side," with gunports facing one another (the interpretation implied in Text A, and by a different phrase in C), but it can *also* mean—and seems to signify in the context here—*firing broadsides* (volleys of cannon fire) at one another.

1   Two fine ships from England did sail
     Blow high, blow low, and so sailed we
   One was the Prince Rupert and the other Prince of Wales
     Cruising down the coast of high Barbary

2   Oh then hail her! then hail her! the Captain he did cry
   Are you a man-of-war or a privateer? says he

3   Oh I am neither man-of-war nor privateer, says he
   But I am a bold pirate and am seeking for a prey

4   Then to broadsides, to broadsides these noble ships did come
   Till at last the English ship the pirates' mast away had blown

5   For more than two long hours this battle lasted as you see
   The ship it was their coffin, their grave it was the sea

C.

"Coast of Barbary." Journal of seaman Horace Wood aboard the whaling bark *Andrews* of New Bedford, 1866-67. Here the phrase "yard arm and yard arm" replaces "broadside to broadside" and is clearly intended to indicate the relative positions of the ships, rather than volleys of cannon fire.

1   There was two lofty ships I would have you understand
Blow you high, blow you low, and so sailed we
The one the Princess Charlotte and the other the Prince of Wales
Cruising down on the coast of Barbary

2   Go aloft, go aloft our noble Captain cries
Look ahead, look astearn [sic], look to windward and to lee

3   There is nothing ahead, there is nothing astern
But a loft[y] ship to wind'ard and a loft[y] ship is she

4   O hail the lofty ship our noble Captain cries
Are you a Man of War or a Privateer said he

5   I am neither a Man of War nor a Privateer said he
But I am a jolly Pirate as ever you did see

6   Yard arm and yard arm the gallant ships did lay
Until the Princess Charlotte shot the Pirate's mast away

7   For quarters for quarters this jolly Pirate cried
But the quarters that we gave them we sank them in the sea

D.

"The Salcombe Seaman's Flaunt to the Proud Pirate." From John Masefield's anthology, *A Sailor's Garland* (1906), compiled before he was made Poet Laureate. Listed among the anonymous poems about piracy, it seems rather a more academic piece than the usual variants of "Barbary"; perhaps the poet polished it up a bit himself. It is included here because it is unusual.

1 A lofty ship from Salcombe came,
Blow high, blow low, and so sailed we;
She had golden trucks that shone like flame,
On the bonny coasts of Barbary.

2 "Masthead, masthead," the captain's hail,
"Look out and round; d' ye see a sail?"

3 "There's a ship what looms like Beachy Head...
"Her banner aloft it blows out red."

4 "Oh, ship ahoy, and where do you steer?...
"Are you a man-of-war, or privateer?"

5 "I am neither one of the two," said she...
"I'm a pirate, looking o'r my fee."

6 "I'm a jolly pirate, out for gold...
"I will rummage through your after hold."

7 The grumbling guns they flashed and roared,
Till the pirate's masts went overboard.

8 They fired shot till the pirate's deck
Was blood and spars and broken wreck.

9 "O do not haul the red flag down...
"O keep all fast until we drown."

10 They called for cans of wine, and drank,
They sang their songs until she sank.

11 Now let us brew good cans of flip,
And drink a bowl to the Salcombe ship.

12 And drink a bowl to the lad of fame,
Blow high, blow low, and so sailed we;
Who put the pirate ship to shame.
On the bonny coasts of Barbary.

SIR WALTER RALEIGH SAILING IN THE LOWLANDS

Sir Walter Raleigh **Sailing in the** Low-lands. *Shewing how the famous Ship called the* SWEET TRINITY *was taken by a false Gally, and how it was again restored by the craft of a little Sea-boy, who sunk the Gally; as the following song will declare.*

(Child #286)

It is doubtful whether this ballad of circa 1635 was ever much in circulation in popular tradition in its original form. In any case, it was entirely supplanted by its much more widely disseminated descendant, "The *Sweet Trinity*" ("The *Bold Trinity*"; "The *Golden Vanity*") [#8], of which an extraordinary number of variants survive. The relationship between the two is so close that Child and Bronson make little distinction between them. Walter Raleigh (circa 1552-1618) was of course the famous Tudor buccaneer and sometime favorite of Queen Elizabeth and her court. His exploits at sea, both the apocryphal and the authentic, are legion. Among other things he was a notorious pirate, though evidently not a very successful one. In 1578 and again in 1579, "He joined his half-brother Sir Humphrey Gilbert in an expedition to explore and discover; in fact, the ships were to engage in piracy on the Spaniards," but they were "driven back" both times, "without appreciable gains." In 1588 he played a principal role in defending England against the Armada; "in 1595 he sailed for Trinidad and ascended the Orinoco in an effort to find treasure," but failed; and in 1616 he was released from the Tower of London, where he had been imprisoned in 1603 under sentence of death for political intrigue—"to command another expedition to Guiana and the Orinoco." However, "the expedition was a failure from the start; ships were lost in storms; his men melted away as the result of disease and desertion; and a group got into a fight with the Spaniards and Raleigh's son was killed. On his return ... the old sentence was invoked and Raleigh was executed" (Barnhart, III:3299). While the older form of the ballad is explicitly about Sir Walter Raleigh, it is not insignificant that in the younger form Raleigh's presence has been obliterated, which implies at least a certain adjustment in the context and meaning of the ballad among those who sang and preserved it over two or three centuries.

The ballad has little to do with Raleigh's own predatory adventuring. Rather, his ship is overtaken on the high seas and captured by "pirates" — that is, foreign patriots. As it turns out, the escape does Raleigh little credit, and his trickery and betrayal of a lowly cabin boy hardly places him in a favorable light. (The captain's cruel character is much worse in some later forms of the ballad, where, when the boy swims back to the ship, while he is still in the water, the captain not only denies him the gold and the bride, but actually forbids anyone to help the lad back aboard; so he bids his shipmates farewell and "sinks into the low-land sea"; or he is taken on board by his shipmates, and expires on deck.) Note the odd substitution of *Gallaly* ["Galilee"?] for *galley,* in this context meaning a sailing vessel with auxiliary sweep oars for maneuverability in a calm (a typical rig of pirates and Turks): in combination with the ship-name *Sweet Trinity,* the substitution vaguely suggests theological allegory. Some 17th-century printed texts indicate the tune "The Sailing of the Lowland," which Simpson does not even mention and which Bronson could not locate; "it may, however, have been the ancestor of the current forms" (Bronson IV: 312). Thus, singers are relegated to using one of the tunes for "The *Sweet Trinity*"—perhaps the one here [#8] or any of the 110 alternatives assembled by Bronson.

1 Sir Walter Raleigh has built a Ship
   in the Netherlands,
Sir Walter Raleigh has built a Ship
   in the Netherlands,
And it is called the Sweet Trinity,
And it was taken by a false Gallaly,
   sailing in the Low-lands.

2 Is there never a Seaman bold
   in the Netherlands?
Is there never a Seaman bold
   in the Netherlands?
That will go take this false Gallaly,
And to redeem the Sweet Trinity,
   sailing in the Low-lands?

3   Then spoke the little Ship boy
        In the Netherlands,
    Then spoke the little Ship boy
        In the Netherlands,
    Master, master, what will you give me?
    And I will take this false Gallaly,
    And release the Sweet Trinity,
        Sailing in the Low-lands.

4   I'll give thee gold, and I'll give thee fee
        In the Netherlands,
    I'll give thee gold, and I'll give thee fee
        In the Netherlands,
    And my eldest daughter thy wife shall be
        Sailing in the Low-lands.

5   He set his breast, and away he did swim
        In the Netherlands,
    He set his breast, and away he did swim
        In the Netherlands,
    Until he came to the false Gallaly
        Sailing in the Low-lands.

6   He had an Augur fit for the nonce
        In the Netherlands,
    He had an Augur fit for the nonce
        In the Netherlands,
    The which will bore fifteen good holes all at
                once
        Sailing in the Low-lands.

7   Some were at Cards and some at Dice
        In the Netherlands,
    Some were at Cards and some at Dice
        In the Netherlands,
    Until salt water flashed in their eyes
        Sailing in the Low-lands.

8   Some cut their Hats and some their Caps
        In the Netherlands,
    Some cut their Hats and some their Caps
        In the Netherlands,
    For to stop the salt-water gaps
        Sailing in the Low-lands.

9   He set his breast and away did swim
        In the Netherlands,
    He set his breast and away did swim
        In the Netherlands,
    Until he came to his own Ship again
        Sailing in the Low-lands.

10 I have done the work I have promis'd to do
        In the Netherlands,
    I have done the work I have promis'd to do
        In the Netherlands,
    For I have sunk the false Gallaly
    And released the Sweet Trinity
        Sailing in the Low-lands.

11 You promis'd me gold and you promis'd me fee
        In the Netherlands,
    You promis'd me gold and you promis'd me fee
        In the Netherlands,
    Your eldest daughter my Wife she must be
        Sailing in the Low-lands.

12 You shall have gold and you shall have fee
        In the Netherlands,
    You shall have gold and you shall have fee
        In the Netherlands,
    But my eldest daughter your Wife
                shall never be
        Sailing in the Low-lands.

13 Then fare you well, you cozening Lord,
        In the Netherlands,
    Then fare you well, you cozening Lord,
        In the Netherlands,
    Seeing you are not as good as your word
        Sailing in the Low-lands.

14 And thus I shall conclude my song,
                Of the sailing in the Low-lands;
    And thus I shall conclude my song,
                of sailing in the Low-lands;
    Wishing happiness to all Seamen,
                old and young
        In their sailing in the Low-lands.

Ballad cut from "Sir Walter Raleigh Sailing in the Low-Lands," reproduced in John Ashton, *Chap Books of the Eighteenth Century* (London, 1882), page 221.

THE *SWEET TRINITY*

[The Golden Vanity; The Bold Trinity; The Mary Golden Tree; The Golden Willow Tree; etc.]

(Child #286)

> The Captain … was all excitement, saying, "He stands up! Only strike that whale and I will give you anything I have, anything except my wife"; and as my iron struck the whale he threw off his hat, saying, "He is fast! Take my wife and all I have!"
>
> I guess he forgot about his offer after we got on board, for I got nothing but the proud satisfaction that I had struck my first whale and proved that a boy only seventeen years old could fill a man's place on a whaleman's deck.
>
> — Nelson Cole Haley, *Whale Hunt*

As "Henry Martin" [#3] is an evolved form of "Andrew Barton" [#2], this famous old ballad, concerning a cabin-boy who rescues his ship from a piratical enemy and is then betrayed by his own captain's treachery, is descended from "Sir Walter Raleigh Sailing in the Lowlands" [#7]. In fact, their relation is so close that Child (#286) does not distinguish between them. Nevertheless, in standpoints of meter, narrative emphasis, historical context, and deployment of the refrain, the two ballads are markedly different. The "*Sweet Trinity*" / "*Golden Vanity*" form is very widely distributed in the British Isles and North America, and from the published field-collections of sea chanteys and sailors' songs it seems also to have been popular among merchant seamen but less so with whalemen, in whose journals only this one text has thus far been encountered (a text that does not much resemble the versions used as a chantey). Among numerous surviving texts there are many variations in the name of the principal vessel, hence variations in the title. Likewise, the nationality of the enemy ship, whether French, Turkish, or Spanish, seems to have varied with fluctuations of politics and the fortunes of war from one era to the next. The ship-names *Sweet Trinity, Golden Vanity,* and *Bold Trinity* each imply symbolic significances, obscure but open to theological speculation. The "lowlands" allusion, where *lowlands* refers to the sea rather than to any "low land," is also found in "The Lowlands of Holland," a contemporaneous Scots ballad about impressment into the royal service to fight a European enemy in the Low Countries, but the actual direction of influence is unknown. In tradition the family of texts has understandably been corrupted with the infusion of lyrics from the popular 19th-century minstrelsy song "Louisiana Lowlands," which it may have inspired. Over the centuries numerous tunes have become attached to the ballad, and variants have been collected from tradition with two- and three-line narrative stanzas, followed by various permutations of a "lowlands" refrain. The two-line stanza seems to have prevailed in the American South, while deepwater ballad and chantey specimens are generally of the three-line type. The Yankee whaleman's manuscript text here — which is actually a substantial fragment—belongs to the two-line species, of which few examples have hitherto been encountered at sea or ashore in New England. Of the many tunes extant, the one here is the only compatible specimen recovered from New England tradition.

The whaleman who recorded Text A was an interesting and ultimately tragic figure. Edward Willson Collins was born in 1809 at Dartmouth, Massachusetts, just outside New Bedford. He and his elder brother Silas were raised with the hope and expectation of going whaling someday; and after Silas completed two voyages in the Dartmouth brig *By Chance* in the 1820s, he gave Edward his shipboard journal. In 1829, in anticipation of taking his own turn before the mast, Edward got the texts of two old ballads from Silas and transcribed them into the volume — "The Lowlands of Holland" and "The Sweet Trinity" — so he could have them with him at sea. Over the next few years he wrote some of his own songs on the blank pages at the back of the volume. It turned out for Edward, as it did not particularly for Silas, that whaling suited him. He was promoted rapidly, was an officer when he married in 1834, and in 1839, at age 30, he was given his first command, the New Bedford ship *Phocion*. A successful voyage (1839-40) led to his appointments as captain of the *Stephania* (1841-44) and then the *Midas* of Fairhaven (1844). But there his luck ran out. Suddenly and mysteriously, he died at sea, aged 35, 230 days out, bound for the Indian Ocean. Captain Collins had had the old journal and the two ballads with him the whole time, and after his death they were sent home for his young son to cherish as keepsakes.

The Collins text [A] tells a story of a sort but omits entirely the captain's treachery, which is usually the heart of the matter and in some manifestations runs to several stanzas. So it turns out to be quite a different story than "Sir Walter Raleigh Sailing in the Lowlands" and the usual "Sweet Trinity" cycle. An interesting variant also recovered from a deepwater informant [B] is likewise quite abbreviated but it provides some unorthodox transformations of nomenclature and it devotes five stanzas at the end to the crew's exacting fatal retribution against the captain for his having betrayed and killed the cabin boy. The actions of the captain and the crew are both capital crimes that would have been punishable as piracy.

I have a gal-lant ship in the North Coun-ter-ies, And she goes by the name of the Bold Trin-i-ty.

And she sails in the low-lands, low-lands low, And she sails in the low-lands low.

A.

"Sweet Trinity." From Edward W. Collins, on the eve of his departure as a green hand in the whaleship *Condor* of New Bedford, 1829-34; in a journal formerly belonging to (and the ballad likely transcribed by) his brother, Silas Collins, brig *By Chance* of Dartmouth, Mass., 1825-28 [Kendall Collection, New Bedford Whaling Museum].

1   I have a ship in the North Countries
     And she goes by the name of the Bold Trinity
     And she sails in the lowlands, lowlands low
     And she sails in the lowlands low

2.   She had not sailed past glasses two or three
     Before she espied a French gallee
     As she sailed in the lowlands…

3.   Then up steps the little cabin boy
     Saying, What will you give the ship to destroy
     And to sink her in the lowlands…

4.   'Tis I will give you gold, 'tis I will give you fee
     And my eldest daughter your wedded wife shall be
     If you'll sink her in the lowlands…

5.   In his hand he carried an auger fitted for his work
     Of which he bored four-and-twenty holes all in a quick
     And he sank her in the lowlands…

B.

"The Cruise in the Lowlands Low." A more complete specimen text from a deepwater source: "'This sea ballad I heard in Black Forest [Pennsylvania] in 1874, sung by John A. Watts, a deep sea sailor before the mast, and I now write it from memory for the first time, and there might be slight errors in the words used to express the tale of poetic justice and gusto of the men 'who went down to the sea in ships!' —John C. French, Roulette [Pennsylvania], 1918" (Shoemaker, *Mountain Minstrelsy of Pennsylvania*, 133). *Mary Golden Tree* is an unlikely name for a Turkish vessel, and in the many texts in which it appears it is almost always the name of the protagonist's ship. Retribution on the captain is not ordinarily a part of the "*Sweet Trinity*" cycle.

1   Our good ship sailed from the north countree—
She went by the name of the "Green Willow Tree."

Chorus—   As she sailed in the lowlands, lowlands—
As she sailed in the lowlands low.

2   We had been out but two days or three,
When we espied a Turk's ship a-lee.

3   Up jumped the cabin boy: "What will you give me
If I sink that pirate a-lee?"

4   "Oh," said our captain, "I'll give you golden store,
And my only daughter you shall wed, soon as we reach the shore,
If you'll sink her in the low lands low."

5   The boy had an instrument, made for the use,
Four and twenty holes, to make at one push.

6   He bent upon his breast and away swam he,
Swam to the "Merry Golden Tree."

7   Some were playing cards and some throwing dice,
When he let in the water and put out their lights.

8   Some took their hats and some took their caps,
To shut out the salt water caps.

9   The boy bent his breast and away swam he,
Swam till he came to the "Green Willow Tree."

10   "Captain, oh captain, take me aboard,
And be unto me as good as your word,
For I sunk her in the lowlands low."

11   "No," said the captain, "I'll not take you aboard,
Nor be unto you as good as my word;
You may sink with them in the lowlands low."

12   The boy bent his breast and down sank he,
Sank by the side of the "Green Willow Tree."

13   We took that captain to the starboard side,
And threw him overboard in the lowland tide.

14   He sank by the side of the "Green Willow Tree,"
And he drowned like the Turk's revelry.

15   We weighed the anchor on our starboard side,
And sailed away with a fair wind and tide.

16   Away and away our good ship did plough,
As we sailed from the lowlands low.

CAPTAIN WARD

The Seaman's Song of Captain *Ward* the famous
Pyrate of the world, and an English-man born

John Ward was the most notorious of the English pirates in the Mediterranean. Born in 1553 at Faversham, Kent, he was first a fisherman and then enlisted in the navy, which he abandoned to prosecute an adventurer's career. He proved to be a great success at it. He "commenced 'rover' about 1604" (Child V:143) by perpetrating a naval mutiny, taking command, and turning the ship to piracy. "By 1606 he commanded a small fleet employing five hundred seamen," specializing in the systematic acquisition of enormous treasures from Venetian merchantmen, eluding efforts to bring him to heel, and living sumptuously in a palace at Tunis; in 1609 he "tried unsuccessfully to obtain a pardon" from King James I (Cordingly 1996, 90). That same year, with Ward still active and thriving in the Mediterranean, his terrible reputation achieved new heights: one Andrew Barker wrote a book about him (Child V:143; Ebsworth VI:423; Logan, 4), and the ballad "Captain Ward" was licensed, making it perhaps the earliest pirate ballad to appear in print in English. Child appears to be mistaken in his contention that Ward "seems not to be heard of after 1609." The authorities never did catch up with him, and, according to Cordingly, Ward died in his bed of natural causes — plague — in 1622, one of the "unusual examples" of pirates "who lived long enough to enjoy their plundered wealth" (Cordingly 1996, 13).

The ballad does not have much of a plot and there are no sea-fights. Yet, its moralistic tone notwithstanding, it does impart a few insights about piracy and a few bits of accurate information about Ward, including his palace at Tunis and heathen henchmen. Even so, its most distinctive features are its mention of sodomy, rarely encountered in any literature of seafaring; and its brief but explicit catalogue of corporeal horrors, unaccountably rare in pirate ballads, if not in ballads generally. The final stanzas are deeper philosophically than most of the usual Victorian glosses that condemn the pirate life: "… His honors [presumably the honors bestowed by public acclaim] we shall find / Shortly blown up in the wind, / Or prove like letters written in the sand."

For both this and the companion ballad "Dansekar the Dutchman" [#10], which appeared on the same sheet at the same time, the tune specified is "The King's Going to Bulloign," now lost. Early editions of "Captain Ward and the *Rainbow*" [#11] call for a tune called "Captain Ward," but that tune cannot be the one intended here, as the *"Rainbow"* ballad and this one are metrically incompatible and cannot be sung to the same tune. Simpson does not even mention "Captain Ward," "Dansekar," or "The King's Going to Bulloign"; Child barely recognizes "Captain Ward" as anything more than archival texts; and Bronson follows suit. They may have a point. There is little evidence that "Captain Ward" has been sung at all during the past three centuries.

1
Gallants, you must understand,
Captain Ward of England,
A pyrate and a rover on the sea,
Of late a simple fisherman
In the merry town of Feversham,
Grows famous in the world now every day.

2
From the Bay of Plimouth
Sayled he towards the south,
With many more of courage and of might;
Christian princes have but few
Such seamen, if they be true,
And would but for his King and country fight.

3
Lusty Ward adventurously
In the Straights of Barbary
Did make the Turkish galleys for to shake
Bouncing cannons fiery hot
Spared not the Turks one jot,
But of their lives great slaughter he did make.

4
The islanders of Malta
With argosies upon the sea
Most proudly braved Ward unto his face,
But soon their pride was overthrown,
And their treasures made his own,
And all their men brought to a wofull case.

5

The wealthy ships of Venice
Afforded him great riches;
Both gold and silver won he by his sword.
Stately Spain and Portugal
Against him dare not bear up sail,
But gave him all the title of a lord.

6

Golden-seated Candy,
Famous France and Italy,
With all the countries of the Eastern parts,
If once their ships his pride with-stood,
They surely were all cloath'd in blood,
Such cruelty was place'd within their hearts.

7

The riches he hath gain'd,
And by bloodshed obtained
Well might suffice to maintain a king;
His fellows all were valiant wights,
Fit to be made prince's knights,
But that their lives do base dishonors bring.

8

This wicked-gotten treasure
Doth him but little pleasure;
The land consumes what they have got by sea,
In drunkenness and letchery,
Filthy sins of sodomy,
Their evil-gotten goods do waste away.

CAPTAIN WARD.

"Captain Ward." Woodcut illustration from the *Forget Me Not Songster* (Boston and New York, 1840s), page 41.

9

Such as live by thieving
Have seldom-times good ending,
As the deeds of Captain Ward is shown;
Being drunk amongst his drabs,
His nearest friend he sometimes stabs;
Such wickedness within his heart is grown.

10

When stormy tempests riseth,
The Causer he despiseth,
Still denies to pray unto the Lord,
He feareth neither God nor devil,
His deeds are bad, his thoughts are evil,
His only trust is still upon his sword.

11

Men of his own country
He still abuseth vilely;
Some back to back are cast into the waves;
Some are hewn in pieces small,
Some are hot against a wall;
A slender number of their lives he saves.

12

Of truth it is reported
That he is strongly guarded
By Turks that are not of a good belief;
Wit and reason tells them
He trusteth not his country-men,
He shews the right condition of a thief.

13

At Tunis in Barbary
Now he buildeth stately
A gallant palace and a royal place,
Decked with delights most trim,
Fitter for a prince than him,
The which at last will prove to his disgrace.

14

To make the world to wonder,
This captain is commander
Of four-and-twenty ship of sayl,
To bring in treasure from the sea
In the markets every day:
The which the Turks do buy up without fail.

15

His name and state so mounteth,
These country-men accounteth
Him equal to the nobles of that land;
But these his honours we shall find
Shortly blown up with the wind,
Or prove like letters written in the sand.

DANSEKAR THE DUTCHMAN
The Song of Dansekar the Dutchman, his robberies done at Sea

Simon Danziker was "Dutch" in the old sense of Deutsch: the surname refers to the then-German seaport of Danzig (now Gdansk). A cohort of Captain Ward [#9], he was hanged at Tunis in 1611, two years after the ballad was first printed. The text is notable for its catalogue of English vessels captured, which, given the journalistic nature of broadsides, may be regarded as fairly accurate.

Sing we sea-men, now and then,
Of Dansekar the Dutchman,
Whose gallant mind hath won him great renown;
To live on land he counts it base,
But seeks to purchase greater grace
By roving on the ocean up and down.

His heart is so aspiring,
That now his chief desiring
Is for to win himself a worthy name;
The land hath far too little ground,
The sea is of a larger bound,
And of a greater dignity and fame.

Now many a worthy gallant,
Of courage and most valiant,
With him hath put their fortunes to the sea;
All the world about have heard
Of Dansekar and Captain Ward,
And of their proud adventures every day.

There is not any kingdom,
In Turkey or in Christendom,
But by these pyrates have received loss;
Merchant-men of every land
Do daily in great danger stand,
And fear too much the ocean main to cross.

They make children fatherless
Wo[e]ful widows in distresse;
In shedding blood they take too much delight;
Fathers they bereave of sons,
Regarding neither cries nor moans,
So much they joy to see a bloody fight.

They count it gallant bearing
To hear the cannons roaring,
And musket shot to rattle in the sky;
Their glories would be at their highest
To fight against the foes of Christ,
As such as do our Christian faith deny.

But their cruel villainies,
And their bloody pyracies
Are chiefly bent against our Christian friends;
Some Christians so delight in evils,
That they become the sons of divels [sic],
And for the same have many shameful ends.

England suffers danger,
As well as any stranger.
Nations are alike unto this company;
Many English merchant-men,
And of London now and then,
Have tasted of their vile extremity.

London's Elizabeth
Of late these rovers taken hath,
A ship well laden with rich merchandize;
The nimble Pearl and Charity,
All ships of gallant bravery,
Are by these pyrates made a lawful prize.

The Trojan of London
With other ships many a one,
Hath stooped sail, and yielded out of hand,
(These pyrates they have shed their bloods,
And the Turks have bought their goods),
Being all too weak their power to withstand.

Of Hull the Bonaventer,
Which was a great frequenter
And passer of the Straits to Barbary,
Both ship and men late taken were
By Pyrates Ward and Dansekar,
And brought by them into captivity.

English Ward and Dansekar
Begin greatly now to jar
About the true dividing of their goods;
Both ships and soldiers gather head,
Dansekar from Ward is fled:
So full of pride and malice are their bloods.

Ward doth only promise
To keep about rich Tunis,
And be commander of those Turkish seas;
But valiant Dutch-land Dansekar
Doth hover near unto Argier [Algiers]
And there his threat'ning colours now displays.

These pyrates thus divided,
By God is sure provided
In secret sort to work each other's woe;
Such wicked courses cannot stand,
The Divel thus puts in his hand,
And God will give them soon an overthrow

CAPTAIN WARD AND THE *RAINBOW*
A Famous Sea-Fight between Captain *Ward* and the *Rain-bow*
(Child #287)

The third in the trilogy of ballads about Ward the Pirate is demonstrably the youngest by two or three generations. It was not part of the original 1609 canon; however, it is the only one of the three that was admitted to the Child canon. It turns out that the basis of Child's implication that "Captain Ward and the *Rainbow*" may also be contemporaneous is mistaken. The twin ballads "Captain Ward" [#9] and "Dansekar the Dutchman" [#10] were registered for publication in April 1609 and are thus certifiably coeval with John Ward's actual career as a pirate. But there is no evidence of an early appearance of "Captain Ward and the *Rainbow*" and plenty to suggest a much later date, not the least of which is the absence of contemporaneous specimens: "The earliest printed editions of ['Captain Ward and the *Rainbow*'] belong to the latter half of the 17th century" (Firth, 342). As Child himself points out, *Rainbow* was "the name of one of [Sir Francis] Drake's four ships in his expedition against Cadiz in 1587," and that ship "is mentioned very often from 1589" (Child V:143). However, the mere existence of a glamorous vessel with a common name in the Armada era is hardly conclusive or compelling — or even relevant — in relation to a character who did not even begin his piratical ravages until "around 1604" (as Child correctly points out on the very same page). By that time much had changed. Not only had Elizabeth been laid to rest and the Stewart dynasty installed in 1603, transforming British naval policy, seaborne trade, and relations with Scotland (now that England had a Scottish king) — changes which in themselves could have had something to do with Ward's turning to piracy the following year. And not only had Spain been supplanted by Holland and France as ascendant rivals to Britain at sea, but, more to the point, by 1604 Drake was already dead eight years (he died in 1596, when John Ward was still an anonymity in the Navy). Of course, Child never argued for a *literal* historical connection between Francis Drake and Ward the Pirate. His supposition — that the legends of Drake and Ward could have been combined in an apocryphal ballad during Ward's actual lifetime — might seem plausible were there any contemporaneous broadside specimens to support it, and were there not a far more compelling explanation.

C.H. Firth, an astute naval historian whose thought was apparently not influenced by Child's muddled nautical incongruities, suggests convincingly that the *"Rainbow"* ballad may be a "legendary version" of an actual British naval expedition to the Barbary Coast commanded by Captain William *Rainborow* in 1637, which resulted in the rescue from slavery of "300 or 400 Englishmen" — hence the transformed name *Rainbow* and the confusion with Ward's notorious earlier career on the adjacent North African coast.

Unlike the two other ballads about Ward the Pirate, "Captain Ward and the *Rainbow*" has been recovered from tradition and there are several tunes associated with it. Early broadsides consulted by Bell, Child, Euing, and Firth call for something called "Captain Ward," which could not be the same tune as for the older ballad of that name [#9]: in fact, it "remains unidentified" (Bronson IV:363) and "does not appear to have survived" (Simpson, 720n). However, "Several eighteenth-century editions of 'A Famous Sea-Fight between Captain Ward and the Rainbow'... are directed to be sung to 'Twas when the seas were roaring'" (Simpson, 720). This is an odd little melody composed by George Frederick Handel that was exploited on the London stage in two of John Gay's musical plays, *The What D'ye Call It: A Tragi-Comi-Pastoral Farce* (1715) and *The Beggar's Opera* (1728); it also "appeared in a host of musical miscellanies" and furnished the melody for "Sir John Barleycorn" and "The Dying Virgin's Farewell," among other ballads (Simpson, 719f). Thus, "'Twas when the seas were roaring" [Tune A] may be the most authentic antiquarian tune that survives for "Captain Ward and the *Rainbow*," especially in light of what Bronson says about the singing heritage of the ballad: "... The melodic tradition is scattered and thin, hardly convincing one that there is any real core. The tunes that have been collected [from tradition] have little in common, and remind one too much of other songs."

TUNE A: "'Twas when the seas were roaring" by George Frederick Handel, per Simpson, 720.

Strike up you lust-y gal-lants, With mus-ic and the beat of drum, For we have de-stroyed a

Ro-ver Up-on the sea is come; His name is Cap-tain Ward, Right well it

doth ap-pear, There has' not been such a rov-er Found out this thou-sand year.

TUNE B: Known as "Captain Ward" or "Ward the Pirate," in North America this appears to be the standard tune for "Captain Ward and the *Rainbow*." It fits the simpler, more vernacular texts of later versions better than it does the early broadside texts but can easily be adapted.

Strike up you lust-y gal-lants, With mu-sic and the beat of drum, For we've de-stroy'd a

Ro-ver Up-on the sea is come; His name is Cap-tain Ward, Right

well it doth ap-pear; There has not been such a rov-er Found out this thou-sand year.

1	**2**
Strike up you lusty gallants	For he hath sent unto the king,
With music and the beat of drum,	The sixth of January,
For we have destroyed a Rover	Desiring that he might come in
Upon the sea is come;	With all his company;
His name is Captain Ward,	And if the king will let me come,
Right well it doth appear,	Till I my tale have told,
There has not been such a rover	I will bestow for my ransom,
Found out this thousand year:	Full thirty tons of gold.

3

"O nay, O nay," then said our king,
 "O nay, this must not be,
To yield to such a rover
 myself will not agree;
He hath deceived the Frenchman,
 likewise the King of Spain,
Then how can he be true to me,
 that hath been false to twain?"

4

With that our king provided
 A ship of worthy fame;
The Rainbow she is called,
 If you would know her name:
And now the gallant Rainbow
 She rolls upon the sea,
Five hundred gallant seamen
 To bear her company.

5

The Dutchman and the Spaniard,
 She made them for to flee,
Also the bonny Frenchman,
 As she met them on the sea.
When as this gallant Rainbow
 Did come where Ward did lie,
"Where is the captain of this ship?"
 The Rainbow she did cry.

6

"O, that am I," says Captain Ward,
 "There's no man bids me lie,
And if thou art the king's fair ship,
 Thou art welcome unto me."
"I'll tell thee what," says Rainbow,
 "Our King is in great grief,
Thou shouldst lie upon the seas,
 And play the arrant thief.

7

"You will not let our merchant ships
 pass as they did before;
Such tydings to our king is come,
 which grieves his heart full sore."
With that, this gallant Rainbow
 she shot, out of her pride,
Full fifty gallant brass pieces,
 charged on every side.

8

And yet these gallant shooters
 Prevailed not a pin,
Though they were brass on the outside,
 Brave Ward was steel within:
"Shoot on, shoot on," says Captain Ward,
 "Your sport well pleaseth me,
And he that first gives over,
 Shall yield unto the sea.

9

"I never wrong'd an English ship
 But Turk and King of Spain,
And the blackguard Dutch man,
 Which I met on the main;
If I had known your king
 But one or two years before,
I would have saved Lord Essex' life
 Whose death did grieve me sore.

10

"Go tell the King of England,
 Go tell him thus for me,
If he reigns king of all the land,
 I will reign king of the sea."
With that the gallant Rainbow shot,
 And shot again in vain,
Then left the Rover's company,
 And home returned again.

11

"O, Royal King of England,
 Your ship's returned again;
For Captain Ward he is so strong
 It never will be ta'en."
"O, everlasting!" says our King,
 "I have lost jewels three,
Which would have gone unto the seas,
 And brought proud Ward to me.

12

"The first it was Lord de Clifford,
 Great Earl of Cumberland;
The second was Lord Mountjoy,
 As you shall understand;
The third was brave Lord Essex,
 From foe would never flee,
Which would have gone unto the seas,
 And brought proud Ward to me."

CAPTAIN EVERY
A Copy of Verses, Composed by Captain Henry Every,
Lately Gone to Sea to Seek His Fortune

Henry Avery (1665 - circa 1728) — alias Henry Every, John Avery, John Every, Long Ben, and Captain Bridgeman — was one of the most colorful of all pirates. Though he is not nearly so well remembered nowadays as Captain Kidd or Blackbeard, "During his own time the adventures of Captain Avery were the subject of conversation in Europe. It was reported that he had married the Great Mogul's daughter, who was taken in an Indian ship that fell into his hands, and that he was about to be the founder of a new monarchy — that he gave commissions in his own name to the captains of his ships, and the commanders of his forces, and was acknowledged by them as their prince" (Ellms, 12). A reputed native of Devonshire in England, he started out as an honest sailor and had already advanced in rank and position before turning pirate. Cordingly summarizes the unpremeditated circumstances of Avery's going "on the account":

> In 1694, Avery was sailing master aboard the *Charles II,* a Bristol privateer hired by Spain to attack French smugglers based on Martinique who were trading with Spanish colonies. En route to the Caribbean the ship stopped at La Coruña for provisions, freight, and passengers. The crew hadn't been paid for eight months and soon after leaving port they mutinied and elected Avery captain. The ship, rechristened the *Fancy* (a name favored by pirates), then set course for the Indian Ocean. (Cordingly 1996, 149)

Avery's wild career in the shipping lanes from Madagascar to Araby lasted only two or three years but sufficed to win him the epithet Arch Pirate. His ravages were sometimes undertaken in partnership with the Rhode Island-born pirate Thomas Tew; he also ran an indeterminate number of other pirate vessels with sub-captains under his general command.

> Notorious names like Black Bart Roberts, Long Ben Avery, Thomas Tew, and Captain Kidd were among those who pirated not only Arab and Mogul vessels sailing between India's Malabar Coast and the Red Sea Ports of Mocha and Jedda, but also richly laden East Indiamen and even ships coming from the west coast of Africa carrying slaves, gold dust, and ivory. They enjoyed the encouragement of North American colonists and developed pirate havens on Madagascar, Mauritius, and the Ile de Bourbon (Réunion). (Ibid, 142)

The conclusion is equally romantic. Captain Avery did not wind up on the gallows like some of his cohorts: "Avery himself was never caught. He had started calling himself Bridgeman and sailed for Ireland, where he vanished. Whatever his end, the legends of the Arch Pirate lived on, inspiring countless others to head for the Eastern seas" (Ibid, 152). The ballad is evidently based on the court proceedings and a published account of the trial of six of his men in 1696 entitled *The Trial of Joseph Dawson &c. for several Piracies and Robberies by them committed in company of Every the Grand Pirate* (London, 1696; cited by Firth, 347) [see #13]. A few years later Avery was "the subject of a play entitled *The Successful Pirate* (1713) by the hack playwright Charles Johnston" (Cordingly 1996, 14). By then the ballad must have been around, too, but it is scarcer than most others of that era, absent from the collections of Child and his heirs, and evidently extinct in tradition. The prescribed tune is "The Two English Travelers": "Its popularity can be judged from the existence of more than twenty broadsides naming the tune for singing, but unhappily the music has not been preserved" (Simpson, 782f).

1   Come all you brave boys, whose courage is bold
     Will you venture with me? I'll glut you with gold.
     Make haste unto Corona: a ship you will find,
     That's called the Fancy, will pleasure your mind.

2   Captain Every is in her, and calls her his own;
     He will box her about, boys, before he has done:
     French, Spaniard, and Portuguese, the heathen likewise,
     He has made a war with them until that he dies.

3   Her model's like wax, and she sails like the wind;
     She is rigg'd, and, fitted, and curiously trimm'd,
     And all things convenient has for his design,
     God bless his poor Fancy, she's bound for the mine [main].

4   Farewell, fair Plimouth, and Cat-Down be damn'd:
     I once was part-owner of most of that land;
     But as I am disown'd, so I'll abdicate
     My person from England to attend on my fate.

5   Then away from this climate and temperate zone,
     To one that's more torrid, you'll hear I am gone,
     With an hundred and fifty brave sparks of this age,
     Who are fully resolved their foes to engage.

6   These northern parts are not thrifty for me;
     I'll rise the Anterise [Antares], that some men shall see,
     I am not afraid to let the world know
     That to the South Seas and to Persia I'll go.

7   Our names shall be blazoned and spread in the sky,
     And many brave places I hope to descry
     Where never a French man e'er yet has been,
     Nor any proud Dutchman can say he has seen.

8   My commission is large, and I made it myself,
     And the capston shall stretch it full larger by half;
     It was dated in Corona, believe it, my friend,
     From the year ninety-three unto the world's end.

9   I honour St. George, and his colours I [wear],
     Good quarters I give, but no nation I spare;
     The world must assist me with what I do want;
     I'll give them my bill when my money is scant.

10   Now this I do say and solemnly swear:
     He that strikes to St. George the better shall fare
     But he that refuses shall suddenly spy
     Strange colours aboard of my Fancy to fly.

11   Four chivileges [sic] of gold in a bloody field.
     Environ'd with green, now this is my shield;
     Yet call out for quarter before you do see
     A bloody flag out, which is our decree.

12   No quarter to give, no quarters to take;
     We save nothing living: alas! 'tis too late;
     For we are now sworn by the bread and the wine,
     More serious we are than any divine.

13   Now, this is the course I intend for to steer;
     My false-hearted nation, to you I declare
     I have done thee no wrong, thou must me forgive;
     The sword shall maintain me as long as I live.

VILLAINY REWARDED; OR
THE PIRATE'S LAST FAREWELL TO THE WORLD
**Who was executed at Execution Dock on Wednesday, the 25th of November, 1696,
being of Every's crew; together with their Free Confession of their most Horrid Crimes**

On the Thames below the City of London, tour guides still point out Execution Dock, a place of hanging or drowning for felons convicted of piracy, murder, mutiny, and other high crimes at sea. In the 17th century British law required that, regardless of where pirates may have been apprehended, they be brought to London for trial and execution. Captain Avery was never taken, but six of his cohorts swung there on 25 November 1696, as related in a contemporaneous narrative on which the ballad "Captain Every" [#12] was later based. "Villainy Rewarded" is a more immediate, journalistic reflection of the event; it was printed for Charles Barnes (London) in 1696, in very close conjunction with the hanging itself [see "The Execution of Five Pirates" (1864), #83 in the Appendix]. The broadside directs that the ballad be sung to "Russell's Farewell," corresponding with which title Simpson identifies three separate tunes and more than fifty ballad texts, many of them — like "Villainy Rewarded" — contrite farewell songs of wrongdoers. The full title, "Villainy Rewarded; Or, The Pirate's Last Farewell to the World," suggests that, of the three melodies, the one properly known as "The Lord Russels Last Farewell to the World" is the one intended here.

1   Well may the world against us cry; for these our deeds most base,
     For which, alas! we now must dye, death looks us in the face,
     Which is no more than what's our due, since we so wicked were,
     And here shall be declar'd to you. Let pyrates then take care.

2   We with our comrades, not yet ta'en, together did agree,
     And stole a ship out from the Groyne, to roam upon the sea;
     With which we robb'd and plundered too, no ship that we did spare.
     Thus many a one we did undo. Let pyrates then take care.

3   Our ship being well stored then for this our enterprise,
     One hundred and eighty men there was in her likewise;
     We pillag'd all we could come nigh, no nation we did spare.
     For which a shameful death we dye. Let pyrates then take care.

4   We robb'd a ship upon the seas, the *Gunsway* call'd by name,
     Which we met near the East Indies, and rifled the same;
     It was gold and silver store, of which all had a share;
     Each man 600 pounds and more. Let pyrates then take care.

5   Thus for some time we liv'd and reign'd as masters of the sea;
     Every merchant we detain'd and us'd most cruelly.
     The treasures took, we sunk the ship, and those that in it were
     That would not to us submit. Let pyrates then take care.

6   Thus wickedly we every day liv'd upon others' good,
     The which, alas! we must repay now with our dearest blood;
     For we on no one mercy took, nor any did we spare.
     How can we then for money look? Let pyrates then take care.

7   We thus did live most cruelly, and of no danger thought,
     But we, at last, as you may see, are unto justice brought
     For outrages of villainy, of which we guilty are,
     And now this very day must die. Let pyrates then take care.

8   Now farewell to this wicked world, and our companions too;
     From hence we quickly shall be hurl'd to clear the way for you;
     For certainly if e're you come to justice, as we are,
     Deserved death will be your doom. Then pirates all take care.

"Captain Avery receiving the three chests of Treasure on board of his Ship."
Anonymous woodcut engraving from Charles Ellms, *The Pirate's Own Book* (Boston, 1837), page 17.

14

CAPTAIN KIDD
Captain Kid's Farewell to the Seas; or, The Famous Pirate's Lament
(Laws #K-35)

William Kidd is the most famous pirate and "Captain Kidd" is the best known pirate ballad. Part of this notoriety devolves from the persistent popularity of a contemporaneous ballad, "Sam Hall."* But much of it emanates from Kidd's terrible reputation and, in North America, his picaresque associations with the American colonies. Unlike Henry Avery, Bartholomew Roberts, or even Edward Teach, "Blackbeard" — and more dramatically and on an even larger scale than Charles Gibbs or Thomas Tew, who were both native Rhode Islanders — Kidd was a pirate of our own. Uniquely among real pirates (as opposed to fictional pirates who exist only in songs), it was Captain Kidd whose song was sung on shipboard by sailors.

In truth, Captain Kidd was only an adoptive American and not such a great pirate. The son of a Presbyterian minister, he was born in Greenock, Scotland circa 1650-55, went privateering in the West Indies, lost his ship to mutiny in 1691, then settled in New York. There he married a wealthy widow and set up as a merchant. In 1696 he obtained a commission to hunt down pirates in the Indian Ocean aboard his *Adventure Galley,* 34-guns, but "after a series of misfortunes" he sort-of turned pirate himself. His one big coup was taking the *Quedah Merchant* in 1698. Laden with a fabulously rich cargo, the vessel carried a French passport, which led Kidd to believe (or construe) made it fair game for a licensed Englishman. But his crew deserted, the government declared him a pirate, and he was never able to force or negotiate his way back to legitimacy. A futile attempt to exonerate himself ended in his arrest at Boston, whence he was taken to London in chains to be tried for piracy and the murder of William Moore, one of his crew. Abandoned by his friends, excoriated by his enemies, reviled by the public, and constrained from mounting a defense, Kidd was summarily convicted and hanged at Execution Dock on 23 May 1701. Bad luck was with him to the last: the procedure failed on the first attempt and had to be repeated. "The grisly corpse was displayed on a gibbet in the Thames Estuary, remaining for several years in order to serve as 'a greater Terror to all Persons from committing ye like Crimes for the time to come.'" Cordingly calls him a "reluctant pirate" because it was not Kidd's intention to repudiate the laws or good graces of England; he was "the best-known pirate in history... and one of the unluckiest" (Cordingly 1996, 152-61; 1992, 123; 1995, Ch. 10; Firth, 347f; H.K. Johnson, 171).

Kidd was constitutionally unsuited to outlawry. His ill-starred plight was brought on more by poor judgment, unfortunate timing, and betrayal than by any premeditated evil design on his part. There is no evidence that he was as ornery or nihilistic as the ballad portrays, but it is the ballad and the legend that define the character for posterity. The ballad appeared around the time of his death in 1701, and, in one form or another, it has been sung ever since, even as a chantey.

---

* The history of this song (also known as "Samuel Hall" and "Jack Hall") has been controversial. Occasionally recovered from tradition (e.g, "Jack Hall [the Chimney Sweep]" in Sharp 1916, 182; and 1920 II:75; "Sam Hall," in Hugill and Colcord), it has often been called a folk song; when collected from cowboys it has been called a cowboy song (Thorp 1908; Lomax 1910; Lomax 1936). Eckstorm & Smyth (248) are correct in their contention that "'Sam Hall' was an English music hall song of the eighteen-fifties, set to the old tune of 'Captain Kidd' and later parodied"; but they are mistaken in their corollary assumption that *therefore* it was *originally* a music-hall song and could not have had "anything to do" with "Captain Kidd" or the "chimney sweep Jack Hall, who was executed in 1701 for burglary." Even the cowboy song collectors realized that, far from not having anything to do with it, "Sam Hall" and "Captain Kidd" are directly related, to the point of parody. And, as the name is more often *Jack* Hall in English tradition, and he is a chimney sweep, why not a provenance going back to the very time when Kidd himself was hanged? Eckstorm & Smyth contend that Kidd's notoriety would have eclipsed any recollection of a mere chimney sweep executed at around the same time; but they fail to appreciate that it is this very contrast — the ridiculous comparison, and the irony of the comparable fates of Kidd and Hall — that may have preserved Jack Hall's name, or at least his surname. In fact, "Chimney Sweep" was printed as a tune as early as 1719 (Simpson, 673). With reference to the music-hall rendition, which at the very least is ultimately founded on "Captain Kidd" and/or "Chimney Sweep": perhaps it was based on an intermediary chimney-sweep song already in circulation. Disher (161) declares quite specifically that a composer named W. G. Ross authored the lines,

My name it is Sam Hall, chimney sweep,
My name it is Sam Hall, I robs both great and small,
But they makes me pay for all—Damn their eyes. —W.G. Ross

Several tunes survive in tradition, but "Coming down," the one named on the original broad side, may be extinct. Simpson quotes a ballad published circa 1660, "The Royall Subject's Joy" (*Roxburghe,* VII:678), which has a "distinctive stanza form" that it shares with "Captain Kidd":

> You Loyall Subjects all
>   *sing for joy, sing for joy;*
> Good news here's at White-Hall,
>   *sing for joy.*
> A second Charles is come,
> Though heavy news to some,
> Let them say no more but mum,
>   *sing for joy, sing for joy.*

"Royall Subject's Joy" calls for a tune named "Sound a Charge," which, as Simpson elegantly demonstrates, survives under various aliases. It is the closest thing there is to a contemporaneous tune for "Captain Kidd" [Tune A]. Simpson further points out that "The stanza pattern of 'The Royall Subject's Joy' is also found in the more recent ballad 'Sam Hall,' with a fine traditional tune," of which two variants are given here: a standard American form given by the Lomaxes [Tune B]; and Hugill's, from shipboard tradition [C]. Joanna Colcord undoubtedly obtained her "Captain Kidd" tune from Helen Kendrick Johnson, but the implication is that it was known at sea [D]. Finally, there is an anonymous American folk hymn of circa 1854, "What Wondrous Love Is This, O My Soul?" — formally known in liturgical music as "Wondrous Love." This, in its finest manifestation, is a mainstay of the so-called "shape-note" or "Sacred Harp" singing-school repertoire that since the mid 19th century has been a feature of low-church rural worship from Alabama to New Hampshire. Sacred Harp melodies and harmonies were thus very widely dispersed, notably in the same kinds of remote communities where traditional songs and ballads also tended to be preserved. As Simpson's "distinctive stanza form" is the same in both, and as a salvation theme predominates in American versions of "Captain Kidd," it seems likely (as Burl Ives claims) that "Wondrous Love" also provided "Captain Kidd" with a tune [E].

TUNE A: "Sound a Charge," from Simpson, *The British Broadside Ballad and Its Music,* p. 673. Transposed from G minor.

My name is Cap-tain Kidd, who has sail'd, who has sail'd, My name is Cap-tain Kidd, who has sail'd;

My name is Cap-tain Kidd, What the laws did still for-bid Un-luck-i-ly I did while I sail'd, while I sail'd.

TUNE B: "Sam Hall," from the singing of Stan Hugill, North Stonington, Conn., May 1981. Transposed from A Major.

Oh, my name it is Sam Hall, it is Sam Hall; Oh, my name it is Sam Hall, it is Sam Hall; Oh, my

name it is Sam Hall and I hate you one and all, Oh, I hate you one and all, God damn your eyes!

TUNE C: "Samuel Hall," from Stan Hugill, *Shanties from the Seven Seas*, p. 449 (not in the abridged reprint edition). "This ballad had innumerable stanzas, but the latter-day sailing-ship man altered these to suit his fancy and turned up a rattling good capstan shanty [anchor-weighing work song] as follows. J. Reed of the ship *St. Mirren* gave me these verses and I have also seen reference to the singing of it at the capstan in the log of a sailing ship bound out to the West Indies." The lyrics appear to be based on "Jack Hall [Chimney Sweep]" but to have been very heavily influenced by "Captain Kidd," to the point of substituting "as we sailed" for "hear our cries" and "damn your eyes" in the refrain. Something like this (rather than like B) is probably the "fine old tune" to which Simpson refers.

Oh, my name is Sam-uel Hall, as we sail, as we sail, Oh, my name is Sam-uel Hall

as we sail. My name is Sam-uel Hall, and I'm on-ly one foot small, Oh, that's bet-ter than

be-ing tall, as we sail, as we sail, Oh, that's bet-ter than be-ing tall, as we sail.

TUNE D: "Captain Kidd," from Helen Kendrick Johnson, *Our Familiar Songs and Those Who Made Them*, 1881, p. 171. Johnson's setting (for which she gives no source) is undoubtedly Joanna Colcord's source, which Colcord (141) does not identify. Transposed from G minor.

You cap-tains brave and bold, hear our cries, hear our cries,

You cap-tains brave and bold, hear our cries. You cap-tains

brave and bold, tho' you seem un-con-troll'd, Don't for the sake of

gold lose your souls, Don't for the sake of gold lose your souls.

"Captain Kidd hanging in chains," from *The Pirate's Own Book* (Boston, 1837).

- 38 -

TUNE E: "What Wondrous Love Is This?" ["Wondrous Love"]: Traditional "shape-note" or "Sacred Harp" singing-school
arrangement of an anonymous American folk hymn of circa 1854, per T. J. Denison, et al., *Original Sacred Harp* (1911), 159.
Compare Christ-Janer, et al, *American Hymns Old and New* (1980), 299.

"Captain Kidd": Standard American text from *The Forget-Me-Not Songster* (circa 1830) and *Forecastle Songster* (1847 and 1850). American songsters and broadsides (see Laws 1957, 159) generally omit references to the *Quedah Merchant* and to Kidd's pirate cohort, Captain Robert Culliford, present in the English broadside; they are clearly the root sources of the versions given by H.K. Johnson, Colcord, and Shay, among whom the specific provenance is not clear (except that Colcord's is from Johnson); and they generally mistake the pirate's name as *Robert* Kidd (the only correction made in the text below).

1   You captains bold and brave, hear our cries, hear our cries,
        You captains bold and brave, hear our cries;
    You captains brave and bold, tho' you seem uncontrolled,
        Don't, for the sake of gold, lose your souls, lose your souls,
        Don't, for the sake of gold, lose your souls.

2   My name was William Kidd, when I sail'd, when I sail'd
    My name was William Kidd, God's laws I did forbid
        And so wickedly I did, when I sail'd.

3   My parents taught me well, when I sail'd, when I sail'd
    My parents taught me well to shun the gates of hell,
        But against them I rebell'd, when I sail'd.

4   I cursed my father dear, when I sail'd, when I sail'd
    I cursed my father dear, and that he did me bear,
        And so wickedly did swear, when I sail'd.

5   I made a solemn vow, when I sail'd, when I sail'd
    I made a solemn vow, to God I would not bow,
        Nor myself one prayer allow, as I sail'd.

6   I'd a Bible in my hand, when I sail'd, when I sail'd
    I'd a Bible in my hand, by my father's great command,
        And sunk it in the sand, when I sail'd.

7   I murdered William Moore, as I sail'd, as I sail'd
    I murdered William Moore, and left him in his gore,
        Not many leagues from shore, as I sail'd.

8   And being cruel still, as I sail'd, as I sail'd
    And being cruel still, my gunner I did kill,
        And his precious blood did spill, as I sail'd.

9   My mate was sick and died, as I sail'd, as I sail'd
    My mate was sick and died, which much me terrified,
        When he called me to his bed-side, as I sail'd.

10   And unto me he did say, "See me die, see me die"
    And unto me he did say, "Take warning now by me,
        There comes a reckoning day—you must die!"

11   "You cannot then withstand, when you die, when you die
    You cannot then withstand the judgment of God's hand
        But, bound then in iron bands, you must die!"

12   I was sick, and nigh to death, as I sail'd, as I sail'd
    And I was sick and nigh to death, and I vow'd at every breath
        To walk in wisdom's ways, as I sail'd.

13   I thought I was undone, as I sail'd, as I sail'd
      I thought I was undone, and my wicked glass had run,
            But health did soon return, as I sail'd.

14   My repentance lasted not, as I sail'd, as I sail'd
      My repentance lasted not, my vows I soon forgot,
            Damnation's my just lot, as I sail'd

15   I steer'd from sound to sound, as I sail'd, as I sail'd
      I steer'd from sound to sound, and many ships I found,
            Most of which I burned, as I sail'd.

16   I spied three ships from France, as I sail'd
      I spied three ships from France, to them I did advance,
            And took them all by chance, as I sail'd.

17   I spied three ships of Spain, as I sail'd, as I sail'd
      I spied three ships of Spain, and I fired on them amain,
            Till most of them was slain, as I sail'd.

18   I'd ninety bars of gold, as I sail'd, as I sail'd
      I'd ninety bars of gold, and dollars manifold,
            With riches uncontrolled, as I sail'd.

19   Then fourteen ships I saw, as I sail'd, as I sail'd
      Then fourteen ships I saw, and brave men they are,
            Ah, they were too much for me, as I sail'd!

20   Thus being o'ertaken at last, I must die, I must die
      Thus being o'ertaken at last, and into prison cast,
            And sentence being past, I must die.

21   Farewell the raging sea, I must die, I must die
      Farewell the raging sea, to Turkey, France, and Spain
            I never shall see you again, I must die.

22   [In] Newgate now I'm cast, and must die, and must die
      To Newgate I am cast, with a sad and heavy heart,
            To receive my just desert, I must die.

23   To Execution Dock I must go, I must go,
      To Execution Dock will many thousands flock,
            But I must bear the shock, I must die.

24   Come all you young and old, see me die, see me die
      Come all you young and old, you're welcome to my gold,
            For I have lost my soul, and must die.

25   Take a warning now by me, for I must die, for I must die
      Take warning now by me, and shun bad company,
            Lest you come to hell with me, for I must die.

15
BOLD KIDD, THE PIRATE

This is essentially a lost broadside-type ballad that is here partly reconstructed from identifiable shards. The lyrics and melody were collected from Rhode Island as a string of mere fragments, published in Flanders & Olney's *Ballads Migrant in New England*. The text is less indebted to "Captain Kidd" [#14] than to "Henry Martin" [#3] and other ballads of actual sea-fights and near misses. Flanders & Olney's tune fragment appears to be a degraded variant of the second half of "The Banks of Claudie" (Laws #N-40), an Anglo-Irish ballad of early 19th-century vintage that also furnished the tune for one of the greatest ballads of the Old West, "The Texas Rangers"; and in its association with "Texas Rangers" the melody is widely circulated. However, "Banks of Claudie/Texas Rangers" is in a pure mixolydian mode, while the Rhode Island fragment of "Bold Kidd" seems to have evolved into a sweet major. The complex interrelationship of ballad airs is so incestuous that the genealogy of the transformed major-key melody may never be disentangled. In any case, even reconstructed and joined to the ancestral tune, the plot of "Bold Kidd, the Pirate" is a simple tale of escape from the perceived threat of Kidd: it is not made clear in the ballad whether the sail spotted from afar actually *is* Kidd; there is no actual engagement and nothing further is said about the pirate himself (there may have been a lot more verses in the original ballad). It is certainly of interest for its relationship to "Texas Rangers"; and the reconstruction is merely an outline with a superb tune, possibly worth tinkering with to fill in a whole story. The modal air is ordinarily sung *a capella* but lends itself to some dramatic modal harmonies.

A.

Fragmentary text and tune collected by Helen Hartness Flanders from Dr. Lucille Palmer, Professor of Modern Languages at State College, Kingston, R.I., 1945; from Flanders & Olney, *Ballads Migrant in New England,* 26f.

"Great God!," cried the first mate, "What e'er shall we do? That is Bold Kidd the Pi-rate, And he'll hove us to."

'Twas the (8th, 12th?) of October
We set out to sea.
(Two lines here, I think)

We'd not been sailing one day
Or two days, or three,
When the watch in the mizzen (?)
A strange sail did see

....
....
And from her ... ?... sail,
Skull-crossbones did fly.
(Or: The flag on her tops'l)

"Great God," cried the first mate (?)
"Whate'er shall we do?
That is Bold Kidd, the Pirate,
And he'll (she'll) heave us to."

"Oh, no," cried the captain,
"That ne'er shall be so;
We'll N?... the top d'gansail (?)
And from her we'll go."

She chased us all night, boys,
And part of next day
Then she pulled in her spanker,
And fared (Sailed?) far away
Skull crossbones did fly.

B.

Tune: "The Banks of Claudie" (Laws #N-40), also known as "The Texas Rangers" (Laws #A-8)"; with the partially reconstructed text of "Bold Kidd, the Pirate."

'Twas the twelfth day of Oc - to - ber that we set out to sea. We'd not been sail - ing

- 42 -

two days, I'm sure it was not three, While the watch up in the miz-zen a strange sail he did

see A - bear - ing down up - on us while we lay un - der lee.

'Twas the twelfth day of October that we set out to sea.
We'd not been sailing two days, I'm sure it was not three three, [1]
When the watch up in the mizzen a strange sail he did see,
A bearing down upon us while we lay under lee [2]

The vessel drawing nearer, 'twas then we did espy
The flag upon her tops'l, skull-crossbones she did fly
"Great God," cried our first mate, "Whatever shall we do?
That is Bold Kidd the Pirate, and he shall heave us to."

"Oh, no," cried our captain,
    "That ne'er shall be so;
We'll set the main t'gan's'l, [3]
    and from her we shall go."
She chased us all the night, boys,
    and part of the next day;
Then she pulled in her spanker,
    and fared off far away.

BELOW LEFT: "Captain Kidd burying his Bible," from Charles Ellms, *The Pirate's Own Book* (Boston, 1837); and RIGHT: a sailor-made scrimshaw sperm whale tooth bearing a copy of the same image (courtesy of the Dietrich American Foundation).

---

[1] Line from several variant texts of "Henry Martin" (q.v., "Sources," #2).

[2] Line adopted from "The *General Armstrong*," in *The Forget Me Not Songster* (Boston, circa 1840s, etc.), 11; *Forecastle Songster* (1850), 254; *The Sailor's Companion, being a collection of the most favorite sea songs now in vogue* (n.d., n.p.) (has "under *her* lee"), per Neeser, 149; etc.

[3] Main top-gallant sail.

16
CAPTAIN THUNDER

This mild-mannered convivial ditty was written by Thomas D'Urfey (1653-1723) for his musical play *The Comical History of Don Quixote,* produced in London during 1694-95. More lascivious than larcenous, it barely qualifies as a pirate song: the Captain appears to be no blackhearted cut-throat, but merely a predatory sea-rogue ashore, crudely propositioning a woman. She answers saucily and holds out for a higher price, alluding to "plunder" only in passing — as if, in true Restoration fashion, to treat piracy casually as a matter of no real moment. After all, D'Urfey's play is a comedy, where stage pirates are required to be amusing and not too fearsome; and she turns out to be plunderer, too. That the Captain alludes to his "pay," to "King's Money," and to certain financial constraints, indicates that his "plunder" is the booty of a conventional naval career — prize cargoes forcibly but legally extracted from the merchant ships of France, Holland, and Spain. Edmunds reports that there were settings by Henry Purcell and Samuel Ackroyde, among others, but the music here is anonymous.

Dear Pinck - a - nin - ny, if half .... a Guin-ny, To Love will win ye, I lay it here down;

We must be Thrif - ty, 'Twill serve .... to shift ye, And I know Fif-ty, Will do 't for a Crown.

Dunns come so bold-ly, King's mon - ey so slow - ly, That by all things Ho - ly, 'Tis all I can say,

Yet I'm so rapt in, The Snare that I'm trapt in, As I'm a true Cap-tain, Give more than my Pay.

1 Dear Pinckaninny,
  If half a Guinny [guinea],
  To Love will win ye,
    I lay it here down;
  We must be Thrifty,
  'Twill serve to shift ye,
  And I know Fifty,
    Will do't for a Crown.

2 Dunns come so boldly,
  King's Money so slowly,
  That by all things Holy,
    'Tis all I can say;
  Yet I'm so rapt in,
  The snare that I'm trapt in,
  As I'm a true Captain
    Give more than my pay.

3 Good Captain Thunder,
  Go mind your plunder,
  Ods wounds I wonder,
    You dare be so bold;
  Thus to be making,
  A Treaty so sneaking,
  Or Dream too of taking,
    My Fort with small Gold.

4 Other Town Misses,
  May gape at Ten Pieces,
  But who me possesses,
    Full twenty shall Pay;
  To all poor Rogues in Buff,
  Thus, thus I strut and huff,
  So Captain kick and cuff,
    March on your way.

Illustration after Robert Cruikshank for "Be Gone, You Saucy Fellow," *Universal Songster* (London, circa 1825-29), III:305.

17
THE DOWNFALL OF PIRACY
[Teach the Rover]

Being a full and true account of a desperate and bloody sea-fight between Lieutenant *Maynard,* and that noted Pirate Captain *Teach,* commonly call'd by the Name of *Black-Beard; Maynard* had fifty Men, thirty five of which where [sic] kill'd and wounded in the Action: Teach had twenty-one, most of which was kill'd and the rest carried to *Virginia,* in order to take their Tryal.

The most curious thing about this ballad is that, while it is almost always printed anonymously, it is attributed to the juvenile authorship of the great American Founding Father, scientist, inventor, ambassador, printer, cabinet minister, aphorist, and *bon vivant,* Benjamin Franklin (1706-1790). Ostensibly written while precocious young Ben, at age 13, was apprenticed to his brother Peter, a Boston printer, it is one of several such early pieces ascribed to the future Sage. The presumption is that the Franklin brothers printed them up themselves as broadsides. However, the case is not certain. As Ellen Cohn of the Papers of Benjamin Franklin at Yale University reports, "Not a single one of Franklin's broadsides has been located, but it is now generally believed that the text was one of 'three excellent New Songs' published almost a half-century later in an English chapbook, *The Worcestershire Garland,*" published at Newcastle-on-Tyne circa 1765. "There it was entitled 'The Downfall of Piracy'…. The text is just crude enough to suggest a young author, and the details follow almost exactly the accounts published in *The Boston News-Letter,*" Boston's only newspaper at the time, on which Franklin is known to have based other juvenile broadsides (Cohn, 297; also C.S. Smith, 170-177).

Unlike Captain Kidd, who went to the gallows in 1701 protesting his innocence and who, not without some justification, characterized himself as a hapless victim of politics and circumstance, Teach the Rover was a dangerous, volcanic rogue who flaunted his piratical ways and died by the sword. Captain Avery [#12] may have been "the Arch Pirate" and Captain Kidd [#14f] may have been more notorious, but Edward Teach — "Blackbeard" — flamboyant, irreverent, impetuous, cruel — was the most ferocious and the most ostentatious, all in all the quintessential blustering pirate. A native of the English port of Bristol, he arrived at Jamaica during Queen Anne's War as a deckhand aboard a British privateer, and "served his pirate apprenticeship" in the brigantine *Ranger* under Benjamin Hornigold, who made Teach a captain and, eventually, a partner in joint piratical enterprises. In Cordingly's words, "During an eighteen-month rampage" in a prize-ship renamed *Queen Anne's Revenge,*

> Blackbeard ranged from Virginia to Honduras, terrorizing shipping and taking at lest twenty prizes. He burned some ships but added others to his growing fleet. Most of the American colonies had turned their backs on the pirates, but struggling North Carolina, lacking the lucrative trade in rice and indigo that made neighboring colonies strong enough to shun traffic with smugglers and pirates still welcomed them.
>
> Blackbeard was a man of imposing stature and frightening aspect. A mane of thick black hair and a long beard, both plaited with colored ribbons, framed his naturally scowling face with its wild-looking deep-set eyes. In battle, armed with three brace of pistols slung in bandoliers, he appeared to be a fury from hell, with smoldering gunner's matches sticking out from under his hat. Blackbeard's awesome figure was matched by his extravagant and impetuous temperament. Even his own men were subjected to terrifying displays calculated to cow the observers. (Cordingly 1996, 114f)

Blackbeard was the epitome of the glowering, explosive, colorful piratical stereotype, who was trained by, partnered with, and dwelled among the most notorious brigands of his day. It is therefore remarkable that his infamy did not inspire a host of contemporaneous ballads and songs, even if his actual pirate career spanned only two or three years. However, there is no shortage of such things nowadays. Since the advent of Hollywood cinema, Blackbeard has regained and even perhaps exceeded the celebrity that attached to him during his lifetime and in the decades after his dramatic demise.

Blackbeard's Atlantic lair was also a quintessence. By 1716 the island of New Providence in the Bahamas had become a "Nest of Pyrates." There,

English pirate chieftains Thomas Barrow and Benjamin Hornigold proclaimed a pirate republic with themelves as governors.... They were joined by leading captains such as Charles Vane, Thomas Burgess, Calico Jack Rackham [ultimately accompanied by Anne Bonny and Mary Read], and Blackbeard. Ex-privateers and outlaws from all over the New World swelled the population of the pirate sanctuary.... After a cruise, pirates looked forward to shore leave on New Providence, which met the recreational requirements of women and wine. It was every pirate's wish to find himself not in heaven after death but back on that island paradise where the resting rovers could laze in their hammocks beneath the palms, swinging gently in the fanning breezes. (Cordingly 1996, 108f)

Nor did Captain Teach ultimately find himself "swinging gently" in a "fanning breeze" of the very final kind that had eventually caught up with Captain Kidd. Blackbeard died with his boots on, sword in hand, in the James River estuary of Virginia on 22 November 1718, in hand-to-hand combat with Lieutenant Robert Maynard, commander of a navy expedition in RMS *Pearl* on orders specifically to dispatch the pirate (Firth, lii). Blackbeard's severed head "was hung below Maynard's bowsprit as proof of his death and taken to Bath and then back to Virginia, where it was stripped of flesh and hung from a pole at the mouth of the Hampton River" as a caveat for other buccaneers "on the account." Meanwhile, thirteen of his pirate cohorts "were tried and condemned to death at Williamsburg [Virginia]" (Cordingly 1996, 116).

"The Downfall of Piracy" commemorates Maynard's exploit and the pirate's demise, forming "a fitting close" to the classic age of piracy (Firth, lii) and to the classic age of pirate balladry. Firth's and Ashton's mutual source was evidently a specimen of *The Worcestershire Garland* in the British Museum (Firth, 351), but, unaccountably, neither Firth nor Ashton reports a tune. However, Carleton Sprague Smith (p. 173) gives a facsimile illustration of the original chapbook which clearly corroborates his assertion (p. 175) that the tune called for in *The Worcestershire Garland* is "What is greater joy and pleasure." According to Chappell, it was first printed in Walsh's *British Musical Miscellany* in 1730, but it is more commonly known by the names of several other texts that later became associated with it: "Welcome, welcome, brother debtor," "Come and listen to my ditty," "The Sailor's Complaint," and especially the sea-song known as "Cease, Rude Boreas." The latter was the incarnation best known to 18th- and 19th-century sailors in connection with lyrics formally entitled "The Storm" (of which "Cease, rude Boreas, blust'ring railer..." is the first line), written by the Scots poet George Alexander Stevens (circa 1710-1784) circa 1754. The setting here is from a circa 1775 edition of the sheet music for "The Storm."

Will you hear of a blood-y bat-tle, late-ly fought up-on the seas? It will make your ears to

rat-tle and your ad-mi-ra-tion cease: Have you heard of Teach the rov-er, and his

knav-er-y on the main; How of gold he was a lov-er, how he lov'd ill got-ten gain?

1 Will you hear of a bloody battle,
    lately fought upon the seas?
It will make your ears to rattle
    and your admiration cease:
Have you heard of Teach the rover,
    and his knavery on the main;
How of gold he was a lover,
    how he lov'd ill gotten gain?

2 When the Acts of Grace appeared,
    Captain Teach and all his men
Unto Carolina steered,
    where they us'd him kindly then;
There he marry'd to a lady,
    and gave her five hundred pound,
But to her he prov'd unsteady,
    for he soon march'd off the ground.

3 And returned, as I tell you,
    to his robbery as before:
Burning, sinking ships of value,
    filling them with purple gore.
When he was in Carolina,
    there the Governor did send
To the Governor of Virginia,
    that he might assistance lend.

4 Then our man-of-war's commander,
    two small sloops he fitted out;
Fifty men he put on board, sir,
    who resolv'd to stand it out.
The lieutenant he commanded
    both the sloops, and you shall hear
How before he landed
    he suppress'd them without fear.

5 Valiant Maynard as he sail'd
    soon the pirate did espy;
With his trumpet then he hailed,
    and to him they did reply:
"Captain Teach is our commander."
    Maynard said, "He is the man
Whom I am resolved to hang, sir,
    let him do the best he can."

6 Teach replied unto Maynard,
    "You no quarter here shall see,
But be hanged on the mainyard,
    you and all your company."
Maynard said, "I none desire
    of such knaves as thee and thine."
"None I'll give," Teach then replied;
    "My boys, give me a glass of wine."

7 He took the glass and drank damnation
    unto Maynard and his crew,
To himself and generation,
    then a glass away he threw.
Brave Maynard was resolved to have
    him, tho' he'd cannons nine or ten:
Teach a broadside quickly gave him,
    killing sixteen valiant men.

8 Maynard boarded him and to it
    they fell with sword and pistol too;
They had courage, and did show it,
    killing of the pirate's crew.
Teach and Maynard on the quarter
    fought it out most manfully;
Maynard's sword did cut him shorter,
    losing his head he did there die.

9 Every sailor fought while he, sir,
    power had to wield his sword,
Not a coward could you see, sir,
    fear was driven from aboard;
Wounded men on both sides fell, sir,
    'twas a doleful sight to see,
Nothing could their courage quell, sir;
    O they fought courageously.

10 When the bloody fight was over
    we're informed by letter writ,
Teach's head was made a cover
    to the jack-staff of the ship;
Thus they sailed to Virginia,
    and when they the story told
How they killed the pirates many,
    they'd applause from young and old.

"Franklin at Ten Years of Age." Anonymous engraving.
Harper's New Monthly Magazine, 20:4 (Jan. 1852), 146.

LONG-SONG SELLER.
" Two under fifty for a fardy'!"

THE BALLAD SELLER

HERE are catches, songs, and glees,
    Some are twenty for a penny;
You shall have what'er you please,
    Take your choice, for here are many.
Here is "Nan of Glo'ster-green,"
    Here's "The Lily of the Valley,"
Here is "Kate of Aberdeen,"
    Here is "Sally in our Alley."

Here is "Mary's Dream"—"Poor Jack,"
    Here's "The Tinker and the Tailor,"
Here's "Bow, wow" and "Paddy Whack,"
    "Tally ho!"—"The Hardy Sailor."
Here's "Dick Dock"—"The hearty Blade,"
    "Captain Wattle" and "The Grinder,"
And I've got "The Cottage Maid,"
    Confound me, though, if I can find her.

Drinking songs, too, here abound,
    "Toby Philpot"—"Fill the Glasses,"
And "Why [sic] stands the Glass around?"
    "Here's a health to all good Lasses,"
Here's "Come, let us dance and sing,"
    And, what's better far than any,
Here's "God save great George our King,"
    "Hearts of Oak," and "Rule Britannia."

ILLUSTRATION: "Long-Song Seller: 'Two under fifty for a fardy'!' [i.e., *48 for a farthing*]," engraved by W.G. Mason after H.G. Hine, in Henry Mayhew, *London Street-Folk* (1851) (*London Labour and the London Poor,* 4 vols., 1851-64, Volume 1), 209. LYRICS: "The Ballad Seller," anonymous, no tune indicated, from *The Universal Songster* (3 vols., London, circa 1825-29), I:9.

Part Two: Broadside Ballads of Bold Rovers

... One of the most peculiar features of [the Booble-Alleys of Liverpool] is the number of sailor ballad-singers, who, after singing their verses, hand you a printed copy, and beg you to buy. One of these persons, dressed like a man-of-war's-man, I observed every day standing at a corner in the middle of the street. He had a full, noble voice, like a church-organ; and his notes rose high above the surrounding din. But the remarkable thing about this ballad-singer was one of his arms, which, while singing, he somehow swung vertically round and round in the air, as if it revolved on a pivot. The feat was naturally unaccountable; and he performed it with the view of attracting sympathy; since he said that in falling from a frigate's mast-head to the deck, he had met with an injury, which resulted in making his wonderful arm what it was.

I made the acquaintance of this man, and found him no common character. He was full of marvelous adventures, and abounded in terrific stories of pirates and sea murders, and all sorts of nautical enormities. He was a Newgate Calendar of the robberies and assassinations of his day, happening in the sailor quarters of the town; and most of his ballads were upon kindred subjects. He composed many of his own verses, and had them printed for sale on his own account. To show how expeditious was his business, it may be mentioned, that one evening on leaving the dock to go to supper, I perceived a crowd gathered about the *Old Fort Tavern;* and mingling with the rest, I learned that a woman of the town had just been killed at the bar by a drunken Spanish sailor rom Cadiz. The murderer was carried off by the police before my eyes, and the very next morning the ballad-singer with the miraculous arm, was singing the tragedy in front of the boarding-houses, and handing round printed copies of the song, which, of course, were eagerly bought up by the seamen.

— Herman Melville, *Redburn* (1849), Ch. 39

Even if the specifics be apocryphal, Melville's characterization is accurate. When he called at Liverpool as a young packet-ship foremast hand in 1838, a visit that formed the partial basis for his urban portrait in *Redburn,* catchpenny ballads and cheap broadsides were having a heyday. From the late 18th century through the first six or seven decades of the 19th, contemporaneously with the Industrial Revolution and the Romantic and Victorian eras, ballads of various kinds were printed up and hawked on street corners for a penny or two, not only in the British Isles — London, Newcastle, Bristol, Glasgow, Dublin, and some of the smaller cities — but also, to a lesser degree, in America and the Colonies — New York, Philadelphia, Boston, Sydney. They were latter-day equivalents of the old blackletter ballads, borrowed from traditional sources, or adapted and versified from the popular press, or written especially for the occasion. Many were coeval with the newsworthy or sensational events they portray, and like the old blackletter ballads, most were set to pre-existing tunes that circulated from ballad to ballad. For some broadside publishers, like the inimitable James Catnach (1792-1841) and his arch rival, John Pitts (1765-1844), ballad-mongering became a successful business, with writers and printers in their regular employ; others, like Melville's ballad-selling entrepreneur in *Redburn,* operated on a far more modest scale. Many of the ballads perished unnoticed and unsung; others were widely circulated, even finding their way into tradition and migrating across the Atlantic.

A surprisingly large proportion concern sailors and seafaring, but only a few involve piracy; and despite that few of them bear any sign of nautical sophistication or technical expertise — suggesting shore origins — many became popular among sailors and appear to have been widely circulated on shipboard well into the 20th century.

Picking up where Francis James Child left off (see "The Old Ballads," above), G. Malcolm Laws formulated a parallel canon of the latter-day English-language broadside ballads manifest in North America. The ones imported from the British Isles are gathered in *American Balladry from British Broadsides* (1959); and in *Native American Balladry* (1964), Laws reports the ones believed to be indigenous. His taxonomy, employing a numbering system that stretches across both camps, is useful in comparing ballads thematically and tracing the extent to which a given ballad may have been disseminated in North America. It is also quite useful in identifying (if nothing else, by their absence from the list) manifestations of ballads that may have fallen out of tradition or become extinct before folklorist-collectors came on the scene to record them. Such manifestations — remnants of ballads that may be known nowhere else — are occasionally found as transcriptions in whalemen's shipboard journals.

18
WILL WATCH, THE BOLD SMUGGLER

Strictly speaking, this is not a "pure" broadside ballad. Rather than making its first appearance in print as a broadside, it had already been published, and presented on the London stage, when it was issued in a cheap, popular format sometime during or just after the Napoleonic era. And instead of the usual anonymous hack authorship typical of broadside ballads, the hack authorship in this case is attributable to one Thomas Cory circa 1806, with the music perpetrated by the professional composer and dramatist John Davy (1765-1824). Nor is it quite a true pirate song, either: Will Watch is merely a smuggler, practicing piracy in its mildest form, if it be piracy at all. On the other hand, cannon fire and funerals were as real for smugglers as for pirates, regardless of what particular transgression may have invited them. This ballad has both, along with clever syntax, a sea fight, and certainly a more cogent moral purpose than many pirate ballads. Writing in 1910, Captain Whall says of it, "Will Watch, the bold smuggler, was a favourite sea hero fifty years ago…. It is quoted by both Marryat and Chamier…. I fear it would sound out of place now alongside the music-hall twaddle usually heard; but in the days when a song, to be appreciated at sea, had to be very professional or very sentimental, this one, somewhat combining the two, was a favourite." The text here is from one of a series of cheap little broadside-like pamphlets entitled *A Garland of New Songs,* published by J. Marshall at Newcastle-on-Tyne circa 1815, with a generic woodcut illustration (as illustrated opposite).

'Twas one morn when the wind from the noth-ward blew keen-ly, While sud-den-ly roar'd the big waves of the main,

A fam'd smug-gler, Will Watch, kiss'd his Sue, then se-rene-ly Took helm and to sea bold-ly steer'd out a-gain.

Will had prom-is'd his Sue that this trip, if well end-ed, Should coil up his hopes, and he'd an-chor a-shore;

When his pock-ets were lin'd, why his life should be mend-ed, The laws he had brok-en he'd nev-er break more.

1   'Twas one morn when the wind from the northward blew keenly,
     While suddenly roar'd the big waves of the main,
   A fam'd smuggler, Will Watch, kis'd his Sue then serenely,
     Took helm and to sea boldly steer'd out again.
   Will had promis'd his Sue that this trip, if well ended,
     Should coil up his hopes, and he'd anchor ashore;
   When his pockets were lin'd, why his life should be mended,
     The laws he had broken he's never break more.

2   His sea boat was trim, made her port, took her lading,
      Then Will Stood for home, reach'd the offing, and cried,
   This night (if I've luck) furls the sails of my trading:
      In dock I can lay, serve a friend, too, beside.
   Will lay too [lay to] till the night came on darksome and dreary,
      To croud every sail then he pip'd up each hand;
   But a signal soon spied, 'twas a prospect uncheering,
      A signal that warn'd him to bear from the land.

A
GARLAND
OF
NEW SONGS.

Will Watch the bold Smuggler
Jockey to the Fair
Come, hafte to the Wedding
The Maid of Bedlam
Jenny Nettles

Newcaftle upon Tyne:
Printed by J. Marfhall, in the Old Flefh-Market.
Where may alfo be had, a large and curious Affortment
of Songs, Ballads, Tales, Hiftories, &c.

3   The Philistines are out, cries
      Will, well, take no head on't,
   Attack'd, whose the man who
      will flinch from his gun;
   Should my head be blown off, I
      shall ne'er feel the need on't,
   We'll fight while we can—when
      we can't, boys, we'll run.
   Thro' the haze of the night a bright
      light flash now appearing,
   Oh! oh! cries Will Watch, the
      Philistines bear down,
   Bear a hand, my tight lads, ere
      we think about sheering,
   One broadside pour in, should be
      swim, boys, or drown.

4   But should I be popt off, you, my
      mates left behind me,
   Regard my last words, see them
      kindly obey'd,
   Let no stone mark the spot; and
      my friends, do you mind me,
   Near the beach is the grave where
      Will Watch would be laid.
   Poor Will's yarn was spun out;
      for a bullet next minute,
   Laid him low on the deck, and he
      never spoke more;
   His bold crew fought the brig,
      while a shot remained in it,
   Then sheer'd, and Will's hulk to
      his Susan they bore.

5   In the dead of the night his last will was complied with,
      To few known his grave, and to few known his end;
   He was borne to the earth by the crew that he died with,
      He's the tears of his Susan, the prayers of each friend.
   Near the grave dam the billows, the winds loudly bellow,
      Yon ash struck with lightning points out the cold bed,
   Where Will Watch, the bold smuggler, that fam'd lawless fellow,
      Once fear'd, now forgot, sleeps in peace with the dead.

19

THE *FLYING CLOUD*
(Laws K-28)

Here a remorseful prisoner confesses his involvement in the two darkest chapters of seafaring, the illicit trade in African slaves and piracy on the high seas. Like many 19th-century broadsides, it is styled as a jailhouse memoir, with a warning to other young lads to steer clear of a life of crime. As such it is the diametrical opposite of "Sam Hall" (the landlubberly counterpart of "Captain Kidd," #14), in which an unrepentant outlaw spits at the world and repudiates expiation. The *Flying Cloud* ballad predates the great Clipper Ship Era of the early 1850s and, by at least a decade or two, the famous clipper ship *Flying Cloud* of New York. The "clippers" alluded to here are the so-called Baltimore Clippers of the early 19th century—sleek, sharp-hulled, heavily-rigged vessels of intermediate size, with raked masts, built for speed and able to outrun most naval and patrol vessels. The Baltimore Clipper was thus the vessel-of-preference for many brigands and illicit traders. (The line in stanza 10, "logging fourteen off the reel," is a calculation of speed, i.e., *fourteen knots,* as measured by the *taffrail log,* a kind of shipboard speedometer. This is indeed fast for a sailing vessel.) Enforcement of prohibitions on slaving, smuggling, and piracy at that time was largely in the hands of the Royal Navy, and the *Dungeness* seems like a good name for a British Navy ship. But according to the definitive inventory compiled by David Lyon, there never was any vessel by that name in the official naval service. Perhaps the vessel was a licensed privateer.

The narrator's name and some of the locales vary among several extant manifestations of the ballad. The given name is usually Edward or William. The surname is often Hallahan or Halloran, and, as these are consistent with the stated Irish ancestry, one of these may be original. Anderson or Hollander is often substituted, especially in American texts. Greig's version puts the tonnage of the *Flying Cloud* at "six hundred and more," rather than "five hundred and more," in either case large for a Baltimore Clipper. But apart from these variations, in essence the text has remained remarkably stable. In most versions the narrator meets Captain Moore and joins the *Flying Cloud* crew in Cuba, is captured by the British ship *Dungeness,* and is incarcerated at Newgate Prison in London. The most dramatic departure appears in one of Doerflinger's texts, where the narrator encounters Captain Moore and the *Flying Cloud* at Valparaiso, they are captured by a Spanish warship named *Dungeon* (a transparent and understandable corruption of *Dungeness,* shared with Greig's Scottish text), and they are taken to an unnamed port in Spanish jurisdiction ("For on the gallows I must die by the laws of a Spanish land").

My name is Ed - ward Hol - lan - der, as you may un - der - stand; I was born in the town of
Wa - ter - ford, in E - rin's hap - py land. When I was young and in my prime, kind for - tune
on me smiled; My pa - rents raised me ten - der - ly, I was their on - ly child.

1 My name is Edward Hollander, as you may understand;
   I was born in the town of Waterford, in Erin's happy land.
   When I was young and in my prime, kind fortune on me smiled;
   My parents raised me tenderly, I was their only child.

2 My father bound me to a trade in Waterford's fair town,
   He bound me to a cooper there by the name of William Brown;
   I served my master faithfully for eighteen months and more,
   Till I shipped aboard the Ocean Queen belonging to Tramore.

3 When we came unto Bermuda's isle, there I met with Captain Moore,
   The commander of the *Flying Cloud,* hailing from Baltimore;
   He asked me if I'd ship with him, on a slaving voyage to go,
   To the burning shores of Africa, where the sugar cane does grow.

4 It was after some weeks' sailing we arrived on Africa's shore,
   And five hundred of those poor slaves, my boys, from their native land we bore.
   The crew they marched them on the deck and stowed them down below;
   Scarce eighteen inches to a man was all they had to go.

5 The plague and fever came on board, swept half of them away;
   We dragged their bodies up on deck and hove them in the sea.
   It was better for the rest of them if they had died before,
   Than to work under brutes of planters in Cuba for ever more.

6 It was after stormy weather we arrived off Cuba's shore,
   And we sold them to the planters there to be slaves for ever more.
   For the rice and the coffee seed to sow beneath the broiling sun,
   There to lead a wretched lonely life till their career was run.

7 It's now our money was all spent, we must go to sea again,
   When Captain Moore he came on deck and said unto us men:
   "There is gold and silver to be had if with me you'll remain,
   And we'll hoist the pirate flag aloft and scour the Spanish Main."

8 We all agreed but three young men who told us them to land,
   And two of them were Boston boys, the other from Newfoundland.
   I wish to God I'd joined those men and went with them on shore,
   Than to lead a wild and reckless life, serving under Captain Moore.

9 The *Flying Cloud* was a Yankee ship of five hundred tons or more,
   She could outsail any clipper ship hailing out of Baltimore.
   With her canvas white as the driven snow, and on it there's no specks,
   And forty men and fourteen guns she carried on her decks.

10 It's oft I've seen that gallant ship with the wind abaft her beam,
   With her royals and her stu'nsails set, a sight for to be seen;
   With the curling waves at her clipper bow, a sailor's joy to feel,
   And the canvas taut in the whistling breeze, logging fourteen off the reel.

11 We sank and plundered many a ship down on the Spanish Main,
   Caused many a wife and orphan in sorrow to remain;
   To them we gave no quarter, but gave them watery graves,
   For the saying of our captain was that dead men tell no tales.

"The Execution of Ten Pirates." Woodcut illustration from Charles Ellms, *The Pirate's Own Book* (Boston, 1837), 403.

12 Pursued we were by many a ship, by frigates and liners, too,
    Till at last a British warship, the *Dungeness,* hove in view;
    She fired a shot across our bow, as we sailed before the wind,
    Then a chain shot cut our mainmast down and we fell far behind.

13 Our crew they beat to quarters as she ranged up alongside,
    And soon across out quarterdeck there ran a crimson tide.
    We fought till Captain Moore was killed and twenty of our men,
    Till a bombshell set our ship on fire; we had to surrender then.

14 It's next to Newgate we were brought, bound down in iron chains,
    For the sinking and the plundering of ships on the Spanish Main.
    The judge he found us guilty, we were condemned to die;
    Young men a warning take by me, and shun all piracy.

15 Then fare you well, old Waterford, and the girl that I adore,
    I'll never kiss your cheek again, or squeeze your hand no more.
    For whiskey and bad company first made a wretch of me;
    Young men a warning take by me, and shun all piracy.

THE BOLD *PRINCESS ROYAL*

(Laws K-29)

Speed was not always on the side of the pirates. Here, a fast vessel and good seamanship save the day when a merchantman is faced with a challenge like the one put by Henry Martin [#3]. This is one of the best of the broadside pirate ballads. Small wonder that it was a favorite aboard American and Canadian ships: the captain's courage and the escape from trouble must have been particularly gratifying to seamen. The ballad was fairly widely disseminated ashore, too, in the British Isles, Maritime Canada, along the New England seacoast, and in the West Indies. Details and place names differ quite a lot in the various texts but the plot remains constant. A splendid melody from Norfolk collected by Ralph Vaughan Williams in 1908 [Tune A] is especially beautiful in his noble piano setting. Tune B, learned from Stan Hugill, typifies the tune prevalent in North American tradition: it is similar to Creighton's and to one of Doerflinger's; Colcord's modal air is quite different. A specimen from the Cayman Islands entitled simply "Pirate Song" [Text B, with a melody of its own] is a unique manifestation along conventional lines.

TUNE A: Collected from tradition in Norfolk, transcribed, and arranged by Ralph Vaughan Williams, 1908 (Sharp 1908, II:40). The guitar accompaniment here can only approximate inadequately Vaughan Williams' brilliant piano accompaniment.

On the four-teen of Ap-ril we sailed from the land, In the bold Prin-cess Roy-al bound for New-found-land, We had for-ty brave sea-men for our ship's com-pa-ny, And bold-ly from the east-ward to the west-ward sailed we.

TUNE B: Attributed to Newfoundland. Learned from Stan Hugill at North Stonington, Connecticut, May 1981.

On the four-teen of Ap-ril we sailed from the land, In the bold Prin-cess Roy-al bound for New-found-land, We had for-ty brave sea-men for our ship's com-pa-ny, And bold-ly from the east-ward to the west-ward sailed we.

1   On the fourteenth of April we sailed from the land,
       In the bold Princess Royal bound for Newfoundland,
       We had forty brave seamen for our ship's company,
       And boldly from the eastward to the westward sailed we.

2   We had not been sailing past days two or three,
       When a man from our foremast a sail he did see,
       She hove down upon us to see what we were,
       And under her mizzen black colours she wore.

3   Now this bloody bold pirate hove up alongside,
       With a large speaking-trumpet, "Whence come you?" he cried.
       Our captain being aft, boys, he answered him so; —
       "I'm out from Gibraltar and we're bound for Callao [*"Caliyo"*]."

4   "Then back your main topsail and heave your ship to!
       For I have some letters to send home by you."
       "When I back my topsail and heave my ship to
       'Twill be in some harbour, not alongside of you!"

5   "Shake the reefs from your topsails, more canvas to spread;
       Fall to with a will, boys, and so heave ahead.
       And loose your t'ga'ns'ls, your royals also,
       And we'll give her all canvas and away we will go!"

6   He chased us to windward for glasses one or two,
       He chased us to loo'ard, but nothing could he do,
       He fired some shots after us, but could not prevail,
       When the bold Princess Royal soon showed him her tail.

7   "Thank God," cried the captain, "the pirate is gone.
       Go down to your grog, boys, go down every one,
       Go down to your grog, boys, and be of good cheer,
       For whilst we have sea-room, no pirate we'll fear."

B.

"Pirate Song." From the singing of Captain Carl Bush, born 1903, a native of South Sound, Cayman Islands. Captain Bush "went to sea from an early age and spent a total of 52 years on ships." He says of the ballad: "That's a true story. We had an old man up here that had been around Europe quite a lot, and when he came he brought that. That's a real pirate song." The name of the ship under attack is *Royal Princess Rufus*, an obvious derivation from *Princess Royal* and *Prince Rupert* [see #6, "High Barbary"]. Textual eccentricities are similar to Creighton's, e.g., the reference to Bordeaux (rather than Callao or Cairo) and, notably, that while the captain is distraught at their prospects ("Oh, what will we do?"), the mate is calm and it is his plan to skedaddle. The tune appears to be reconstituted from several ballad airs, including "Bold *Princess Royal*." Except for minor punctuation changes in stanza 6, the words, music, and accompaniment here are as printed in *Traditional Songs from the Cayman Islands*.

'Twas the eigh-teenth of Jan-ua-ry we sail'd from the Strand, There was fif-ty bold sea-men bound out from Cay-man.

There was fif-ty bold sea-men, our ship's com-pa-ny, As we sail'd from to the west-ward, to the east-ward sail'd we.

1 Twas the eighteenth of January we sailed from the Strand,
There was fifty bold seamen bound out from Cayman,
There was fifty bold seamen, our ship's company,
As we sailed from to the westward, to the eastward sailed we.

2 We had not been sailing for many a long mile,
When the man from our mast he'd sing: "Sail-ho," he cried,
"Come sail-ho, come sail-ho, sing sail-ho," he cried,
"Here come's a bold tops'l schooner on the weather 'bout side."

3 And whither ye, and whither ye, our captain," he cried,
"Here come's a bold tops'l schooner on the weather 'bout side."
So our old captain took a spyglass to see what he could see,
And on her fore topmast he spied a black flag.

4 "Oh, dear me! Oh, dear me! Oh what shall we do?
Here comes some bold pirates gonna rob us I know,"
Our chief mate he answered, "These things shall not be,
Watch, you shake out those reef points and away we shall flee."

5 So in less than ten minutes, she pulled up along side,
With a loud voice speaking trumpet say, "Where are you from?"
Our captain being bold he answered him so,
"We are just from Gibraltar bound up to Bordeaux."

6 "Watch your back, your main topsails and heave your ship two [sic],
For I'm some bold pirate has a message for you."
"I'll back my two top sails, I'll heave my ship to,
To have been so close to harbour not alongside of you."

7 So he chased us to windward that whole live-long day,
She chased us to windward till our ship would not stay,
That old pirate he fired a blank shot thinking that would prevail,
As the bold *Royal Princess Rufus* showed the pirate her tail.

8 Since the pirate has left us, we've nothing to fear,
With a glass of good whiskey likewise good beer,
Go down to your hammock, I say, every seaman,
With a glass of good whiskey and the best of red rum.

9 That pirate, that pirate, that pirate alone,
That pirate has left us plenty of sea room,
Go down to your hammock, I say, every seaman,
With a flask of good whiskey, likewise England's rum.

THE BOLD PIRATE
(Laws K-30)

This rare ballad has been collected in Maine, New Brunswick, and Nova Scotia, however it was not common; it was even scarcer in Britain and it does not appear in period songsters. But as the extant texts specify a "royal" ship with a British crew and Bristol as the port of embarkation, and as it certainly has the flavor of an English broadside, the presumption (in which Malcolm Laws implicitly concurs) is of British origin. Fanny Eckstorm and Mary Smyth call it "a fine old pirate song," and their composite text, from Maine, is by far the best—though, lamentably, they do not provide music. The tune from New Brunswick [A], almost the only one extant, is unusual, even bizarre. Collector Edward Ives' informant was evidently unable to sing very well and the melody is obviously flawed, notwithstanding Ives' efforts to restore it by "conjecture." The restoration here [Tune B] — also conjectural — leans more towards modal orthodoxy. The text from Maine also tends towards orthodoxy. In the New Brunswick version the narration is almost wholly in the pirate's voice, but a third-person narrative voice takes over just in time to relate the pirate's demise. The Maine text conforms more to the usual format: a first-person narrator sustains it all the way through, with intermittent interruptions for the ship-to-ship hallooing and catcalls that characterize pirate ballads since "Sir Andrew Barton" [#2]. Interesting features are a fair degree of nautical sophistication, suggesting sailor authorship or sailor-driven textual refinements that are consistent with its life in maritime North America: references to walking the plank (stanza 5) and to taking the pirate ship as a prize (stanza 14), which certainly makes better fiscal sense than scuttling or burning it; and, at the end, the resolve not to go to sea again, which, in one form or another, typifies literally dozens of sailors' ballads and chanteys.

TUNE A: Edward D. Ives's partly conjectural transcription, collected in New Brunswick.

TUNE B: The durations of notes slightly adjusted to accommodate Eckstorm's lyrics; and slightly revised (i.e., the flatted seventh restored throughout, resulting in a purer six-tone mixolydian mode).

'Twas on the eigh-teenth day of March we sail'd from Bris-tol town, And we sail'd all that live-long day till the night came rol-ling on. And then we saw a bold pi-rate sail-ing three foot to our one; He hail'd us in Eng-lish and ask'd us whence we come.

1   'Twas on the eighteenth day of March
      We sailed from Bristol Town,
  And we sail-ed all that livelong day
      Till the night came rolling on.

2   And then we saw a bold pirate
      Sailing three foot to our one;
  He hail-ed us in English,
      And asked us whence we come.

3   We told him we was from Bristol Town,
      And on our course was bound,
  And ask-ed of him the reason why
      He ran us so fast down.

4   Up spoke this bold old pirate,
      "I soon will let you know!
  Haul down your fore and main courses
      And let your ship lie to,

5   "And if you fire one shot at me,
      This instant you I'll sink,
  And every man you have on board
      This day shall walk the plank."

6   Then up spoke our brave commander,
      And says, "No such thing can be
  While we have twenty-eight brass guns
      To bear us company.

7   "Besides we have three hundred men,
      All British seamen bold,
  Who value more their honor
      Than a miser does his gold."

8   Then this bold pirate boarded us
      With three hundred of his men;
  With pistols, pikes, and cutlasses
      We soon did slaughter them.

9   He haul-ed down our ensign flag,
      Thinking our royal ship to take;
  We ran them such a rig, my boys,
      Made their very hearts to ache.

10   Then this bold pirate boarded us
      With the remainder of his men;
  By the word of our commander bold,
      We soon did slaughter them.

11   And out of that five hundred men
      We reduc-ed them to three [*two*],
  And down on their knees for mercy cried,
      But none it was their due.

12   Then this old pirate strove from us,
      And tried to run away;
  But a broadside from a rounded gun
      Caus-ed him to stay.

13   We h'isted out our boats from the buoys
      And boarded her immediately;
  And there we saw this bold commander
      With both legs shot off to his knees.

14   We took her all in tow, my boys,
      What a glorious sight to see!
  We towed her in to the sight of land,
      Beside the Bristol quay.

15   Where each one had his fortune made
      And we each got safe on shore,
  We'll ask one another to dine together
      And not plough the sea any more.

KELLY THE PIRATE (I)
(Laws K-31)

In his splendid, illustrated journal of a whaling voyage aboard the ship *Lucy Ann* of Wilmington, Delaware in the 1840s, John F. Martin describes shipboard musical activities in charming detail. Amateur theatricals and musical soirees performed by the crew were not uncommon aboard whaleships to relieve the tedium of long months at sea. Sometimes these involved elaborate costuming and even handwritten concert bills, listing the order of performance, cast, and other credits. Martin provides particulars about an evening performance held on deck on 16 February 1842 in which many of the crew participated as singers, musicians, and comics. One of the songs on that occasion was "Kelly the Pirate," sung by a sailor pseudonymously listed only as "King David." Apparently the pirate song was so well received that it was performed again on March 30th—this time by a shipmate named Chub and the ship's steward, who "sang together holding on to each others hands & when they came to the part we'll clap a few Yankee pills into her tail they throw their hats & Jackets on deck with furious looking countenances which never fails to produce a roar among the crew." *Clap a few Yankee pills into her tail* is a double or triple entendre, the literal meaning of which is *to fire some American cannonballs into the stern of the pirate ship.* The secondary libidinal meanings, and tertiary medical implications, are not difficult to imagine, especially given that *clap* and *tail* are the operative words, and the crew were a couple of dozen young lads in their teens and twenties cooped up on a ship for months at a time.[1]

There are two quite similar ballads about "Kelly the Pirate." This one, undoubtedly the older form, is found in British broadsides (one of which was printed by John Pitts, perhaps as early as the 1780s and in any case before 1810) and has survived in tradition in England, Ireland, and Nova Scotia. The other [#23] is found in American songsters and less often in tradition. The version sung aboard the *Lucy Ann* was clearly an American adaptation of the British broadside text here: the passage quoted is from the third stanza ("We'll give her a few English pills in her tail") and does not appear in the other form of "Kelly the Pirate." Creighton points out that in a text she collected from Terence Bay, Nova Scotia, "Nova Scotia place names have been substituted for those in the old English song": in her variant the line corresponding to the one quoted by the whaleman is, "Then we clapped a few *Terence Bay Quills* in her tail" (italics added). In whatever form, this line seems to be one of the distinguishing features of this form of the ballad; the others are that it is presented as a sailor's Come-All-Ye and has no refrain.

George Kelly was an imaginary pirate; however, an interesting feature of the broadside is the allusion to John Paul Jones (1747-1792), whom Americans call a naval hero of the Revolutionary War but about whom there is a British ballad called "Paul Jones the Pirate" (Logan, 38).

Come bold Brit-ish tars, give an ear to my song, If you'll pay at-ten-tion, I'll not keep you long,

It is of a staunch frig-ate, a ship of great fame, How she fo't that great pi-rate George Kel-ly by name

1 Come bold British tars give an ear to my song,
   If you'll pay attention I'll not keep you long,
   It is of a staunch frigate, a ship of great fame,
   How she fought that great pirate, George Kelly by name.

---

[1] Martin's full concert program is printed and annotated in my *Jolly Sailors Bold* (Camsco Music, 2010), Appendix V, pp. 456ff.

2   Our jolly ship's crew all took to our glass,
    Likewise the lieutenant to see what she was,
    Our captain jump'd up and view'd her all round,
    George Kelly the pirate, I'll lay fifty pound.

3   We sail'd along till we came within shot,
    The bold pirate seem'd for to value us not,
    We sail'd along till we came within hail,
    We gave her a few English pills in her tail.

4   Yard-arm to yard-arm close we did lie,
    Our shots from our great guns thro' her rigging did fly,
    With round and grape metal we pepper'd her bones
    Crying out jolly tars, we're a second Paul Jones.

5   The prize we have taken and found out her name:
    The noted George Kelly, from Dunkirk she came,
    We made them both captives that very same day,
    And straight to Newcastle we sail'd away.

23
KELLY THE PIRATE (II)
(Laws K-32)

KELLY THE PIRATE.

Sometimes accompanied by a crude woodcut illustration (the one here is from the *Forget Me Not Songster* circa the 1840s), this is the "Kelly the Pirate" ballad found in American songsters and occasionally in Nova Scotia tradition. The defining characteristic feature of "Kelly the Pirate (II)" seems to be that it opens with specific orders received from an admiral and ends with a salute to the frigate and crew who vanquished the pirate. The frigate is sometimes named—*Antelope, Hart, Stag* —and sometimes not. Mackenzie's contention is that "Kelly (II)" may be "an American composition derived from" the English precursor is less than convincing; in fact, the evidence is that *both* are British. First of all, there were no American admirals at that time: commodore was the highest rank in the U.S. Navy; flag rank was specifically excluded until Congress authorized it during the Civil War. Moreover, "Kelly" as sung aboard the American whaler *Lucy Ann* in 1842 is clearly an American adaptation of the British "Kelly (I)" [#22], while the lyrics recovered from Pennsylvania tradition (Shoemaker, 177) are just as clearly a British rendition of Mackenzie's so-called "American" form, which has the refrain "And it's oh, Britons, Stand true: / To your colo[u]rs stand true!"

It is also likely that to reinstate the original context of the songster text here, the phrase "to cruise the channel" (stanza 1) should be rendered "to cruise the Channel" —i.e., the English Channel— as there is no American equivalent that would make proper sense in context. Similarly, "And straight to new prison" (stanza 7) may want to be restored to "And straight to Newgate Prison"— unless this line be merely a corruption of the same line in the British broadside, "And straight to

Newcastle." It is British in either case. Thus, both forms of "Kelly" appear originally to have been British and to have been only minimally (if at all) Americanized in print or in tradition. To fit the excellent melody, the refrain has to be spliced on again, but it could be altered to "Then it's all *Yankees* stand true... ," as it would have been in the last century had Yankees sung it.

Our Ad-mir-al gave or-ders on the same day, To cruise in the chan-nel for our en-e-my,

To pro-tect all our mer-chants from the brave foe, And all in-ter-lop-ers. as you may sup-pose,

Then it's all Bri - tons stand true,   *Stand true to your col - ors stand true.*

1   Our Admiral gave orders, on the same day,
        To cruise the channel for our enemy,
        To protect all our merchants from the brave foe,
        And all interlopers, as you may suppose.

2   On the 21st of January, so clear was the day
        A man from the mast-head a sail he spied;
        A sail, O a sail, he loudly did cry,
        She is a large cutter, and seems to lay by.

3   Our noble commander, he pulled out his glass;
        So did our lieutenant, to see what she was;
        Our captain jumped up, and survey'd her all round—
        It's Kelly, the pirate, I'll lay fifty pound.

4   Do you see that proud villain? he cried: Make sail,
        We'll soon overhaul him, my boys, I'll give bail;
        Jump up and shake out your bags, all snug and clear,
        And up with your helm and after them steer.

5   We sailed 'till we came within gun shot;
        Bold Kelly he seemed to value us not;
        With a loud voice, like thunder, Bold Kelly he did say,
        Bend your guns, blow your matches, boys, and fire away!

6   We engaged with this cutter for four hours and more,
        Till the blood from the scuppers like water did pour;
        With round and grape metal we pepper'd her hull,
        Till down came her ensign, staff, colors, and all.

7   We have taken this prize all on the same day,
        And straight to new prison sent Kelly away.
        Here's a health to our captain, and lieutenant, too,
        Likewise the Hart frigate, and all her crew.

24
BOLD DANIELS
(Laws K-34)

Of this rare ballad about an encounter with a Caribbean pirate Laws reported no broadsides, it is not in any songsters, and all of Laws' citations (including Colcord's *Songs of American Sailormen*) trace to Minnesota and the singing of one Michael C. Dean. Another specimen is reported from Labrador by MacEdward Leach, who says of its shorter text, "The ballad gains by this compression." It appears to have been influenced by "The Bold *Princess Royal*" [#20]. "La Guire" ("La Guayra" in some texts; corrupted to "Maguire" in at least one) refers to *La Guira*, founded in 1588, the seaport for Caracas, Venezuela, which is indeed "under the Spanish Main."

On the twen-ty sec-ond of Feb-ru-ar-y from old Eng-land we set sail, Bound down to La Guire with a sweet and a pleas-ant gale. Our cap-tain called all hands right aft, and un-to us did say, "There's mon-ey for you to-day, my boys, to-mor-row we'll sail a-way.

1   On the twenty-second of February from Old England we set sail,
    Bound down to La Guire with a sweet and a pleasant gale.
    Our Captain called all hands right aft, and unto us did say,
    "There's money for you today, my boys; tomorrow we'll sail away,"

2   We had not been long sailing all under Callanding shore,
    When [to] a man [in] our main mast head a strange sail did [appear]
    With a black flag on her mizzen peak came bearing down this way.
    "I'll be bound she's some pirate," Bold Daniel he did say.

3   In the space of twenty-five minutes, my boys, this pirate ranged alongside,
    With a loud and speaking trumpet, "Where are you from?" he cried.
    "The *Roaming Lizzie* we are called; Bold Daniel is my name;
    We sailed from La Guire just under the Spanish Main."

4   "Come, back your fore main topsails and heave your ship to under my lee."
    "O no, O no!" cried Daniel, "I would rather sink at sea."
    So up went their bloody flag, our lives to terrify;
    With their great guns to our small arms at us they then let fly.

5   We mounted [five six-pounders] to fight one hundred men,
    And when this action first began, it was about half past ten;
    We mounted [five six-pounders], our crew being twenty two.
    In the space of twenty-five minutes, my boys, those pirates cried, "Mirbleu."

6   So now we fought 'em and taken [a] rich prize all under Callanding shore,
    A good old place in America; we named it Baltimore;
    We'll drink success to Daniel; likewise his jovial crew
    Who fought and be[a]t those pirates with his noble twenty-two.

25

BOLD MANAN THE PIRATE
[Bold Manning; Manan the Pirate]
(Laws D-15)

The syntax and especially the melody of this piece impart to it a much more modern feel than the usual broadside ballad imported from the British Isles. A text recovered from Nova Scotia with a New Brunswick provenance is entitled "Bold Manning," while two tracing to Maine are entitled "Bold Manan." Of these, only the Canadian one has a tune. Uniquely among the pirate ballads, Laws classifies it as of North American origin. However, allusions to Rodney in both of the Maine texts (absent in the Canadian specimen) suggest at least three things: that it may be considerably older than it appears; that it may be based on a British or colonial precursor, not found; and that it may refer to some actual event, not discovered. George Brydges Rodney (1719-1792), a renowned British admiral whose exploits include important naval victories against America's Dutch and French allies during the War of the Revolution, had earlier served as Royal Governor of Newfoundland (1748-52) and intermittently as a fleet commander in the West Indies (1761-79). Rodney was well known in the Colonies, and while he is one of the most illustrious in the pantheon of British naval heroes he was no favorite of the American patriots. Inexplicably, it is the Canadian text that omits his part in the ballad and the American ones that retain it.

When Laws summarized "Bold Manan" in *Native American Balladry* he was unaware of the third manifestation of the ballad from Nova Scotia (which was yet to be collected and published by William Main Doerflinger); thus, he premised his comments on the two texts from Maine:

> The pirates capture and ransack the *Fame* from New York and murder her crew. To stop an argument among his men, Manan severs the head of a young lady on board whose fate they had been discussing. A merry celebration of the victory follows. The next day, Manan mistakes a warship under Captain Rodney for an East Indiaman. In the ensuing battle the pirate ship is sunk. (Laws 1950, 168)

"Bold Manning," the Nova Scotia specimen, is undoubtedly a manifestation of the same ballad, sharing turns of phrase and narrative characteristics, but it does not conform to Laws' description. Apart from being the only one of the three with its tune intact—and apart from the fact that the tune itself is unique among pirate ballad melodies—it exhibits two other standout features. One is the pirate bosun's revelation (in stanza 2) that the ship they are pursuing is his own father's vessel, and "he felt his blood run cold." Unfortunately, this intriguing premise leads nowhere in the fragment that survives (such as the bosun intervening in his father's behalf), but as a theme it harkens back to the improbable dramatic coincidences and incestuous complexity of some of the old English and Scottish Popular Ballads. The texts from Maine proceed according to formula, the only surprise being that what the pirates initially think is an East Indiaman turns out to be the Navy's leading strongman. In fact, the whole point of "Bold Manan" seems to be that Bold Rodney decimates and sinks the brutal pirates in the end, implying (as broadside ballads often do) that such is ever the fate of outlaws and renegades. But in "Bold Manning" there is no Rodney, no Navy, no denouement: the naval episode is absent, the pirates just go along on their merry way, singing. Perhaps a few lines are missing: the Maine texts run to thirteen and fourteen stanzas; "Bold Manning" has only twelve. But there may be something more subtle going on here, having to do with the late vintage of the text, romanticism, and a rebellious repudiation of imperial naval authority, vis à vis the American and African-American elements in the ballad's provenance.

Finally, the tune is a bit odd—perfectly cogent when sung *a capella,* as it was by the Black ship's cook who sang it while scouring pots in a New Brunswick logging camp, and as it was by the shantyboy who learned it from him and sang it for Bill Doerflinger; but oddly resistant to any consistent musical accompaniment. However, simply by changing two notes (perhaps thereby restoring the tune to its original condition) it falls into a fairly standard, very engaging ragtime-era pop-song progression that is fun to play, shows off some of the African influence that may be indigenous, and characterizes it as unique among pirate-ballad tunes. Still, the pirates' attitude and the tune are a tad too lilting and merry for the gruesome details to which they are attached.

TUNE A: "Bold Manning," from Doerflinger, *Songs of the Sailor and Lumberman,* p. 139: from the singing of John Apt of Greenland, Nova Scotia, who learned it from a Black former ship's cook working in a New Brunswick logging camp.

Bold Man-ning was to sea one day, And a drear-y day it was, too, As drear-y

day as ev-er you see, All wet with fog and dew. They spied a large and lof-ty ship, A-

bout three miles a-head. "Come h'ist up our main-tops'l, boys, And af-ter him we'll speed.

TUNE B: "Bold Manning," after Doerflinger, p. 139, but slightly altered: by changing one note in measure 12, and one note in measure 16—in both cases from D to E—a ragtime/blues quality is restored.

Bold Man-ning was to sea one day, And a drear-y day it was, too, As drear-y

day as ev-er you see, All wet with fog and dew. They spied a large and lof-ty ship, A-

bout three miles a-head. "Come h'ist up our main-tops'l, boys, And af-ter him we'll speed.

"Bold Manning": composite text, following the Nova Scotia format, including the bosun's revelation (stanza 2) and doubling of names (William Craig is the name of both the pirate bosun and the merchant captain because they are father and son), omitting the naval episode at the end, but incorporating lines and phrases from "Bold Manan the Pirate" (the Maine texts) to flesh out the imagery and enhance the story.

1   Bold Manning was to sea one day, and a dreary day it was, too,
     'Twas thick as any buttermilk among the fog and dew;
     They spied a large and lofty ship about three leagues ahead.
     "Come h'ist up our main-tops'l, boys, and after her we'll speed."

2   He called unto his bosun, whose name was William Craig:
     "Oh Craig, oh Craig, come up on deck and h'ist up our black flag!"
     His bosun was a valiant man, his heart was stout and bold,
     But when he saw his father's ship, he felt his blood run cold.

3   Now, Manning's ship you all do know, no finer ship e'er swam,
Bold Manning being like a hungry shark, he plowed the raging main
With five hundred and fifty men on board, and brass guns forty-nine,
As brave and crafty fellows as ever you could find.

4   They bore right down upon her, and sheered up alongside.
With his loud speaking trumpet, "Whence come you?" he cried,
"Where are you from," cried Manning, "I pray you tell me true,
For if you tell to me a lie 'twill be the worse for you."

5   And then those frightened mariners, not knowing what to do,
And then these frightened mariners, they up and told him true,
"We are the *Fame,* to New York sailed, for Liverpool we're bound,
Our Captain's name is William Craig, a native of that town."

6   "Oh no! Oh, no!" cried Manning, "These things can never be true!
So heave your main yard to the mast and let your ship lay to.
And if you think my orders are not fit for to obey,
With grape shot and with canister I'll sink you where you lay!"

7   Those poor affrighted seamen, not knowing what to do,
They hove their main yard to the mast and let their ship lay to.
These bold and crafty pirates, with broadsword in hand,
They went on board of the merchant ship and slaughtered every man.

8   Some they shot and others they stabbed, and all of them they drowned,
And most of these poor fellows lay bathing in their blood.
They hunted the ship all over and ransacked everything,
Until they came to a female in the after mess cabin.

9   She, not hearing of the murders or knowing what was done,
Played upon her own guitar. True sweetly she sung:
"Home, home, sweet home, there is no-place like home;
'Tis for an absent lover that caused me to roam."

10   Some did stomp and some did swear they would make her their bride [wife];
"Stand back, stand back!" said Manning, "An end to all your strife!"
He boldly rushed upon her, without fear or dread,
He boldly rushed upon this female and severed off her head.

11   These bold and crafty pirates, not caring what they done,
They went on board of the pirate ship and merrily they sung,
With a keg of rum on the capstan, so boldly they did sing,
To the mid watch of that night you might hear their echoes ring:

12   "We pirates lead a merry, merry life, and a merry, merry life lead we!
"And when a strange sail heaves in sight, we haul her under our lee.
When the jolly, jolly grog is flowing, ri fol the dol i day!
It is under the black flag we'll fight, till we conquer or we die!

26

CAPTAIN COULSTON
[Captain Colsten; Captain Colstein]

Irish sea-song anthologist James N. Healy has called this obscure piece "a splendid, neglected ballad," and it has certainly been scarce in the 20th-21st centuries. It is probably rooted in 18th-century Irish tradition, but the few surviving specimens evidence revisions and transformations from the 19th century, especially in the version here, collected in Ireland (sampled in Text B). The ballad was reportedly popular in Wexford but has been rare elsewhere, and no printed broadside is recorded on either side of the Atlantic. Healy's text of nine stanzas is from Ireland; Huntington & Herrmann have another, from Sam Henry's collection. Edith Fowke recovered a version in North America: seven stanzas from an Anglophone singer in Quebec. The variants differ in several ways, but most notably in the two very strange stanzas that are present in Healy's rendition, where they appear as the second and third verses, but are absent in Fowke's (they are appended here as Text B). The outstanding, distinctive feature common to both of these, however, is that it is not Captain Coulston or some other "bold hero," but rather one of the women passengers who dispatches the pirate captain by pistol-shot. Healy calls his version a "gorgeous ballad" with "a fine tune," and so it is. Edith Fowke's text and tune, as rendered by Ellen Cohn, are even better.

TUNE A — from James N. Healy, *Irish Ballads and Songs of the Sea* (1967), p. 34, which Healy does not identify except in association with his text of "Captain Coulston."

TEXT and TUNE B of "Captain Colstein," from the singing of Ellen Cohn, after the version collected by Edith Fowke (uniquely in North America), in *Traditional Singers and Songs from Ontario* (1965): sung by O.J. Abbott (1957), who learned it from Albert Tapp, a sailor and sometime lumberman from Gaspé, Quebec.

You inhabitants of Ireland that's bound to cross the sea, Come join with Captain Colstein, that hero brave and free; Come join with Captain Colstein, that hero brave and bold Who fought his way all on the sea and never was controlled.

1.   You inhabitants of Ireland that's bound to cross the sea,
     Come join with Captain Colstein, that hero brave and free;
     Come join with Captain Colstein, that hero brave and bold
     Who fought his way all on the sea and never was controlled.

2.   From the eleventh till the twenty-first we ploughed the raging sea,
     For ten long days of merriment, bound for Americay;
     Our merriment being over and going to bed at night,
     Our captain went all round the deck to see if all was right.

3.   "Oh, don't go down," our captain cried, "There is no time for sleep,
     For in less than half an hour we'll be slumbering in the deep.
     The pirate ship is coming up from the wide western sea
     To rob us of our property, bound for Americay."

4.   The pirate ship came up to us and bid for us to stand:
     "Your gold and precious loading, this moment I demand;
     Your gold and precious loading, this day resign to me,
     Or not a soul will you ever bring into Americay."

5.   Then up spoke Captain Colstein, that hero brave and bold:
     "It's in the deep we all shall sleep before we'll be controlled."
     'Twas then the battle it began, the blood in streams it flowed;
     Undaunted was our passengers till the pirate was overthrown.

6.   There was a lady on the deck with her true love by her side;
     With courage bold she fought her way along the bulwark side,
     Saying, "Don't you fret, my bonny boy, we'll shortly end the strife";
     And with a pistol ball she took the pirate captain's life

7.   The cries of women and children, whilst in the hold they lay;
     Our captain and his passengers, they showed them Irish play;
     The pirate ship surrendered just at the break of day,
     And we marched them back as prisoners into Americay.

B.

Excerpts from a text entitled "Captain Coulston," from James N. Healy, *Irish Ballads and Songs of the Sea* (1967), pp. 43f, about which Healy provides no further particulars. These stanzas are absent from Edith Fowke's variant, collected in Canada.

2.   The number of his passengers was three hundred and sixty-two;
     And they were all teetotallers, excepting one or two,
     The lemonade was passed around, to nourish them at sea,
     And Father Mathew's medals they wore unto Amerikay.

3.   The weather it was charming as ever you saw before;
     For twenty days of pleasure we never thought of shore.
     The captain and his lady fair, were seen on deck each day
     To crown our hearts with merriment while sailing on the sea

HICKS THE PIRATE
Tune—The Rose Tree

This is a contemporaneous ballad about an actual historical figure whose trial, conviction, and execution briefly created a sensation on the eve of the Civil War, then faded into obscurity. The words are preserved in a cheap broadside printed by De Marsan in New York when the hubbub was at its height, and the melody is a fairly well known traditional Irish air to which other lyrics have occasionally been written, including by Thomas Moore, who used it for "I'd mourn the hopes that leave me," which was one of his better known songs in its day.[2]

By his own admission, Albert Hicks was a criminal and a murderer, but he can be called a pirate only on a technicality, being that the three murders for which he was hanged were committed on shipboard at sea. While neither the story nor the ballad is remarkable, what is remarkable is that the authorship of the lyrics is attributed. John Thorn identifies him as Henry Backus (1798-1861), a prolific folk balladist from the town of Saugerties in New York's Hudson River Valley.[3]

> Hicks was a waterfront thug, not a pirate, who in March 1860 was drugged by a rival gang member and woke up to find himself "shanghaied" onto the oyster sloop *E. A. Johnson* and bound for Virginia. Knowing from past practice just what to do, he murdered the entire crew—the skipper Captain Burr and the brothers Watts—with an axe, gathered up their clothing and valuables, and threw them overboard. Managing the sloop badly as he turned it back toward New York, he collided with the schooner *J. R. Mather,* outbound for Philadelphia. Hicks lowered a boat piled high with his victims' belongings and made for shore at Staten Island.

Thorn reports that "the wrecked *E. A. Johnson* was brought ashore awash in blood," and Hicks was "chased from New York to Providence," where he was apprehended and brought back to New York on federal charges of piracy on the High Seas. Convicted for the three murders, he was hanged on Bedloe's Island in New York harbor on July 13, 1860.

> His procession from jail to gallows took on the aspect of a circus, and a general holiday atmosphere prevailed. Excursion boats had been lined up beforehand for the twelve thousand spectators (a *New York Times* estimate) ... "HO! FOR THE EXECUTION" read the headline on one classified ad (1860). Peanut vendors and lemonade stands did a brisk business to the beat of the fife and drum. The thirsty "imbibed lager-beer," reported the *Times,* and in rowboats there were "ladies, no, females of some sort, shielding their complexion from the sun with their parasols, while from beneath the fringe and the tassels they viewed the dying agonies of the choking murderer."

According to Thorn, Hicks (typically of the some notorious convicts awaiting execution) "hired a writer to make his confession suitably bloodcurdling to sell to a publisher, with the proceeds to go to his widow"; viz, "I have killed men, yes, and boys too, many a time before, for far less inducement than the sum I suspected I should gain by killing them; and I had too often dyed my murderous hands in blood in days gone by, to feel the slightest compunctions or qualms of conscience then." Later, grave robbers stole his body and sold it for medical dissection, and P.T. Barnum installed a wax effigy of Hicks among the notorious figures in his American Museum.

As for the air, O'Hea & Carey call it an "exquisite love melody said to have been composed about 1650 by Thomas O'Connellan (c. 1625-1700), the famous Irish harper." The original title was "Móirín Ní Chuillonáin [Little Mary Cullenan]," from a text by the poet, John O'Tuomy (1706-75), but it was also known by several other names, including "The Gimlet," "The Irish Lilt," "The Dainty Besom Maker," "Old Lee Rigg," and "Killeavy." An opera by John O'Keeffe, *The Poor Soldier* (1783), may have been the first appearance of the title "The Rose Tree."[4]

---

[2]   The tune has been unequivocally identified and has been widely anthologized, notably by J.L. Molloy in *The Songs of Ireland* (London: Boosey & Co., 1873, p. 21).

[3]   John Thorn, "The Saugerties Bard," *Voices: The Journal of New York Folklore,* 31, Fall-Winter, 2005. His principal citation is "Execution of Hicks, the Pirate," *New York Times*, July 14, 1860, page 1.

[4]   J.F. O'Hea & John Carey, *Gem Selection Songs of Ireland* (Dublin: Valentine & Sons), pp. viii and 48.

1

A mournful tale heart rending,
   To you kind friends I will relate:
The solemn truth intending
   Of three that met a tragic fate:
An Oyster Sloop was sailing
   Upon the oceans sparkling tide,
In the healthful breeze regaling,
   She moved upon the waters wide.

2

But upon this Oyster vessel,
   A pirate bold had found his way,
With wicked heart this vassal
   The captain and two boys did slay;
He seized the gold and silver,
   Which this poor captain had in store;
His watch and clothes did pilfer,
   While he lay struggling in his gore.

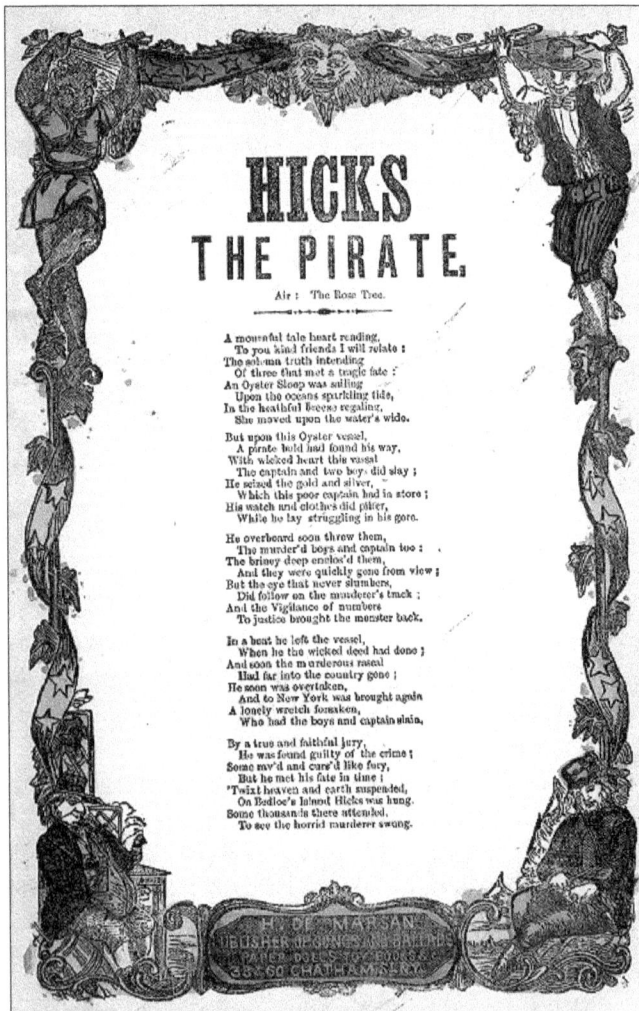

3

He overboard soon threw them,
   The murder'd boys and captain too:
The briney deep enclos'd them,
   And they were quickly gone from view;
But the eye that never slumbers,
   Did follow on the murderer's track;
And the Vigilance of numbers
   To justice brought the monster back.

4

In a boat he left the vessel,
   When he the wicked deed had done;
And soon the murderous rascal
   Had far into the country gone;
He soon was overtaken,
   And to New York was brought again
A lonely wretch forsaken,
   Who had the boys and captain slain.

5

By a true and faithful jury,
   He was found guilty of the crime;
Some rav'd and curs'd like fury,
   But he met his fate in time;
'Twixt heaven and earth suspended,
   On Bedloe's Island Hicks was hung.
Some thousands there attended,
   To see the horrid murderer swung.

"Hicks the Pirate." Broadside printed by H. De Marsan of New York in March 1860 on the occasion of the arrest and trial of Albert Hicks for piracy and murder, but before he was actually hanged. The lyrics are attributed to Henry Backus. "The Rose Tree," a traditional Irish air, is specified; and the stanzas are framed with De Marsan's characteristic and entirely generic border ornaments.

THE *BROOKLYN*

This is one of two obscure ballads about the USS *Brooklyn,* a steam-screw sloop-of-war that was in service from 1859 to 1889. William Edward Johnson's application for a Navy pension in 1910 traces the genesis of the other, earlier ballad to a shipmate with whom he served in the Union Navy. Johnson's father was a slave and his mother a Free Black. Born in Virginia in 1842 and raised in Pennsylvania and the Midwest, he was employed on Mississippi River steamboats before enlisting under the alias Edward Cendyrlin. From August 1862 to September 1863 he was cabin cook on the *Brooklyn,* commanded by Henry Haywood Bell, and in a deposition (generously provided by W. Jeffrey Bolster) he reports, "William Densmore was Chief coxswains mate, he was kind of a poet and he wrote quite a piece in regard to the 'Brooklyn' and the Civil War, I will repeat a few lines of it.

> It was in December 1861, As you shall understand
> Seceshes gloom had overcast Columbia's happy land
> Craven was our Capt.s name, as you shall understand
> As brave a naval officer as any in the land
> Down through the Gulf of Mexico, 'the Brooklyn' she did steer
> ----- in search of privateer"

More than a decade later, whaleman/merchant seaman Frederick Merrill transcribed the other *Brooklyn* ballad into his journal and signed it "F.M." No tune is specified but it appears to be derived from a British ballad cycle known by several titles but which appears in Captain Whall's anthology as "Shakings," while textual and rhythmic resonances link it also to "The Girls Around Cape Horn" ("Rounding the Horn"), which was well established in British and American shipboard tradition in the mid 19th century. The straightforward story is similar to "High Barbary" [#6] and several others. It may or may not have some basis in truth. Both before and after the Civil War the U.S. Navy intermittently tried to eradicate the illicit slave trade to Cuba. Charlestown, mentioned in the text, was the site of Boston's Navy base. However, the real USS *Brooklyn* was never based at Boston and was never dispatched to chase after slavers or pirates. The 1878 Arctic voyage on which Merrill transcribed the lyrics had an unusual purpose. After a conventional Atlantic whaling voyage as a green hand in the New Bedford bark *Janus* (1875-76), he was in the schooner *Eothan* of New York, commanded by Thomas Barry (former mate of the New Bedford whaler *Glacier*), to deliver American Army officer Frederick Schwatka and his party to Hudson Bay, where they planned to search for Sir John Franklin's lost Arctic expedition. Lt. Schwatka distinguished himself not only by traversing large tracts of hitherto uncharted territory and making the longest sledge journey up to that time, but discovering tangible evidence of the fate of the Franklin expedition, which had sailed in 1845 and disappeared in 1847.

TUNE A – "Rounding the Horn", from Ralph Vaughan Williams and A.L. Lloyd, *The Penguin Book of English Folk Songs,* 1959, 90: collected in Lancashire, 1907.

TUNE B -"The Girls Around Cape Horn": composite. Compare Colcord 1938, 177.

Em | Am Bm Em | D7 | G G7 | C (Em) Am Em Dm | G C

TUNE C - "Shakings," from W.B. Whall, p. 113f.

C | Am Em Dm (F) | Am | F | Am Em Dm

E | F | Am Em Dm | F | Am C | F C Dm | Am

"THE BROOKLYNN." Transcribed by Frederick Merrill, green hand, whaling bark *Janus* of New Bedford, 1875-76; and seaman, schooner *Eothen* of New York, 1878. In the journal the text lacks division into lines or stanzas; it is here divided into lines and stanzas, with minor corrections to grammar, spelling, and punctuation.

1. There is a bark, a gallant bark, which lies in Boston Bay,
   Awaiting there for orders, her anchor for to weigh,
   She is bound for the coast of Cuba, boys, our gallant ship shall go,
   We are bound to sink and to destroy, where ever we may roam.

2. We had not sailed but 30 leag[ue]s or 40 leag[ue]s or more,
   When we espied a large ship, and down upon us bore,
   Shes hailed us in a Spanish voice, and asked us whence we came,
   We just set sail from Charlestown, and the Brooklynn is our name.

3. Are you a man of war sir? pray tell you unto me.
   I am no man of war, sir, but private, as you see;
   Then brace away your fore yards, and let your ship come to;
   Then hoist your tackles and lower your boats, or else I will sink you.

4. Up Spake our Capt[ain] bold, unto his men did say,
   Cheer up, my lively lads, we are sure to gain the day;
   If it had not been for my own brother, this battle would never been tried,
   Let every brave man, stand to his gun, and we give to them a broadside.

5. The broadside was given, w[h]ich coursed them all to wonder,
   To see therefore the gallant mast come rolling down like thunder;
   We showed them no quarter boys, they could no longer stay
   When we gave ha[r]d and the red has stoo[d] and showed them American play.

6. Now we bid this pirate a dew [adieu], to America we will steer,
   And when we arrive on American shores, those girls they will us cheer;
   They will call us there bold hero[e]s and prais[e] our officers, to[o];
   They will drink success to the Brooklynn and all her jolly crew.   F.M.

* The first of five steam-screw warships authorized by Congress in 1857, the *Brooklyn* was designed and built in New York by Jacob A. Westervelt & Son (launched 1858; commissioned 1859). Her first captain was David G. Farragut, and when the reputed balladeer Densmore was chief coxswain's mate (1862-63) the *Brooklyn* was with Farragut's force against New Orleans and Vicksburg, She was rammed by the Confederate gunboat *Manassas* and participated in blockade and search-and-destroy missions at Mobile Bay and on the Texas and Florida coasts under successive command of Thomas T. Craven, Henry H. Bell, Chester Hatfield, and George F. Emmons, capturing several vessels along the way. After the war she was in South America and the Mediterranean, served as flagship of the South Atlantic and Asiatic Squadrons, and completed a circumnavigation in 1889, after which she was permanently decommissioned. (Source: Robert J. Cressman, U.S. Naval Historical Center, 2005).

LIVERPOOL PLAY

This English piece has striking affinities with "The *Brooklyn*" [#28], and perhaps the two ought to be considered variants of the same ballad. The words and music here were collected separately in 1910 by the eminent composer and pioneer folksong collector Ralph Vaughan Williams from two different sources in the English shires of Norfolk and Suffolk, and were anthologized by Roy Palmer in his superb selection of *Folk Songs Collected by Ralph Vaughan Williams* (London, 1983). Palmer calls it a "song for all seasons, or rather for all contingencies." Variants specify a different date (or mention no date), different ship-names (or specify no ship-names), and different ports (or do not identify the port). The nationality of the pirate and geography of the cruising ground also vary from text to text. Presumably, so does the melody. But Palmer neither mentions any American manifestation (which could be "The *Brooklyn*") nor says which ballad may be descended from which. As "The *Brooklyn*" is based on an actual American vessel, and was written down a generation before "Liverpool Play" was collected, a substantial case can be made for the American ballad being the original and the British ballad being a derivative variant.

1. It was the fourth of November, boys, in
     Liverpool Straits we lay,
   A-waiting for fresh orders, our anchor
     for to weigh.
   Bound down to the coast of Africa, our
     orders they did run so;
   We're bound to sink and destroy, my
     boys, wherever we do go.

2. Now we had not been sailing scarce
     sixty leagues or more,
   Before we espied a large French ship,
     and down on us she bore.
   She hailed us in French colours to ask
     from whence we came.
   "We've just come down from Liverpool,
     and the Dolphin is our name.

3. "Are you a man of war, sir? Pray tell me
     what you be".
   "I am no man of war, sir, but a pirate
     you do see.
   So heave up your fore and main yards,
     and let your ship come to,
   For our tackles are all hauled and our
     boats all lowered—or else we will
     sink you."

4. Now our captain being an English man
     on the quarter-deck did say:
   "Let every man stand true to his gun and
     we'll show them Liverpool play.
   If it had not been for my own brother
     this battle would never've been tried;
   Let every man stand true to his gun and
     we'll give them a broadside."

5. So broadside to broadside, which caused
     all hands to wonder,
   To see her French and lofty spars come
     rolling down like thunder.
   We shot them from our quarter-deck till
     they could no longer stay;
   Our guns being smart we played a good
     part, and we showd them Liverpool
     play.

6. This large French ship was taken to
     Liverpool Docks and moored;
   We fired shots at our sweethearts and
     fancy girls ashore,
   We lowered down the French colours
     and let fly the red, white, and blue;
   We drank success to the Dolphin and all
     her gallant crew

ABOVE: *Alwilda, the Female Pirate.* This fanciful image of the semi-legendary 5th-century Scandinavian female pirate appeared in *The Pirate's Own Book,* anonymously authored by Charles Ellms (Boston, 1837). It was widely copied in whalemens' scrimshaw and may have inspired the character of Fanny Campbell. RIGHT: *Fanny Campbell, the Female Pirate* graces the cover of a spurious "biography" entitled *Fanny Campbell, the Female Pirate Captain: A Tale of the Revolution* (Boston, 1845). Allegedly based on an historical personage, a native of Lynn, Massachusetts, her fictitious exploits and even her costume were partly modeled after the literary success of Alwilda and became analogously popular: the image also appears frequently on contemporaneous scrimshaw. The author was "Lieutenant Murray," pseudonym of Maturin Murray Ballou (1820-1895), who produced at least two other pirate romances that same year, *Red Rupert, the American Buccaneer* and *The Naval Officer; or, The Pirate's Cave.* He later achieved prominence as editor of *Gleason's Pictorial Magazine* and *Ballou's Pictorial Magazine.*

Part Three: Women in Buccaneers' Clothing

When it comes to ballads and songs, female pirates are a difficult subject. Real women "on the account," though few in number, are more than a mere footnote in the history of freebooting.

Grace O'Malley (circa 1530-1603), known as Granuaile,[1] practiced coastwise piracy and ran a protection racket on the coast of Galway (Chambers, 170; Cordingly 1995, 72). Called a pirate often enough, she was a colorful local tycoon, a successful merchant, and is reputed to have been a competent navigator. Why not also a smuggler and a buccaneer? But Grace is also a legitimate Irish patriotic heroine, and the songs and poems about her are filled with castles and land battles and a famous audience with Queen Elizabeth, not much about ships and nothing about piracy.[2]

The two most prominent historical female pirates were sometime shipmates and rivals who, in 1720 at Port Royal (Jamaica), were tried for piracy and sentenced to be hanged. Anne Bonny, the natural daughter of a prominent Irish attorney, was the consort of pirate captain "Calico Jack" Rackham. Pregnancy saved her from the gallows; she then disappears from view. Mary Read, raised as a boy in London, was from working-class stock. She masqueraded in drag her entire career, served in infantry and cavalry in Flanders before going to sea, and at age 19, pregnant, is said to have died in prison of natural causes before she could be hanged or reprieved.[3]

None of these historical pirate women is immortalized in pirate balladry. Nor did female pirates of fiction and lore fare much better, ballad-wise. The semi-legendary Norse pirate Alwilda, scourge of the Skaggerat in the fifth century, was a frequent subject of whalers' scrimshaw fourteen hundred years later. Yarns about her circulated at sea, but no ballads in English have emerged. The same is true of the apocryphal Yankee buccaneer Fanny Campbell, who is still venerated in her native Lynn, Massachusetts, as if she had really existed. Her exploits would seem ripe for balladry, but no ballad of Fanny Campbell has come to light.

Which leaves us with fanciful ballads about women who go to sea disguised as men and engage in sea fights, but who are not necessarily pirates themselves. The heroine of the songster version of "The Female Warrior" [#32] battles an English admiral, but the text is equivocal about her status and nationality — whether she is an Irish rebel, a Scottish Jacobite, an American patriot, or perhaps an English traitor. In a variant of the same ballad recovered from tradition in Canada [#34], and in "The Female Smuggler" [#30], the women are not pirates but courageous pirate-fighters (their smuggler upbringing is only to provide background color).

FANNY CAMPBELL,
THE FEMALE PIRATE CAPTAIN.

Portrait of the Female Pirate.

BY LIEUTENANT MURRAY.

BOSTON:
PUBLISHED BY F. GLEASON, 1 1-2 TREMONT ROW,
1845.

Jones, Printer, 12 Congress Street.

There is also a fragment that folklorist Frank Kidson believed to be a rare ballad about a woman combating the infamous pirate Captain Ward: however, "As We Were A-Sailing" [#33] turns out to be strictly generic, merely a hybridized corruption of "The Female Warrior." The greatest ballad about female pirate-fighter is "Captain Coulston" [#26], in the previous chapter.

Though the meager selection here does not include any songs about historical female pirates and does not even constitute a satisfactory ratio of female presence, it is probably a statistically accurate approximation of the actual incidence of females fighting with or against pirates at sea.

---

1. Cordingly gives the name *Granuaille,* but her biographer (Chambers) and most Irish sources give it *Granuaile.*
2. Chambers (pp 180-199) reproduces the texts of several of these. There are a few modern compositions intended for singing that incorporate aspects of Granuaile's nautical activities: note, for example, *"Grá innu Mhaol* (Grace O'Malley)," which has words (partly in Gaelic) by P.J. McCall, to the traditional air *"Mo Theaglach"* (Healey, *Irish Ballads and Songs of the Sea,* 50).
3. Cordingly 1995, 117f; Cordingly 1996, 57-65; Shay 1934, passim. *The Oxford Dictionary of National Biography* reports that Anne Bonny's father secured her release from prison, whereupon she emigrated to South Carolina, married, raised a family, and lived until 1782.

THE FEMALE SMUGGLER

The implication — according to W.B. Whall, the British master mariner who produced the first authoritative anthology of sailors' songs (1910); also according to Frank Shay, who put together one of the first American collections of deepwater songs (1924) and wrote a fictional biography of Mary Read, entitled *Pirate Wench* (1934) — is that "The Female Smuggler" was actually sung on shipboard by merchant sailors in the 19th century. But Shay lifted his text and tune directly from Whall; and Whall never actually says, as he does in many other cases, that he heard it performed at sea. It is always sung to tune of "The Dark-Eyed Sailor" (Laws #N-35), which is described as "one of the most widely known ballads on the 'broken ring' theme" (Fowke 1965, 166), "among the most popular songs on both sides of the Atlantic" (Karpeles, 283), and "one of the most stable songs in folk tradition" (Manny & Wilson, 230). "Dark-Eyed Sailor" was surely enormously popular at sea and has been recovered both from sailors' singing tradition and from shipboard manuscripts. But there is little evidence that "Female Smuggler" enjoyed a similar popularity at sea or ashore. Whatever its provenance among mariners, it seems to be a spinoff of "Dark-Eyed Sailor." A shortened text was published with the "Dark-Eyed Sailor" tune in *Beadle's Dime Melodist* (1859), a peculiar feature of which is the use of "salieur" for *sailor,* "mothier" for *mother,* and other affected devices to imitate the stilted "regulation pronunciation" of sailors that Captain Whall takes pains to explain (the style is akin to what can still be detected in the fine singing of Louis Killen, a native Geordie from Gateshead-on-Tyne, County Durham):

> O come list a-whidle adnd you soodn shadll hear;
> By the rodling sea lived a maiden fair;
> Her father followed the rum-smuggling trade
> Like a wardlike hero,
> Like a wardlike hero that never was aff-er-aid.

The ballad is somewhat confused as to who are the pirates and who the lawful authorities. At first Jane is fighting pirates, later defending herself in court against a charge of piracy, then pardoned, betrothed, and wed like a society debutante. An odd vestige of a real female pirate haunts the ballad. Mary Read was raised as a boy and dressed herself in male garb during her entire career in the army and as a pirate at sea. But legend has it (and so does Frank Shay in his speculative "biography") that for her trial at Port Royal in 1720, perhaps as a ploy to obtain a lenient judgment, she showed up in splendid feminine finery, undoubtedly pillaged from victims of her nefarious trade. In real life she did not marry the prosecutor; and while pregnancy might have saved her from the gallows, she died of a "fever" before the issue could be decided.

Come list' a while, and you soon shall hear, By the rol-ling sea lived a maid-en fair, Her fa-ther

fol-lowed the smug-gling trade, Like a war-like he-ro. Like a war - like he - ro that ne-ver seemed a-fraid.

1   O Come list' a while, and you soon shall hear,
    By the rolling sea lived a maiden fair,
    Her father followed the smuggling trade,
    Like a warlike hero.
      Like a warlike hero that never seemed afraid.

2   Now, in sailor's clothing young Jane did go,
    Dressed like a sailor from top to toe;
    Her aged father was her only care
    O[f] this female smuggler.
        Of this female smuggler who never did despair.

3   With her pistols loaded she went aboard.
    And by her side hung a glittering sword,
    In her belt two daggers; well armed for war
    Was this female smuggler,
        Was this female smuggler, who never feared a scar.

4   Now they had not sailed far from the land,
    When a strange sail brought them to a stand.
    "These are sea robbers," this maid did cry,
    "But the female smuggler,
        But the female smuggler will conquer or will die."

5   Alongside, then, this strange vessel came.
    "Cheer up," cried Jane, "we will board the same;
    We'll run all chances to rise or fall,"
    Cried this female smuggler,
        Cried this female smuggler, who never feared a ball.

6   Now they killed those pirates and took their store,
    And soon returned to Eng-a-land's shore,
    With a keg of brandy she walked along,
    Did this female smuggler,
        Did this female smuggler, and sweetly sang a song.

7   Now they were followed by a blockade,
    Who in irons strong did put this fair maid,
    But when they brought her for to be ter-ied,
    This young female smuggler,
        This young female smuggler stood dress-ed like a bride.

8   Their commodore against her appeared,
    And for her life she did greatly fear.
    When he did find to his great surprise
    'Twas a female smuggler,
        'Twas a female smuggler had fought him in disguise.

9   He to the judge and the jury said,
    "I cannot prosecute this maid,
    Pardon for her on my knees I crave,
    For this female smuggler,
        For this female smuggler, so valiant and so brave."

10 Then this commodore to her father went,
    To gain her hand he asked his consent.
    His consent he gained, so the commodore
    And the female smuggler,
        And the female smuggler are one for evermore.

THE SMUGGLER'S BRIDE

One of few pirate songs cast in the tragic-romantic mode, this ballad endorses a strange standard of patriotism: even while they flout Britain's laws and fire on King's ships, the smuggler and his bride take particular pride in fighting and dying "like Britons." The lyrics in Ashton's *Modern Street Ballads* (1888) are closely related to "The Female Smuggler" [#30]; they benefit from the fancy saileur-vocalization described by Captain Whall for that ballad and can be sung to the same air. But "Smuggler's Bride" was evidently intended to be sung to a tune composed by E.J. Loder (1813-1865) for a poem by H.F. Chorley (1808-1872) entitled "The Brave Old Oak"; the melody was also used for "The Demon of the Sea" [#43]. For the music, see page 93.

1
Attention give and a tale I'll tell,
Of a damsel fair in Kent did dwell,
On the Kentish coast, when the tempest rolled,
She fell deep in love with a smuggler bold.

2
Upon her pillow she could not sleep,
When her valiant smuggler was on the deep,
While the winds did whistle she did complain,
For her smuggler ploughing the raging main.

3
When Will arrived on his native coast,
He would fly to her that he valued most,
He would fly to Nancy, his lover true,
And forget all hardships he'd lately been thro'.

4
One bright May morning the sun did shine,
And lads and lasses all gay and fine,
Along the coast they did trip along,
To see the wedding, and sing a cheerful song.

5
Young Nancy then bid her friends adieu,
And to sea she went with her lover true,
In storms and tempests all hardship braves,
With her valiant smuggler upon the waves.

6
One stormy night when the winds did rise,
And dark and dismal appeared the skies,
The tempest rolled and the waves did roar,
And the valiant smuggler was driven from shore.

7
Cheer up, cries William, my valiant wife,
Says Nancy—I never valued life,
I'll brave the storms and the tempests through
And fight for William with sword and pistol
too.

8
At length the cutter did on them drive,
The cutter on them did soon arrive,
Don't be daunted, though we're but two,
We'll not surrender—like Britons true.

9
Cheer up, says Nancy, with courage true,
I will fight, dear William, and stand by you,
They like Britons fought, Nancy stood by the gun
They beat their enemies, quick made them run

10
Another cutter bow hove in sight,
And joined to chase them with all their might;
They were overpowered, and soon disarmed,
It was then young Nancy and William were
alarmed.

11
A shot that moment made Nancy start,
Another struck William to the heart,
This shock distressed sweet Nancy's charms,
When she fell and died in William's arms.

12
Now Will and Nancy to life bid adieu,
They lived and died like two lovers true,
Young men and maidens, now faithful prove,
Like Will and Nancy, who lived and died in
love.

THE FEMALE WARRIOR (I)
(Laws #N-4)

This is one of the broadside-and-songster texts that found its way into tradition, where the ballad as a whole and the woman's role in it underwent significant transformations. This form, "Female Warrior (I)," is a songster version published in New York circa 1830 and in Baltimore in 1836, and is definitely American in context. Though it has been *called* a pirate song, it is not really a pirate song at all; rather, it concerns a woman-disguised-as-a-man who saves the day in a naval engagement after the captain is slain; and except for the Americanized context, it is consistent with Laws's taxonomic description: "After learning the mariner's art, a damsel dresses in men's clothing and ships on board a British warship as mate. During a fierce battle with a French ship, the captain is slain. The girl takes his place, leads the crew to a victory, and returns to England, where she is rewarded by the Queen and marries her true love." A substantial fragment recovered from tradition in Yorkshire [#33, "As We Were A-Sailing"] seemed to folklorist Frank Kidson, who collected it, to be about a female who fights pirates — but only because Kidson was misled by Child and believed the "enemy" to be pirates, rather than conventional French or Spanish foreigners: there is no evidence in the text itself that they are outlaws. An excellent variant collected by William Main Doerflinger from a retired Canadian sea captain really is about fighting pirates [#34]; and "Captain Coulston" [#26] has an analogous denouement with a heroine who saves the day. The metric scheme of the ballad here, from *The American Songster* (circa 1830), hardly seems consistent and regular enough to sing, and the tune is not known; but the narrative fills out the circumstances of Kidson's fragment.

1   A Story, a story, to you I will tell,
       Concerning a damsel in Baltimore did dwell,
       As beautiful a creature as ever you did see,
       And she ventur'd her life for the sake of her dear.

2   She dress'd herself in men's array, all fitting for the sea,
       On board of the Union, she shipp'd herself away,
       She served three years, and of the fourth a part,
       'Till at length she had learned the mariner's art.

3   And its first when she landed on the brave Scottish shore,
       Where the drums they do rattle and, cannons loudly roar,
       She espied a British admiral, a playing on the main,
       Which caused her to haul on her topsails again.

4   The first salutation she gave them a broadside,
       The second salutation her brave captain was slain;
       She fought them couragcously, with both sword and gun,
       That at length through the port holes the blood began to run.

5   For quarters, for quarters, the enemy did cry,
       No quarters, no quarters, the damsel did reply,
       The very best quarters that I can afford,
       Is to fight, sink, or swim, my boys, or jump overboard.

6.   And 'tis now we've gained the victory, let's take a glass of wine,
       Here's a health to your true love, and not forgetting mine;
       And here's also a health to the girl renown'd by fame,
       She's a captain on board of the ship Union by name.

AS WE WERE A-SAILING
(Laws #N-4)

The eminent Yorkshire folklorist Frank Kidson found this fragment in his home county and published it in 1893. He was unable to account for its origin or for the female warrior—certainly the most distinctive feature of the ballad—and, because of the *Rainbow* reference at the end, he supposed it to be about a battle against the pirate Captain Ward. But what Kidson did not realize is that this ballad is merely a foreshortened and hybridized form of "The Female Warrior" [#32], missing a first stanza to set up the scenario. As it stands, there is not much in the text to suggest that it is about pirates rather than a conventional Spanish enemy. Even though "Spanish shore" is sometimes taken to refer to the Barbary Coast, across the straits and to the south of Spain, the enemy here are clearly "Spanish lads," not the "pirates" or "Turks" one expects to find in British pirate ballads. The text additionally appears to be related to, or to have been influenced by, another English ballad known as "Captain Mansfield's Fight with the Turks at Sea" or "The *Royal Oak*," which is based on a successful British naval engagement against seven Algerine ships in December 1669 (Firth, 344), but which has no female character.

As we were a-sail-ing un-to the Span-ish shore, Where the drums they did beat, my boys, and loud can-non did

roar, We spied our lof-ty en-e-mies come bear-ing down the main, Which caus'd us to hoist our top-sails a-gain.

As we were a-sailing unto the Spanish shore
Where the drums they did beat, my boys, and the loud cannon did roar,
We spied our lofty enemies come bearing down the main,
Which caused us to hoist our topsails again.
… … … … … … … … … … … … … … … … … … … …

Oh! broadside to broadside, to battle then we went,
To sink one another it was our intent;
The very second broadside our captain got slain,
And this damsel she stood up in his place to command.

We fought four hours, four hours so severe,
We scarcely had one man aboard of our ship that could steer
We scarcely had one man aboard could fire off a gun,
And the blood ran from our deck like a river did run.

For quarter, for quarter, those Spanish lads did cry,
"No quarter! No quarter!" this damsel did reply;
"You've had the best of quarter that I can afford,
You must fight, sink, or swim, my boys, or jump overboard.

So now the battle's over, we'll take a glass of wine,
And you must drink to your true love, and I will drink to mine;
Good health unto this damsel who fought all on the main,
And here's to the royal gallant ship called Rainbow by name.

THE FEMALE WARRIOR (II)

This descendant of "The Female Warrior" [#32] was collected by William Main Doerflinger "from the singing of Captain Henry E. Burke of Toronto, Ontario, and formerly of Lunenburg, Nova Scotia." The original "Female Warrior" ballad concerns conventional warfare conducted by an unconventional heroine, and the sea-fight is between a British warship and a conventional French or Spanish enemy. But this derivative narrates a full-scale engagement against French pirates, in which a woman masquerading as a man takes over from the slain captain and wins the battle. The tune is pedestrian and derivative, and in its present form cannot be as old as the text. Some of the missing stanzas can be imported and adapted from #32 and #33.

This dam-sel was bro't up to read and to write, But this dam-sel was ne-ver bro't up for to fight, But be-ing gal-lant-ly dressed in her roy-al es-tate, She shipp'd on board of the *Un-ion* as mate.

1 This damsel was brought up to read and to write,
  But this damsel was never brought up for to fight,
  But being gallantly dressed in her royal estate,
  She shipp'd on board of the *Union* as mate.

2 When she served a twelvemonth, a twelvemonth or more,
  Till at last we grew close to the old England shore,
  There we saw a French pirate a lying down by the main,
  And it caused us to hoist up our tops'ls again.

3 We hoisted our tops'ls and bore down alongside,
  But the first salutation we got was a broadside.
  We gave them another just as hot as they sent.
  Now for to sink each other was our full intent.

4 This first salutation the captain was slain,
  And this damsel was chosen, master to remain,
  [*lines missing*]

5 Then she fought this French pirate for several hours severe,
  Till she scarcely had a man on her deck that could steer,
  Till she scarcely had a man that could handle a gun,
  While the blood from her scuppers like water did run.

6 For quarters, for quarters, this French Turk did cry;
  But "No quarters! No quarters!" this damsel replied.
  "You've had all the quarters that I can afford.
  You must fight, sink, or swim, or die by the sword."

THE CORSAIRS FAREWELL.

The cover illustration for "The Corsair[']s Farewell" sheet music published in New York by George Endicott (1802-1848) [song #53] was drawn, lithographed, and printed by Endicott himself circa 1837-39 (author's collection). However, the scene is actually a dramatically enriched adapted of an engraving by Joseph Goodyear (1797-1839) entitled "Conrad and Medora," after a painting by Francis Philip Stephanoff (1788-1860), illustrating an episode in the tragic ballet "Le Corsaire," produced on the London stage in 1837 with music by exiled French harpist Nicholas Charles Bochsa (1789-1856) and choreography by another exiled Frenchman, François Albert (1787-1865). The ballet was, in turn, based upon Byron's poem "The Corsair" (1814). Whaleman William A. Gilpin of Wilmington, Delaware (previously known only as the anonymous *Ceres* A Artisan), produced at least three finely engraved, reversed-image scrimshaw adaptations of the same scene on sperm whale teeth, at sea circa 1837-43 (New Bedford Whaling Museum, ex collection of Captain Michael Rodgers; and two private collections).

Part Four: Victorian Parlor Songs of Rovers and Romance

In the Victorian era, on both sides of the Atlantic, prodigious quantities of popular ditties were produced by professional tunesmiths and lyricists for the domestic parlor and the music-hall stage. Caroline Moseley's succinct definition characterizes these so-called parlor songs as "short, lyric compositions, published and sold as sheet music or in books and songsters, and sung within the domestic circle"; they "could be heard in the theatres and concert halls... but were sung primarily at home," across the entire spectrum of 19th-century economic and social strata — not only in America, as Moseley points out, but also in the British Isles, Canada, and the Antipodes.

Each of Moseley's operative terms speaks volumes about how parlor songs differ from the folk songs and broadside ballads of the preceding chapters. Parlor songs are *short* compared to the ballads, which frequently entail convoluted narratives and can run to dozens of stanzas. In concept and dimension, parlor songs are characteristically *lyric,* rather than *epic;* simple and romantic, rather than complex or realistic. Moreover, they are *compositions* in the specific sense of being the self-conscious, purposeful contrivances of songwriters-for-hire, calculated to appeal to popular taste, with its Victorian penchants for blithe nicety, euphemistic discretion, saccharine romance, and maudlin sentimentality. They were *published,* almost always under registered copyright, to suit a commercial marketplace, typically by comparatively sophisticated companies specializing in the production, sale, and national distribution of printed music. The publishers commonly employed their own songwriters, paid some form of royalties, or purchased properties outright; they utilized state-of-the-art typesetting and lithographic printing methods, and entailed significant capital risk with expectation of profit, often in partnership with distributors in other cities, domestically and abroad. Songs were promoted and marketed as proprietary commodities in accordance with emerging advertising methods, new in the middle 19th century. To maximize appeal, popular pieces were characteristically issued in a selection of formats devised for home consumption, theatrical performance, and organized group singing; they were pitched for high, medium, and low male or female voices, and were given settings for accompaniments on a variety of musical instruments — typically piano, parlor organ, flute, and guitar.

The lyrics were likewise characteristically pitched to the popular taste, aimed at some vague common denominator, risking little, frequently bland and placatory, as music or as poetry seldom venturous or profound. In Moseley's words, when they broached seafaring themes, "Such songs indicate how Americans regarded the oceans which bounded them, and this, in turn, tells us something about how they regarded themselves. The sea in these songs is decorative, harmless, man-centered"; the songs are "benign" and "unrealistic." In fact, Moseley may be too modest in limiting her remarks to a single nationality when she says, "This was a way, I believe, of taming the ocean and bringing it into the parlor; of permitting Americans — those by the fireside and those aboard ship — a spurious sense of mastery over an alien and threatening environment." For if this be true at all, it is certainly as true of the parlor songs of English, Scottish, and Irish composition as it is of the ones originating on the western shores of the Atlantic; and with regard to the widespread popularity of many Victorian parlor songs throughout the English-speaking world in the 19th century, there is little to differentiate the respective nationalities.

So, too, the handful of pirate songs in the parlor song genre. They are comparatively few; and apart from "I'm Afloat, I'm Afloat" ("The Rover of the Sea") [#46], with words by Eliza Cook and music by Henry Russell, most of them do not appear ever to have been candidates for the hit parade. Still, even a couple of the obscure ones were known by sailors at sea. The national origins of the words and music appear to be fairly evenly distributed among English, Irish, Scottish, and American perpetrators. Most were written and published in the early Victorian period, in the late 1830s and 1840s; by the '50s the fashion for creating new ones, such as it was, seems to have passed, as American visions of adventure and derring-do turned increasingly away from the sea and towards the western frontier.

THE PIRATE LOVER

In standpoint of the lyrics, cast here in a woman's voice, this American parlor piece is among the best of all "composed" songs about pirates because it actually faces piracy head on, and does so without sentiment and without surrendering the essential air of romance that imparts a measure of dramatic tension. It is a genuine pre-Victorian period piece, less saccharine than many that came along in the generation to follow. The words are by poet James G. Percival (1795-1856), a graduate of Yale College who lived and worked in New Haven; and the pleasant melody is by James Aykroyd, music teacher, arranger, and musical instruments dealer in Nashville, Tennessee, in the 1820s and in New Bern, North Carolina, in the 1830s-'40s. Two Philadelphia publishers issued separate editions of sheet music at around the same time: G. Willig (Wolfe #376) and G.E. Blake (N° 69 in *Blake's Musical Miscellany* series; Wolfe #377), both circa 1824. The lyrics were reprinted in a Boston edition of *The Forget Me Not Songster* (in the 1840s) and *The New Song Book* (Hartford, 1851). Here, as in "The Corsair's Bride" [#36], but to an even greater extent, the female voice expresses more than sappy, doe-eyed admiration for her pirate lover. Rather, it exhibits the extraordinary features of skepticism and regret regarding the pirate's evil deeds. She says, "I cannot behold thee / In plunder and gore" and still "fold thee in fondness": she is repelled by his deeds, disappointed that rather than the hero she initially thought him to be, he is primarily motivated by greed; she fears he will be killed; she is ashamed of his livelihood; and though she cannot help loving him, she calls him "false, mean, and cruel."

1
Thou art gone from thy lover,
  Thou lord of the sea!
The illusion is over
  That bound me to thee;
I cannot regret thee,
  Tho' dearest thou wert,
Nor can I forget thee,
  Thou lord of my heart.

2
I lov'd thee too deeply
  To hate thee and live,
I am blind to the brightest
  My country can give;
But I cannot behold thee
  In plunder and gore,
And thy Minna can fold thee
  In fondness no more.

3
Far over the billow
  Thy black vessel rides;
The wave is thy pillow,
  Thy pathway the tides;
Thy cannons are pointed,
  Thy red flag on high,
The crew are undaunted,
  But yet thou must die.

4
I thought thou wert brave,
  As the sea-kings of old;
But thy heart is a slave,
  And a victim to gold;
My faith can be plighted
  Thy low heart has blighted
To none but the free;
  My fond hopes in thee.

5
I will not upbraid thee;
  I leave thee to bear
The shame thou hast made thee,
  Its danger and care:
As thy banner is streaming
  Far over the sea,
O! my fond heart is dreaming
  And breaking for thee.

6
My heart thou has broken,
  Thou lord of the wave!
Thou has left me a token
  To rest in the grave:
Though false, mean, and cruel,
  Thou still must be dear,
And thy name, like a jewel,
  Be treasured up here.

THE CORSAIR'S BRIDE

The lyrics of this lament are ascribed to "The Lady of a Noble Duke"—a deliberate obfuscation. What *grande dame* of the British peerage would want her good name sullied by such a tawdry association with the theatre? The music is by the minor British composer Leander Zerbini, and the ensemble was published by Hewitt at New York circa 1830-32 (after an undated London edition of 1830): a cover illustration by the Pendleton company shows a woman sitting on a rocky seashore, with a Celtic harp alongside and a sleek schooner attacking and burning another vessel in background. As in "The Pirate Lover" [#35], but to a lesser extent, the woman here voices regret at having sacrificed everything to follow her pirate paramour, but this song is more about her loss and her homesickness and self-pity than about recoiling from the violence and cruelty of piracy at sea. The sheet music advertises that it was sung by "Madame Vestris" and "Miss Bartolozzi," who were actually the same person, the London-born contralto, actress, and impresario Lucia Elizabeth née Bartolozzi (1797-1856), daughter of Gaetano Stefano Bartolozzi (1757-1821), a music teacher and fencing master. She married ballet master Auguste Armand Vestris in 1813, he deserted her after four years, she had a series of modest triumphs on the stage, and beginning in 1831 she was London's first female theatre manager. In this she was a major success, famous for her stage sets, realism, and pioneering innovations. "The Corsair's Bride" came along in this period, at the height of her celebrity. In 1838 she married Charles James Mathews, with whom she was involved in various other theatrical ventures, all the while continuing on the stage.

1. For thee I left a Father's arms, and many a kindred Smile;
    Gay scenes that had a thousand charms, for this lone sea girt Isle,
    Now seated in a moss grown cave, I watch the foaming tide,
    And mourn the hour that I became a ruthless Corsair's bride,
    A ruthless Corsair's bride.

2. In specious guise a Warrior brave, his armour glittering bright;
    He wooed and wooed me by his smiles, my artless faith to plight;
    With well stor'd caskets, for my dow'r, the stormy waves defied,
    But little dream'd that fatal hour, made me a Corsair's bride,
    Made me a Corsair's bride.

3. Betrayéd by his seeming love, thro' mournful scenes to roam;
    While memory so keen points out, my much regretted Home.
    Lay still my harp, with chords unstrung tho' once you were my pride;
    The willow wreath does best become the Corsair's weeping bride.
    The Corsair's weeping bride.

THE PIRATE'S DESERTED BRIDE

This English parlor song of circa 1830 is catalogued in the British Library under its proper title and also, erroneously, as "The Corsair's Deserted Bride," in obvious confusion with the preceding [#36]. The mention of Conrade [sic] suggests that it may also be related to Byron's poem, "The Corsair" (1814), which in 1837 was adopted as the basis of the ballet "Le Corsaire," consisting of French music and French choreography on the London stage, with leading characters named Conrad and Medora. The popularity of the ballet inspired "The Corsair's Farewell" [#53]. The lyrics of "The Pirate's Deserted Bride" were written by Harry Stowe Van Dyke, the score is an early work by William Christian Selle (1813-1898), sometime chapel organist at Hampton Court and professor of music and Doctor of Music at Richmond (England), and the song was popularized in England by chanteuse Eliza Inverarity (1813-1846), who also toured it in the USA. The American sheet music, published in New York by J.L. Hewitt circa 1830-32, has an Endicott lithograph that closely parallels Pendleton's cover for "The Corsair's Bride": a woman sits on a rocky seashore (here without a Celtic harp), while a lateen-rigged pirate schooner sails away in the background.

1. Far o'er the sea the bark is gone, with her blood red flag above;
    And I am left to weep alone, my sorrows and my love;
    My fears rise with the rising gale, for my heart is on the main;
    Oh! I ne'er shall see that spreading sail and blood red flag again.

2. Far o'er the sea whilst waves roll high, the bark outstrips the wind
    And Conrade gives perchance no sigh, for her he leaves behind;
    Yet oh! for him my sighs shall burst, and for him my warm tears flow
    That love is faithful which is nurs'd midst bitterness and woe.

3. Soon the fair rose which pleasure wears, in the height of transport now
    Shall love the flatt'ring bloom it bears, and wither on her brow;
    But sorrow's mournful express wreath, is more constant tho' less fair,
    It courts the brow in life, and death still finds it clinging there.

THE ROVER'S BRIDE

In this melodramatic parlor song by two of Britain's most prolific songsmiths, the poetry by Irish-born songwriter Thomas Haynes Bayly (1797-1839) does not divide into stanzas; therefore, the melody by Scots composer Alexander Lee (1802-1852) is through-composed without repeats. The words and music here are from the American sheet music by James Hewitt (New York, circa 1830-35); the punctuation and scattershot quotation marks are verbatim as found there; so too the abrupt ending.

"Oh if you love me, furl your sails, draw up your boat on shore,"
"Come tell me tales of midnight gales but tempt their might no more,"
"Oh stay!" Kate whisper'd, "stay with me!" "Fear not!" the Rover cried,
"Yon' bark shall be a prize for thee, I'll seize it for my bride."
The boat was in pursuit, it flew; the full sails bent the mast!
Poor Kate well knew the Rover's crew would struggle to the last
And ceaselessly for morning's light she prayed upon her knees,
For all the night, the sounds of fright were borne upon the breeze!
And morning came, it brought despair! The Rover's boat was gone!
Kate rent her hair, one bark was there, triumphant but alone!
She sought the shore she braved the storm, a corpse lay by her side!
She strove to warm the Rover's form, then kiss'd his lips and died.

39
THE ROVER'S HOME

This British parlor song has words by the prolific Irish songwriter Thomas Haynes Bayly (1797-1839) with music through-composed by John Feltham Danneley (1786-1836), a church organist and music teacher in Ipswich (England). The setting and accompaniment are very elaborate, with a mere twelve lines that run to five full pages in the sheet music. The song was popularized by a basso known as Signor Giubelei, who circulated in high echelons of British society and married into the aristocracy. The American sheet music was published by Firth & Hall at New York in the 1830s, with a cover by the Endicott firm that has a Mediterranean-looking bearded brigand in cape, cloak, skirts, and turban-like head-dress, holding a cutlass, standing on a seaside promontory, pointing seaward towards a topsail schooner underway. The structure is ABAC, with a long B section, after which the A section repeats, followed by a much shorter C section.

Oh   talk no more of the tran-quil shore, of the charms of hill and dale,   We   love   to float in the

Ro-ver's boat, Borne on by the north - ern gale.   We   look be - low where the wa- ters flow,   and we

look to skies a — bove, Then tell me not of the lands — man's lot, for this is the life we

love.   Fear-less we view the e-ne - mies crew, When their proud flag waves before us, We dread not wreck

on the Ro-ver's deck, Tho' storms are how-ling o'er us, You trem-ble to hear of   the Ro - ver's ca- reer,

Track'd by the white sea foam.   Tem-pests and strife are the charms of life, And the deep is the Ro-ver's

home...   love, for   this is the life we love, for

this is the life we   love...   the   life   we love.

THE PIRATE'S BARK

If the claims on the sheet music be believed, this British parlor song, now nearly extinct, must have enjoyed at least a brief moment of popularity in England in the middle 1830s. Neither the lyricist, J. Burrington, nor the composer, John W.L. Ash, is remembered for any other contribution to the arts, but other names on the sheet music would have counted as testimonials in promoting it. It was "published for the composer" in London by Z.T. Purday, as "sung by Miss Sherriff, Mr. Purday and Mrs. Wood." "Miss Sherriff" was actually Jane *Shirreff* (1811-1883), soprano, who debuted in 1831, toured America in 1838, then married and retired. "Mr. Purday" was Charles Henry Purday (1799-1885), prolific hymnologist, secular composer, and baritone from the same family of musicians as the publisher, who was also a retail dealer in musical instruments. "Mrs. Wood" was Mary Anne Patton (1802-1864), a child prodigy soprano from Edinburgh who as an adult became a "major luminary" of the London concert stage. Even after she married Lord William Pitt Lennox (1824) she continued using her maiden name professionally; and after they divorced (1831) she married tenor Joseph Wood and assumed his surname. As for the song, it varies little from the vaguely romantic fluff of the era, with a slightly livelier-than-usual tune.

1. Lightly thou art bounding
    My bark upon the Sea
Like an Eagle on the Mountain
    Thou'rt rapid and as free
Thy snowy sails are lending
    Their surface to the breeze
Thy pliant spars are bending
    With a Niad's graceful ease.

Yet swifter swifter speed thee
    My wild sea bird away
An enemy doth heed thee
    He marks thee for his prey
Then haste my Bark O haste thee
    On thy pearly ocean track
Tho' the water demons chase thee
    They can never bring thee back

2. Thou hast born me ocean's daughter
    With the Tempest raging high
In safety tho' its waters
    Hath commingled with the Sky
When the billows gathered round thee
    And the waves dash'd o'er thy prow
Ever faithful still I found thee
    And thou wilt not fail me now.

On! on my beauty speed thee
    Another bound and then
No danger shall impede thee
    In thy passage o'er the Main.
Hurah Hurah my Rover
    We're fleeting past the wind
The fancied danger's over
    Thou'st left them far behind.

COME, BRAVE WITH ME THE SEA, LOVE

This art song by the Italian composer Vincenzo Bellini (1801-1835) is from his 1834 light opera *I Puritani* ["The Puritans"]. It appeared in various American sheet music editions in the 1830s and '40s. At least one, published in Boston, has the lyrics in both English and Italian, including the ostensibly original Italian title, "Suoni la Tromba Intrepido" (Keith's Music Publishing House, circa 1834-37). A slightly later New York edition has a piano accompaniment by one S. Milon (James L. Hewitt & Co., 1837). The plot of the opera, as described by Brewer, concerns the Puritan revolution in England in the 1640s and seems only obliquely related to the duet, if at all:

> *Puritani (I),* "the puritans," that is Elvira, daughter of Lord Walton, also a puritan, affianced to Arturo (*Lord Arthur Talbot*), a cavalier. On the day of their espousals, Arturo aids Enrichetta (*Henrietta, widow of Charles I*), to escape; and Elvira, supposing that he is eloping, loses her reason. On his return, Arturo explains the facts to Elvira, and they vow nothing on earth shall part them more, when Arturo is arrested for treason, and led off to execution. At this crisis, a herald announces the defeat of the Stuarts, and Cromwell pardons all political offenders, whereupon Arturo is released, and marries Elvira.

There is also a more explicitly piratical version by John Watson, a Scots arranger who was also responsible for the much better known "John Anderson my jo, John." The American sheet music for this was issued at Philadelphia by Fiot, Meignen & Co. in 1837, and must have proven fairly popular, as it continued in print in separate Fiot and Meignen editions after their partnership was dissolved in 1839. Watson had clearly worked it up for his performing family members, notably *Mrs.* Watson (there was also a *Miss* Watson), and it takes liberties. First of all, the sheet music describes it as "the celebrated Duett sung by Mrs. Watson & Mr. Plumer, With most enthusiastic applause in the Favorite Opera *The Pirate Boy,* Performed at the New York, Philadelphia & Boston Theatres, Adapted & Arranged from Bellini's opera *I Purtani,* by J. Watson." *The Pirate Boy* is actually a different opera, keeping Bellini's music but with a different plot and characters; and the setting of "Come, Brave with Me" itself becomes quite complicated, being through-composed for two voices, the rover Templemore and his sweetheart Clara, who sing consecutive solos (the rover's invitation followed by the lady's answer). They next alternate lines, then sing simultaneously, but singing slightly different words and at cross-purposes. To accomplish this, somebody had to write a new libretto and had to tinker with the lyrics, adding lines in the voice of Clara that are not indigenous to the Bellini opera nor to the original (anonymous) translation.

TUNE: "Come, Brave With Me the Sea, Love." From two editions of the sheet music: Keith's Music Publishing House, Boston, n.d., circa 1834-37 (Lester S. Levy Sheet Music Collection, Johns Hopkins University); and Fiot, Meignen & Co., Philadelphia, 1837 (author's collection).

The original English lyrics, from three editions of the sheet music: Keith's Music Publishing House, Boston, n.d., circa 1834-37 (Lester S. Levy Sheet Music Collection, Johns Hopkins University); James L. Hewitt & Co., New York, 1837 (Levy Collection); and Fiot, Meignen & Co., Philadelphia, 1837 (author's collection).

Come, brave with me the sea, love,
The empire of the free, love!
There shalt thou dwell with me, love,
My blessing and my pride.
Come hasten with me there, love,
While yet the wind is fair, love!
Where sparkling billows foam, love!
Where fate may bid us roam, love!
My ship shall be thy home, love,
And thou a Sailor's bride!

'Tho fair the earth may be, love,
It is not like the sea, love!
Where soars the spirit free, love,
As on its breast we ride.
Come then dwell with me there,
Come while the wind is fair, love,
While sparkling billows foam, love,
So boundless and so wide,
With me all dangers dare, love,
As should a Sailor's bride.

Come, brave with me the sea, love,
And o'er its breast we'll ride.
With me all dangers dare, love,
As should a Sailor's bride.

B.

Additional lyrics from the light opera *The Pirate Boy*, arranged by John Watson, which is said to be "based on" Bellini's *I Puritani*, "...as sung by Mrs. Watson & Mr. Plumer." These lyrics styled as responses in the voice of the rover Templeman's paramour, Clara. (Philadelphia: Fiot, Meignen & Co., 1837.)

Ah! no I may not roam, love,
From father, friends and home, love,
Where sparkling billows foam, love,
So boundless and so free.
For dangers dread are there, love,
When tempests rend the air, love;
'Tho beautiful the sea, love,
When winds and waves are free, love;
The fair green earth for me, love,
Still there I must abide.

No, not with thee there, love,
Altho' the wind is fair, love,
I may not dangers dare, love,
Altho' a sailor's bride.
The fair green earth for me, love;
I may not dangers share, no, no, no!
I may not dangers dare, love,
Altho' a sailor's bride.

"The Pirate Lover." Wood engraving by W.illiam J. Pierce, "Drawn and engraved expressly for The Novelette," 18:3 (a tabloid magazine published in Boston by Elliott, Thomes & Talbot, circa 1848) illustrating a story by Sylvanus Cobb, Jr., entitled, "The Texan Cruiser; or Calypso the Wanderer, A Tale of the Mexican War."

[Drawn and engraved expressly for The Novelette.]   THE PIRATE LOVER.   [See page 11.]

THE BUCCANEER'S BRIDE
[Away, away o'er the boundless deep]

This obscure piece is based on "Away! Away We Bound o'er the Deep," with words and music by Joseph Rodman Drake (1795-1820). It was well known on shipboard. Huntington recovered transcriptions from whalemen's journals of the New Bedford ship *Hillman* (1854-57) and bark *Pacific* (1870-72), there is a fragment from the bark *Oak* of Nantucket (1869), and the song is mentioned but not quoted in William H. Keith's journal of whaling and merchant voyages aboard Boston and Wellfleet vessels (1865-71). Whether it had a melody of its own is not established. The tune and accompaniment here are Drake's, for the parent song, as published in the popular sheet music setting by T.V. Wiesenthal (Baltimore, circa 1834). The words are taken from a broadside, sloppily entitled "Bucanier's Bride" and crudely printed on cheap paper by Henry DeMarsan (New York, circa 1855-60). The rhyme scheme and spelling leave much to be desired. To fit the lyrics to the melody requires adjustments of text or tune, including various repetitions.

1   Away, away o'er the boundless deep,
         We merrily, merrily roam;
     Come, man your breaks, while the mermaids sleep,
         With a song of the highland home.

2   On the deck I stand, with my gallant bark,
         To guide my love o'er the sea;
     To the spicey isles, where the bright sun smiles
         With its golden fruits for you.

3   To the land of the rose where the ruby grows
         With its thousand gems so bright
     I'll deck thy brow as the morn doth now
         With its fairy beams of light

4   Sleep on, sleep on, my virgin bright,
         Nor dream of your highland home;
     We brothers will watch by the bucanier's bride,
         'Till the dew on the twilight is gone.

THE DEMON OF THE SEA

This songster-like piece has plenty of action and a suitably moralistic outcome. It has evidently not been anthologized and is primarily known in only two examples, one from singing tradition in New Brunswick and the other from a shipboard copybook aboard a New Bedford whaler circa 1847. The sailor text was published by Huntington, who could find no tune for it so he used one of the melodies for "Captain Ward and the *Rainbow*" [#11]. He also points out that the last King Edward of England prior to the 20th century died in 1553, implying that the presence of the name is a corruption; but he does not try to account for a scenario that might explain it. Certainly any of the seven medieval Edwards (the Martyr, the Confessor, and five with numbers) would have been too early to figure into a ballad of this ilk; and Edward VI, the Boy King, the frail son of Henry VIII who died in 1553, is an improbable reference. *Edward* could be a simple two-syllable substitution for *Henry,* harkening back to Henry VIII and his campaign against Scotland [see "Sir Andrew Barton," etc., #2-4]; or *King Edward* could be a corruption of *Prince Edward,* a ship-name that figures in at least two pirate ballads — including some renditions of "High Barbary" [#6]; and "Bold Sawyer," a ballad that narrates an action of a British naval squadron led by Captain James Sayer against the French in 1758 (Ashton 1891, 48; Firth, 212).

On the other hand, in this case any attempt at such solutions proves pointless. Surprisingly, a fragment of evidence actually survives concerning the origin of both "The Demon of the Sea" and "The Pirate of the Isle" [#44]. In *London Street Folk* (1851), the first of four volumes in his massive *London Labour and the London Poor* (1851-64), Henry Mayhew quotes an anonymous London street author, identified only by the initials J.H., to the effect that the informant wrote both ballads in the 1830s, this one to the tune of "The Brave Old Oak" by E.J. Loder:

> "Above fourteen years ago I tried to make a shilling or two by selling my verse. I'd written plenty before, but made nothing by them. Indeed I never tried. The first song I ever sold was to a concert-room manager. The next I sold had great success. It was called 'The Demon of the Sea,' and was to the tune of 'The Brave Old Oak.' Do I remember how it began? Yes, sir, I remember every word of it. It began: 'Unfurl the sails, / We've easy gales; / And helmsman steer aright. / Hoist the grim death's head / The Pirate's head / For a vessel heaves in sight!' That song was written for a concert-room, but it was soon in the streets, and ran a whole winter. I only got 1 s[hilling] for it. Then I wrote 'The Pirate of the Isles,' and other ballads of that sort. The concert rooms pay no better than the printers for the streets." (Mayhew, I:302f)

Given such circumstances of authorship, any relevance to the actual sequence of kings named Edward and Henry can hardly be the point. The situation also suggests that it may sometimes be unwise to put too fine an historical edge on textual criticism of parlor songs and street ballads.

A.

"The Demon of the Sea," from the copybook of William Histed, ship *Cortes* of New Bedford, circa 1847. Tune: "The Brave Old Oak" by E.J. Loder (1813-1865), composed for a text by H. F. Chorley (1808-1872) (Duncan I:306; McCaskey II:103; etc.).

1 "Come spread your sails with steady gales,
   And, helmsman, steer her right!
   Hoist the grim death flag," the pirate cries,
   "For a vessel heaves in sight.
   Run out your guns, in haste bear down,
   From us she must not slip;
   Cheer, cheer, lads, cheer, we know no fear
   On board the demon ship."

Chorus: Then huzza for a life of war and strife
               Oh the pirate's life for me!
               My bark shall ride the foaming tide,
               For I am demon of the sea.

2 Two ships of war came from afar,
   From Edward, England's king;
   "Go fetch," he said, "alive or dead,
   The captain of the pirate's bring."
   But his pride I shook, his ships I took
   And I sunk them in the wave:
   Six hundred and ten of proud Edward's men
   Met with a watery grave.

3 And yon ship, too, I mean shall sue,
   That ever my bark saw;
   For by her rig she seems to be
   A British man-of-war.
   "Give a broadside!" the pirate cried,
   "Show them a pirate's fare;
   Fire red hot balls, destroy them all,
   And blow them in the air!"

4 Two ships engaged in equal rage,
   In dreadful murderous scene;
   The die was cast, for a ball at last
   Had struck her magazine.
   Now one and all did stand appalled,
   And seemed in great despair,
   For the captain, too, and all his crew
   Were blown high in the air.

Final   Then no more will he ride the foaming tide,
Chorus: No more a dread will he be;
               For the pirate's dead, low lays his head
               In the deep and dark blue sea.

B.

"The Demon of the Sea": after the singing of James Cameron, Bloomfield Ridge, New Brunswick, collected and published by Edward D. Ives. This variant lacks a refrain and is distinctive for being cast mostly in the pirate's voice. "Since Cameron only hoarsed out one stanza before reciting the rest, parts of the tune are conjectural"; so, too, the three revisions here: in measure 6, a B natural is replaced with a C; likewise in measure 10; and the last two entire measures, which effectively changes the key from major-modal to minor (the original ending is also shown). A textual jumble in stanza 3 ("My men are brave, no man can knave / As noble as band as I") has also been corrected.

"Furl your sails through the pleas-ant gale, And helms-man steer her right. Hoist a- grimm's our flag," our pi - rate cries. "There's a ves - sel hove in sight." hove in sight."

1   "Furl your sails through the pleasant gale,
    And helmsman steer her right.
    Hoist a-grimm's our flag," our pirate cries.
    "There's a vessel hove in sight."

2   "Now run out your guns! In haste bear down!
    From us she must not slip!
    Come to a large cheer, for we know no fear
    On board of the demon ship.

3   "My men are brave, no man or knave
    Has as noble a band as I.
    And at my nod fear naught nor God,
    And even Fate defy.

4   "Two ships of war sailed from afar
    And proudly roamed the sea.
    To take me tried, but I defied;
    There's none can conquer me.

5   "Then two men of war were fitted out
    By Edward, England's King.
    'Go bring,' he said, 'alive or dead,
    That pirate captain bring.'

6   "Their ships I took, their pride I shook,
    With all their crew so brave.
    And six hundred and ten of King Edward's men
    In the ocean found their grave.

7   "And yon ship too, we'll make her rue
    When first my barque she saw.
    For I do not think in fact she floats
    As an English man-of-war.

8   "Run out your guns! Fire full broadside!
    Give them a pirate's fare!
    With red-hot balls, destroy them all
    And blow them into the air!"

9   Two ships engaged in equal rage
    And equal slaughtery,
    'Til the die is cast, the ball at last
    It reached the magazine.

10   And Captain Moore he trembles now,
    For he stands in deep despair;
    And the pirate captain and all his crew
    Were blown into the air.

11   No more he'll roam the swelling foam,
    No more a dread he'll be;
    For the pirate's dead, and the ocean's red
    With the Demon of the Sea.

44
THE PIRATE OF THE ISLE

The narrative here concerns the defeat of a self-confident pirate by a British man-of-war. It was evidently written for the London music halls in the 1830s by the same anonymous London street poet who authored "The Demon of the Sea" [#43]. It has a lovely melody, suitable for a tenor or baritone solo of the kind that Richard Henry Dana, Jr., and Herman Melville describe in their shipboard narratives. It was certainly in tradition among square-rig sailors in the mid 19th century, whence it remained comparatively stable. Captain Harlow's version, "sung by Wm. R. B. Dawson, an old-time chanteyman," is virtually the same as the one given by Admiral Luce, including the presence of a final chorus; their tunes are also related and harmonically compatible. There are three substantially older texts in whalemen's manuscripts—one from William Histed's copybook of the ship *Cortes* of New Bedford, circa 1847 (Huntington, 74); one transcribed by George E. Sanborn of Lowell, Massachusetts, in the journal of his shipmates, George M. Jones and Albert F. Handy, aboard the New Bedford bark *Waverly* circa 1859-63; and the third written down by George W. Piper of Concord, New Hampshire, aboard the ship *Europa* of Edgartown, Massachusetts, 1868-70 (the latter two manuscripts are in the Kendall Collection, New Bedford Whaling Museum). These vary from the printed texts in subsidiary features only, stanza for stanza following the same general scheme and adopting some of the same stilted syntax, with such esoterically "artistic" lines as "Proud Gallia's sons and Spanish dons...." The melody is from an anonymous American compilation of 1883 entitled *Naval Songs,* where the song is presented without comment. The text here is whaleman George Piper's, circa 1868-70.

Oh! I com-mand a stur-dy band of pi-rates bold and free, No laws I own, my ship's my throne,

My king-dom is the sea: My flag flies red at the top-mast head, And at my foes I smile, I no

quar-ter show wher-e'er I go, Un-til the prize I take in tow. My men are tried, my bark's my pride,

My men are tried, my bark's my pride, I'm the pi-rate of the isle, I'm the pi-rate of the isle.

1 I command a band a sturdy band
   Of pirates bold and free
   No laws I own my ship is my throne
   My kingdom is on the sea
   My flag flies red at my royal mast head
   And at my foes I smile
   No quarters show where so ever I go
   For soon the prize we will take in tow

Chorus   For my men I have tried, my bark is my pride
For my men I have tried, my bark is my pride
I'm the pirate of the isles, I am the pirate of the isles
I am the pirate   I am the pirate
I am the pirate of the isles

2   I love to sail in a pleasant gale
On the wide and raging sea
With a prize in view we will heave her to
And haul her under our lee
Then we will give three cheers and for home we will steer
While fortune on us smiles
For there is none dare cross that famed Le Ross
Unto his flag they will strike of course

3   Proud galleon sons and Spanish Dons
With pride and fury burn
They have crossed the seas for to fight with me
But never more again returned
Then England too doth me pursue
But at her threats I smile
Her men I have slain her ships I have ta'en
I have burned and sank them in the main

4   At length there is in sight a ship of might
An English man of war
She hails Le Ross and stops his course
And a broadside unto her she poured
The pirate he returned the fire
And proudly he did smile
But a fatal ball soon caused him to fall
And loud for quarters his men did call

Chorus for the last verse
      In the briny deep he is laid to sleep
In the briny deep he is laid to sleep
Once the pirate of the isles
Once the pirate of the isles
Once the pirate   Once the pirate
Once the pirate of the isles

THE WILD ROVER

Not to be confused with the traditional Irish ballad of the same name — which has nothing to do with piracy or seafaring — this "Wild Rover" is a shallow parlor piece cast in the woman's voice, declaring that she would love nothing better than to be a freebooting pirate's bride, as though pirates commonly took their genteel wives to sea with them. The poetry is forced, formulaic, and mannered, and the "plot" is a kind of seagoing equivalent of the universal theme of the "Gypsy Davy," "Three Gypsies," and "House Carpenter" ballads, in which a lady abandons her comfortable, conventional, respectable, middle-class luxuries to join an untamed band of brigands, or a freebooter of the road or forest (such as a Romany rover or highwayman), or to take a lover far beneath her station (as in the "House Carpenter" ballad). Such a dialectic resonates with notions of sexual liberation and of repudiation of a State of Civil Society for something superficially resembling a State of Nature, or at least a state of rebellion and the absence of suppression. In this case, she is prepared to sacrifice her home, her dowry, and her pride of social position, but in pre-Victorian manifestations of the Gypsy Lover ballads it sometimes amounted to abandoning an already existing husband and baby, often also a castle and estate. Interestingly, the woman's willing attitude in this song, and her resolve to be fearless, are exactly the opposite of the lady's timid response in version B of "Come, Brave with Me the Sea, Love" [#41].

"The Wild Rover, A Ballad Arranged for the Guitar by Leopold Meignen." From the sheet music (Philadelphia: Fiot, Meignan & Co., n.d., circa 1835-39). N° 34 in Fiot and Meignen's Enterpeiad series

1.   I will rove from the land where my forefathers lie,
From the land of my birth with my own love I'll fly,
All, all I'll give up, both my dow'r and my pride,
To be with my first love the wild Rover's bride;
I will watch when he sleeps, I will smile when he wakes,
I'll feel prouder than him at each prize that he takes,
For my love is as boundless and pure as that sky,
And as deep as the sea which so stirless doth lie,
All, all I'll give up, both my dow'r and my pride,
To be with my first love the wild Rover's bride (2x).

2. In the calms I will sit by his side and I'll sing
    A song, of that land where the Lotuses spring;
    In the storms I'll not tremble, I cannot know fear,
    When my first love, my dear love, my own love is near.
    Then farewel[l] to the home of my childhood! we'll go
    From the land of the Cedar where bright Rubies grow,
    O'er you deep blue sea in thy bark we will sail,
    And sweet odours will come in each wandering gale.
    All, all I'll give up, both my dow'r and my pride,
    To be with my first love the wild Rover's bride (2x).

46
I'M AFLOAT, I'M AFLOAT
[The Rover of the Sea]

"The Rover of the Sea," a famous poem by Eliza Cook (1818-1889) that begins, "I'm afloat, I'm afloat," was set to music by Henry Russell (1812-1900) around 1840. The sheet music was widely circulated in several editions, and in 1844 the lyrics were printed in *The Sheet Anchor,* a Christian temperance magazine for seamen. The song has occasionally been encountered in tradition, there are several transcriptions in whalemen's journals of the 1840s and '50s, and we have the testimony of Admiral Luce and the anonymous editor of *Naval Songs* (1883) that it was also popular in the 19th-century navy. The orthodox lyrics here were transcribed at sea by whaleman Charles C. Evans in the journal of his shipmate, Daniel A. Chapel, cooper aboard the ship *Benjamin Tucker* of New Bedford, in 1851.

I'm a-float, I'm a-float on the fierce rol-ling tide, The o-cean's my home and the barque is my pride;

Up, up with my flag, let it wave o'er the sea, I'm a-float, I'm a-float, and the Rov-er is free.

I fear not the mon-arch, I heed not the law; I've a com-pass to steer by, a dag-ger to draw,

And ne'er as a cow-ard or slave will I kneel, While my guns car-ry shot or my

belt bears a steel. Quick, quick, trim the sails, let the sheets kiss the wind, And I'll war-rant we'll

soon leave the sea-gulls be-hind; Up, up with my flag, let it wave o're the sea; I'm a - float,

I'm a - float and the Rov-er is free; I'm a - float, I'm a - float, and the Rov-er is free.

1   I'm afloat I'm afloat on the fierce rolling tide
     The ocean is my home and the barque is my pride
     Up up with my flag let it wave o're the sea
     I'm afloat I'm afloat and the Rover is free

2   I fear not the monarch I heed not the law
     Ive a compass to steer by Ive a dagger to draw
     And never as a coward or a slave will I kneel
     While my guns carry shot or my belt bears a steel

3   Quick Quick trim the sails let the sheets kiss the winds
     And I'll warrant we ll soon leave the seagull behind
     Up up with my flag let it wave o're the sea
     I'm afloat I'm afloat and the Rover is free

4   The night gathers o're us the thunder is heard
     What matters our vessel skims on like a bird
     What cares she for the storm-ridden main
     She had braved it before and she'll brave it again

5   The light gleaming flashes around us may fall
     They may strike they may cleave but they cannot appall
     With lightnings above us and darkness below
     Through the wide wast[e] of waters right onward we go

6   Hurrah my brave boys may ye drink may ye sleep
     The storm fiend is hushed we're alone on the deep
     Our flag of defiance still waves o'er the sea
     Hurrah boys hurrah boys the Rover is free

May 14th 1851   well what of it   Chas C Evans

THE ROVER OF THE SEA (II)

That this song is known only from a ballad slip by George Walker & Son of Durham (England) suggests that it properly belongs among the broadside ballads. However, the title is indebted to the popularity of "The Rover of the Sea," also known as "I'm Afloat! I'm Afloat" (#46), of which Walker also printed a broadside under the title "I'm Afloat," in the same series, circa 1845-60 (see page 146); and the tone of the lyrics is more akin to the carefree yeo-ho-ho rhetoric of parlor songs than to the customarily narrative structure and often greater realism of the broadside ballad genre. As usual with such ephemeral publications, the lyrics are anonymous and the tune is not named. A modicum of redeeming social value is encapsulated in the last line.

I'm rover of the seas,
    And chief of a daring band,
Who obey all my decrees,
    And laugh at the law of the land.
Wherever my swift bark steers,
    Desolation and rapine are spread,
And the names of the famous buccaneers
    Fill the bosoms of all with dread.
        For I'm Rover of the Seas —
            Ha ! ha !
        For I'm Rover of the Seas.

King of the waves am I
    And rule with despotic sway,
As over the waves I fly,
    In search of my lawless prey.
No mercy I ever show
    To any I chance to meet —
But 'neath the billows they go,
    For dead men no tales repeat.

I'm the terror of the main,
    For none yet has conquered me,
And every victory I gain
    Makes me firmer the lord of the sea;
In storm, or in calm or in fight,
    I ever am the same,
And dearly have earn'd the right
    To claim my blood-stain'd name.

I envy no king on shore,
    For there's none has power like me,
They're bound by the oath they swore
    While I am reckless and free;
And tho' danger I meet each day,
    Yet merry my life is pass'd
For let there come what may
    I can but die at last.

Broadside by George Walker & Son., Durham (England), undated, circa 1845-60; from the same series as the example on page 146.

THE PIRATE'S LIFE FOR ME
Tune—Some love to roam.

The *Pirate's Songster* specifies the tune "Some love to roam," but the full title is actually "Some love to roam o'er the dark sea foam," a landlubberly text by Charles Mackay (1814-1889) for which Henry Russell (1812-1900) composed the music. It was published at New York and Baltimore in 1836 and several subsequent editions.

Some love to roam o'er the dark sea foam,
Where the shrill winds whistle free;
But a chosen band in a mountain land,
And a life in the woods for me,
When the shrill winds whistle free;
But a chosen band in a mountain land,
And a life in the woods for me,
When morning beams o'er the mountain streams
Oh! merrily forth we go
To follow the stag to his slippery crag
And to chase the bounding roe.
To follow the stag to his slippery crag
And to chase the bounding roe.
Ho! ho! ho! ho! ho! ho! ho!
Ho! ho! ho! ho! Ho! Ho! Ho! Ho!

Some love to roam o'er the dark sea foam,
When the shrill winds whistle free;
But a chosen band in a mountain land,
And a life in the woods for me!
And a life in the woods for me

And a life in the woods for me
I love to ride o'er the foaming tide,
Where the winds and waves play free,
With a daring band, with a blade in hand,
Oh, a pirate's life for me;
Our craft's broad sails, breast, breeze or gale,
And merrily forth she flies,
To follow each bark, o'er waves so dark,
And seek the glorious prize.
Yeo ho! yeo ho! &c.

Each gallant bark, we quickly mark,
And we follow in her track,
Though guns appear, we will bear near,
We range up for attack.
Our hot gun's blaze sweep shroud and stays,
Amid death and horror's cries,
Our boarding pikes! she strikes,
We merrily seize our prize.
Yeo ho! yeo ho! &c.

THE RED ROVER'S SONG

A musical setting by the 19th-century composer Chevalier Sigismund von Neukomm (1778-1858) for an old poem by the baroque English bard Edmund Smith (1672-1710) was published at New York by Edward Riley & Co., circa 1836-42. Neukomm was a pupil of Franz Joseph Haydn and a friend of Tallyrand and Dom Pedro I, Emperor of Brazil. The lithographic cover by Endicott & Co. (illustrated below) has a solitary bearded pirate on deck amidships, forward of a hatch that seems to have a mast or spar protruding from it, with a dismembered cannon and cannon shot at his feet; he wears a cocked hat, navy-style officer's coat, short, flowing skirts, and a brace of pistols, with cutlass raised, holding the halyard of a very large skull-and-crossbones flag. What it lacks in strict nautical accuracy it makes up for in drama.

1. A merry life is ours, I trow, while o'er the billows' surge we go.
   Our birthright joy! to care unknown, for time and pleasure are our own.
   O'er bounding main we boldly dash, 'mid thunder's peal and lightning's flash.

2. The skies may frown, or be they fair, we little look, and less we care.
   And gaily sail, our track to keep, upon the proud and peerless deep.
   The land we loathe, the Sea we love, For joys it hath all joys above.

3. We joy to see the Dolphins play, beneath the sun-lit sparkling ray.
   To mark while on our course we run, the splendor of the setting sum.
   But oh! our greatest joy will be: to feel, to know we're brave and free.

THE RED ROVER'S SONG,!

↑ Cover illustration from "The Rover's Flag" (next page).

THE ROVER'S FLAG

Edwin Ransford (1805-1846), the English baritone and lyricist who popularized this parlor song, may have written the words, as he did for many of the songs he sang. He was also a music publisher in London, doing business as Ransford & Son. In the British sheet music the words and music are anonymous but the arrangement is credited to Sidney Nelson (1800-1862), better known for "The Rose of Allandale" and "The Pilot." It was published by Nelson's former business partner, Charles Jefferys (1807-1865) of Jefferys & Co., successors to Jefferys & Nelson, with a full-page scene of a pirate chief in a swashbuckling pose (see page opposite). Jefferys was also a prolific lyricist, and it was Nelson who set many of Jefferys's words to music (their most famous collaboration was "Jeannette and Jeannot"). An American edition of "The Rover's Flag," published by Edward Riley & Co. in Philadelphia circa 1836-42, credits the music to Montague Corri (1784-1849), son and partner of Domenico Corri (1746-1825), Italian-born composer and music dealer in Edinburgh and London. It has a nifty half-page cover illustration by the Endicott firm, of an armed square-topsail schooner of 20 guns, flying the infamous black flag (Levy Collection).

- 1 -

O ever a Rover's life for me,
A gallant bark and a rolling sea;
On my own proud deck, like a King I'll stand
Where brave hearts bow to their Chief's command.
With canvas spread where'er I roam
The deep deep sea to me's a home,
And my heart on that would ever be
With the black flag roving gallantly,
The deep deep seas to me's a home,
And my heart on that would ever be
With the black flag roving gallantly
The black flag roving gallantly
    The black flag roving gallantly.

- 2 -

Thro' thunder storm and lightning flash
Onward my bark will proudly dash,
Swift as the flight of the Hawk she'll sail
And bravely ride thro' the wildest gale.
We'll shun no foe and strike to none
With bright sword gleaming or mounted gun
But we'll meet them still on the broad blue sea
With our black flag roving gallantly
The black flag roving gallantly
Oh! we'll meet them still on the broad blue sea
With our black flag roving gallantly
The black flag roving gallantly
    The black flag roving gallantly.

THE WRECKER'S SONG

Stories have been told the whole world 'round of landbound pirates deliberately luring ships to destruction on a lee shore, so that shipwrecked cargoes could be plundered on the beaches. In the British Isles the nefarious practice is particularly associated with remote stretches of wild coast-line in the West Country and the North, also in the vicinity of treacherous currents, tides, and shoals on the seacoasts Scotland, Ireland, and Wales. In the USA, it is inseparable from popular stereotypes of the Outer Banks of North Carolina. Tradition has it that Nag's Head, N.C., was named for the old horses (*nags*) to which counterfeit running lights were fastened at night, such that the animals' loping gait walking the dunes would broadcast to approaching ships the false impression of vessels bobbing at safe anchorage. Outer Banks historian David Stick suggests that an artist-writer for *Harper's New Monthly Magazine* who visited the region in 1860 may have been the first to commit the much older story to paper: "Nag's Head derives its name, according to the prevalent etymology, from an old device employed to lure vessels to destruction. A Banks pony was driven up and down the beach at night, with a lantern tied around its neck. The up-and-down motion resembling that of a vessel, the unsuspecting tar would steer for it."

The same article in *Harper's* is also quoted as saying that the Banks-dwellers' "kindness and hospitality to wrecked seamen is unfailing and unlimited," and Stick suggests that there are "other explanations" for the naming of Nags Head "which date back even further." However, these all have to do with three places in England named Nags Head, and there is nothing in Stick's arsenal to explain how the Nags Heads in England were named; and nothing to suggest that Nags Head, N.C., was not named for Nags Head, England, precisely because of analogous piratical practices luring ships onto the dunes. There were certainly plenty of wrecks at and around Nags Head, N.C., chronicled by Stick himself in *The Outer Banks of North Carolina* (1958) and *Graveyard of the Atlantic* (1952). But "The Wrecker's Song" is a British piece about this type of land-bound piracy. The sheet music, published at London in 1838, has words by a W.H. Baker, a turgid melody by one William Aspull, and an introductory paragraph to set up the background.

On several parts of the British Coast there used to reside individuals whose occupation was to parade the Sea Shore in search of plunder from the Vessels wrecked upon those parts of the Coast. These individuals, hardened by lawless privilege, were often known to delude Mariners by false lights to seek shelter from the raging Tempest only to meet certain destruction on those dangerous Shores; and if saved from a watery grave, murder was their inevitable doom for the sake of possessing the valuables they might have about their persons.

1. When sinks the sun in the distant sea,
   And night steals o'er the sky,
   And heavy gulls all sluggishly,
   To rocky caverns hie,

Refrain:
   Then I with my staff walk the ocean's side,
   To look out for prey in the rolling tide.
   Then I with my staff walk the ocean's side,
   To look out for prey in the rolling tide.
   In the rolling tide, in the rolling tide,
        the rolling tide
   Then I with my staff walk the ocean's side,
   To look out for prey in the rolling tide.

2. When India's fleet is bound for home,
   And Biscay's bay is cross'd;
   And in a billowy sea of foam,
   Some hapless bark is lost

3. When loud the signal gun at night,
   Burst on the stormy air,
   I cheat the crew with treacherous light,
   And laugh at their despair.

52
THE PIRATE'S SERENADE

The sheet music published in 1838 bills this as "A Popular Ballad AS SUNG BY MR. HENRY HORNCASTLE. Composed by J. Thomson. Sung by Mr. J. H. Horncastle." The lyrics may have been inspired by "The Pirate's Song (III)" [#75] by Scottish poet Allan Cunningham (1784-1842), an earlier parlor-poem of a sea-rover's wooing in which the suitor likewise (but somewhat more articulately) offers a lady a carefree life of luxury and adventure as a pirate's bride. The music is by the Scots composer John Thomson (1805-1841). Even though "Pirate's Serenade" is better than many of its ilk, it never achieved much popularity in its own time and remains obscure today. The lyrics were mangled in *The American Sailor's Songster*, the sheet music is scarce, and evidently the words and lyrics were not anthologized together in the Age of Sail. The elaborate melody must have been intended as a vocalist's showcase and requires quite a lot of acrobatics properly to accompany it on the guitar.

My boat's by the tow'r, my barque's in the bay, And both must be gone ere the dawn-ing of day; The

moon's in her shroud, but to guide thee a-far, On the deck of the dar - ing's a love light-ed star.

Then wake, la - dy, wake, I am wait - ing for thee, And this night or nev-er my bride thou shalt be. Then

wake, la - dy, wake, I am wait - ing for thee, And this night or nev-er my bride thou shalt be.

1 My boat's by the tower, my barque's in the bay,
And both must be gone ere the dawning of day;
The moon's in her shroud, but to guide thee afar,
On the deck of the daring's a love lighted star.
Then awake, lady, wake, I am waiting for thee,
And this night or never my bride thou shall be.
        Then awake, lady, wake, I am waiting for thee,
        And this night or never my bride thou shall be.

2 Forgive my rough mood, unaccustom'd to sue,
I woo not, perhaps, as you land lovers woo,
My voice has been tuned to the roar of the gun,
That startle the deep when the combat's begun.
And heavy and hard is the grasp of that hand,
Whose glove has been ever the guard of our band,
                Then wake, lady, &c.

3 Oh, islands there are, on the face of the deep,
Where the leaves never fade, and the skies never weep,
And there, if thou wilt, our love bower shall be,
When we leave for the greenwood our home on the sea.
And there thou shalt sing of the deeds that were done,
When we loos'd the last blast and the last battle won.
                Then wake, lady, &c.

4 One hundred shall serve the best of the brave,
And the chief of a thousand shall kneel to thy slave,
Thou will reign queen, and thy empire shall last
Till the red flag by inches be torn from the mast.
But think not of these, and this moment be mine,
The plume of the proudest shall ever be thine.
                Then wake, lady, &c.

5 Oh! haste, lady, haste, for the fair breezes blow,
And my ocean bird poises her pinions of snow;
Now fast to the lattice these silken cords twine,
They are meet for such feet and such fingers as thine:
Then signal my mates—ho! hurrah for the sea!
This night and forever, my bride thou shalt be.
                Then signal, &c.

THE CORSAIR'S FAREWELL

The American sheet music for "The Corsair's Farewell" was published circa 1839 in New York by George Endicott, the artist and lithographer, as Nº 7 in his series of "Illustrated Songs, Ballads & Duets." (It may also have been issued as Nº 4 in the same series.) The cover (see page 80) features an exotically-clad, mustachioed Turkish- or Algerine-style piratical figure, armed with musket, sword, pistol, and dirks, with an exotically-clad woman clinging to his side as he points out a window seaward, where there is a boat standing by a crenellated castle turret on the shore and one or two lateen-rigged sailing vessels in the offing. The words and music by George Linley (1798-1865), an English composer of light operas, are unremarkable.

1. Good bye! my Love, good bye!
      Our bark is in the bay,
    And we must gain Isle Idra,
      Before blush of day.
    Nay! Weep not tho' I go
      To peril o'er the main,
    My blood red flag ere long
      shall meet thy gaze again.
    List! tis the well known signal gun –
      Days bright orb his course hath run;
      Days bright orb his course hath run.

    One kiss, good bye! One kiss, good bye!
      Good bye! my Love, good bye,
    Our bark is in the bay,
      And we must gain Isle Idra,
    Before blush of day.

    Nay! Weep not tho' I go
      To peril o'er the main,
    My blood red flag ere long
    Shall meet thy gaze again!

2. The breeze is blowing freshly,
      My crew but wait for me,
    And yonder, like some wild bird,
      My bark's white wings I see;
    Ne'er whisper, love, of danger,
      Dry up that timid tear,
      Thou are a Corsair's Bride,

      And shouldst not harbor fear,
    Hark again, the signal gun!
      Fare thee well, my lovely one!
    One kiss, good bye! &c. &c.

BLOW ON! BLOW ON! THE PIRATE'S GLEE

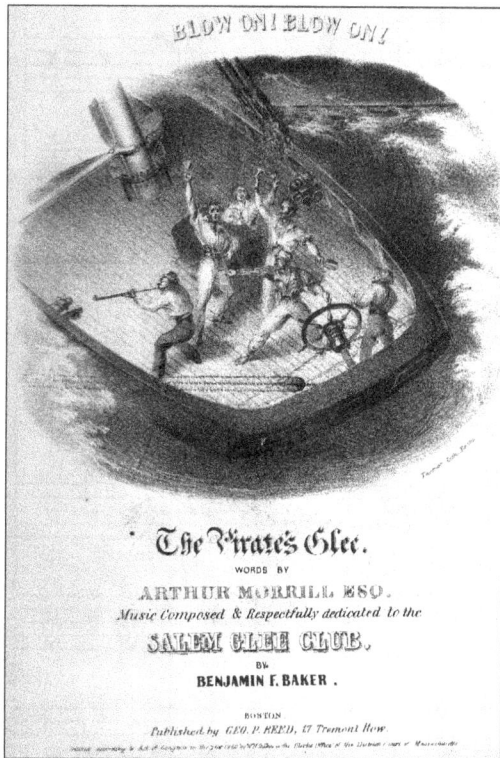

In the *Liberty Minstrel* songster (1846) and *Forecastle Songster* (1850) the lyrics are unattributed and the tune unspecified. But the sheet music, published by George P. Reed of Boston in 1840, attributes the words to Arthur Morrill, Esq., who is otherwise unidentified, with music "Composed & Respectfully dedicated to the Salem [Massachusetts] Glee Club" by Benjamin Franklin Baker (1811-1889), a choirmaster, singer, composer, editor, and teacher of music, whose most enduring composition is the beautiful air for Henry Wadsworth Longfellow's poem "Stars of the Summer Night." The "Pirate's Glee" setting is for male voices in four parts. It has a fairly long stretch sung in octaves in unison, and seems to depend more upon a syncretic blend of the several parts than designed to be carried by the tenors. Singing it can be tricky, as it has an A-B-A structure, with the second A section designated as a *D.C. al coda* repeat (but with no actual coda symbol in the sheet music), while the B section ends in a strangely elongated cadence that moderates around, then terminates in a dominant chord, thus setting up (and virtually requiring) the repeat of the A section.

1 Blow on! blow on! we love the howling
      Of winds that waft us o'er the sea;
   As fearless as the wolf that's prowling
      Upon our native hills are we.
   The doom'd in terror fly before us;
      We've nailed the black flag to the mast!
   It there shall float triumphant o'er us—
      We will defend it to the last!

2 Roll on! roll on! we love the motion
      Of waves that bear us on our way:
   No swifter bark e'er sail'd the ocean;
   Nor skiff more lightly skims the bay.

   The lightning from the sky is flashing;
      The thunder's distant roar we hear;
   But, while o'er waves we thus are dashing,
      We waves, nor winds, nor lightnings fear.

3 Flash on! flash on! we love the gleaming
      That through the darkness shows our way;
   The black flag still is proudly streaming,
      As proudly as it floats by day.
   The waves' roar with the thunder mingling,
      Is music that we love to hear;
   The lightning's flash, at midnight shining,
      Shows us a scene forever dear.

THE FREEBOOTER!

Billed as "A Glee As Sung By W.B. Oliver, L. Marshall & A. Lothrop at the secular concerts of the Boston Musical Institute, and by the Euterpean Vocalists," this obscure piece was composed by Englishman John Jolly (1794-1838) and arranged by Sidney Pearson in an American edition published at Boston by William H. Oakes in 1841. Neither the Boston Musical Institute nor any of the singers has been identified, and do not seem to have exerted any visible musical influence in Boston or elsewhere, highbrow or low. The asymmetrical lyrics are anonymous, it has no real stanzas, no real melody or lead voice, and the through-composed music works only if the song be sung in all three parts, with multiple repeats of each line of text. The lyrics are included here, as they may be of minor interest to history and popular culture, but the complicated musical setting is so overlong, artsy, and gymnastic that it is deemed of insufficient value to consume four or five pages of print here. It can be found in the American Memory Collection of the Library of Congress, on their website at http://memory.loc.gov/ammem/mussmhtml/mussmTitles151.html.

> How merry is the life of the Freebooter bold,
> His pouch is filled with the glittering gold;
> His heart gay and light is devoted to love and his own lady bright,
> His drink is red wine.
> How merry is the life of the Freebooter bold,
> With their wine and their fair ones,
> Their glaves and their gold:
> > How merry is the life of the Freebooter bold.

"The crews of Blackbeard's and Vane's vessels carousing on the coast of Carolina."
Anonymous woodcut illustration from Charles Ellms. *The Pirate's Own Book* (Boston, 1837), page 339.

PIRATE'S CHORUS

Sometime during 1865-71, William Keith of Mattapoisett, Massachusetts, wrote the single stanza of "Pirate's Chorus" into his shipboard journal. Written by the Irish-born violinist, baritone, and composer Michael William Balfe (1808-1870) for his light opera *The Enchantress* (1845), it is not the sort of thing that sailor stereotypes suggest would have interested a common foremast hand. But of the 79 songs Keith transcribed in his journal, there are no chanteys (worksongs), no deepwater sailors' ballads, only two or three generic ballads ("Henry Martin" among them), and only six or seven that can be called traditional folk songs; and of these, most appear to have been copied from printed sources. The overwhelming majority—71—are parlor songs and other popular compositions by professional songwriters, produced for the stage and printed by commercial publishers, including "Old Folks at Home" and "The Man on the Flying Trapeze." There is little to suggest that Keith, born in 1844, was in any way unusual in his musical and poetic tastes, and much to suggest that his anthology typifies the predilections of merchant sailors and whalemen. According to a rare annotation in his journal, when Keith went to sea he brought along a small inventory of essentials: a "Pocket Clasp Bible"; a copy of "Worcester's Comprehensive Diction ery [sic]," evidently as yet unread; "Sargent's Fifth Reader"; a blank book "for songs" (used as a journal and copybook); lead pencils, watercolor paints, and an ivory ruler. Some of his songs were actually transcribed by shipmates George R. Worth of Nantucket and Henry Gibson of Tremont, Massachusetts; others were written down by Charles M. Kinney, who evidently took the volume with him on a later whaling voyage. Like most Yankee whalemen of the era, they were all young—in their twenties—and much influenced by whatever was current on the hit parade. Balfe's music burned brilliantly for a while and had more staying power than most; these sailors may even have sung some of it at sea. Balfe's arrangement here takes at least two pirates to sing it properly. For a richer effect, try tinkering with Balfe's prescribed harmonies and chords.

Ev - er be hap - py and light as thou art, Pride of the Pi - rate's heart!

Long be thy reign o'er land and main, By the glaive, by the chart, Queen of the

Pi - rate's heart! Queen! Ev - er be hap - py and light as thou art, Pride of the Pi - rate's

heart! Pride, pride of the Pi - rate's heart! Pride, pride of the Pi - rate's heart.

Ever be happy and light as though art
Pride of the pirate's heart!
   Long be thy reign
   O'er land and main:
By the glaive, by the chart,

Queen of the pirate's heart.
Ever be happy and light as though art
Pride of the pirate's heart
[*Pride of the pirate's heart*]
[*Pride, pride of the pirate's heart*]

HO! FOR A ROVER'S LIFE; OR THE SONG OF THE PIRATE

This "descriptive ballad" is through-composed, the music is highly stylized and repetitive to the point of redundancy, the rhythm is irregular, and the lyrics are not divided into actual stanzas. It was written and composed by John H. Hewitt (1801-1890), a native of New York City, graduate of the U.S. Military Academy at West Point, sometime infantry officer, and performer on the flute, composer, musical arranger, poet, lyricist, dramatist, and literary editor in Baltimore, Washington, and various cities in South Carolina, Georgia, and Virginia. (He once won a poetry competition in which Edgar Allan Poe took second place, much to Poe's enduring consternation, even though Poe won the short-story prize in the same competition.) The song is altogether not much suited to modern tastes, but in its day it must have been quite a showcase for the celebrated Anglo-American baritone Henry Russell, whose name appears on the title page of the sheet music (published by the author-composer in association with Firth & Hall, New York, 1843). As is the case with many parlor songs about pirates, the lyrics romanticize the carefree way of life "on the account"; however, here a warship appears — implying a mortal threat — and the song ends equivocally, with the pirate ordering his men to "stand to their guns" and that the flag be nailed to the mast, meaning that it cannot be "struck," thus leaving no chance for surrender. The assumption must be that the Navy was ultimately victorious, which is the outcome that most audiences and all sailors would have expected and preferred.

Ho! for a rover's life,
Battle and stormy strife!
Fearless he braves Wild wind and waves,
Like a prison's bird set free!
Seeking the stormy deep,
Where mountain billows leap,
He's the monarch of the sea,
The monarch of the sea.

Moor'd in the friendly cove,
Oft turn his thoughts to love;
The dark-eyed maid Hears his serenade,
And is charm'd by his wild minstrelsy.

Listen sweet maid to thy lover's guitar,
While he worships thy beauty,
thou bright southern star!
Come brave the ocean, belov'd one with me,
There's joy on the billows
when smile'd on by thee.

A gun is heard! All hands on board,
A sail appears out on the sea,
And we give her chase right merrily.

Hurrah! my boys, our guns tell true,
She strikes! Hurrah for the pirate crew!

Ho! for a rover's life,
Battle and stormy strife;
Fearless he braves wild wind and waves,
A rover's life for me, A rover's life for me.

Thus sung the proud chief of the pirate crew,
As his trim schooner
danc'd o'er the waters blue;
But soon thro' the mist was a warship spied,
With her teeth grinning death on either side.

"Stand, stand your guns!
Nail our flag to the mast!"
Was the cry of the chief
as the thunder roll'd past.
He falls! while the blood
down his pale forehad runs,
And his sinking craft groans, he cries
"Stand to your guns!
Stand to your guns, my boys,
Stand to your guns, stand, stand,
Stand to your guns."

58
THE *MALEK ADEHL*
Tune—*Will Watch.*

This rousing sea chase, cast in the voice of one of the pirates and using plenty of sailor lingo, is based upon an actual incident. The *Malek Adehl*—actually, *Malek Adhel*—was a brig, named after a sultan of Turkey, built in 1840 as a merchantman by the celebrated New York shipbuilder William Webb for Mexican owners. Shortly thereafter she was prosecuted for piracy:

On or about 30 June, 1840, the brig *Malek Adhel* sailed from New York bound to Guayamas, in California, under the command of Joseph Nunez. The vessel was armed with a cannon... ammunition, and... pistols and daggers on board. It appeared from the evidence... that she stopped several vessels upon the high seas, and at length put into the port of Fayal, where she remained for some days. Departing thence, she arrived at Bahia, in Brazil, about the twenty-first of August, 1840, where she was seized by the *Enterprise,* a vessel of war belonging to the United States, and sent into the port of Baltimore for adjudication. A libel was there filed against vessel and cargo upon five counts... to punish the crime of piracy.... Two other counts were afterwards added.... (United States v. the Brig Malek Adhel, 43 U.S. 210, 1844; ref: http://supreme.justia.com/us/43/210/)

The USS *Enterprise* was a brig of 10 guns, built at New York in 1831 and commanded at the time by Lt. Louis Goldsborough (1805-1877), who was later a rear admiral in the Union Navy. After the prosecution the *Malek Adhel* was briefly in the Pacific trade, and in 1846 she entered the Mexican Navy as a 10-gun brig in the war against the United States. Captured at Mazatlan on 6 September 1846 by the USS *Warren* under Comdr. Joseph B. Hull, she was taken into the U.S. Navy, served the remainder of the war on the California coast, and was sold off in 1848. The tune specified in the songsters is "Will Watch" [#18], composed by John Davy (1765-1824) for lyrics by Thomas Cory.

1. Up with the black signal, and brace for the battle,
    A United States cruiser ploughs upon our lee,
    There's a wild flap of death in her sail's thrilling rattle,
    There's danger when Yankee tars fight on the sea.
    Out guns and blades, boys, quick, make fast your hatches
    She'll pour a broadside by the next foamy swell,
    Prime well your lee guns and stand by with your matches
    To sink or to die for Malek Adehl.

2. Ha! the blaze sweeps our mizzen, she still pours upon us,
    Her stars light the sky, and her guns light the sea,
    Fight on—should they take us, they'll mercy have on us,
    For noble are Yankees by land or by sea.
    We cut down their yard, yet their broadside will sink us,
    That shout from her crew now sounds like our death knell
    Our fore deck is gone! — Ere the ocean shall drink us,
    Strike! strike, the black flag of Malek Adehl.

TO THE MAST NAIL OUR FLAG: THE PIRATE'S SONG

This narrative song is unusual among popular pieces about pirates, as it captures some of the bitterness and brutality of the piratical life. It is the only song text in *The Pirate's Own Book* (1837) and also appears in the *American Sailor's Songster* (1848), two editions of the *Forecastle Songster* (1847 and 1850), and Rinder's *Naval Songs* (London, 1895). Rather than waxing rhapsodic about how much fun it is to be a freebooter (or a freebooter's bride), the bitter lyrics, which are signed only "L.E.L.." actually make explicit reference to theft, violence, cruelty, and the antisocial nature of life "on the account." The melody by Horatio Dawes Hewitt (1829-1894) is less compelling. The sheet music was published by George P. Reed of Boston in 1846, with a Bufford & Co. lithograph of a sleek topsail schooner with raked masts, flying the Jolly Roger flag and heeled far over in a stiff blow on a heavy sea.

TO THE MAST NAIL OUR FLAG.

THE PIRATE'S SONG.

The words by L.E.L. Music composed

respectfully inscribed to MISS ELIZA GAITHER of Washington, D.C. by

HORATIO D. HEWITT.

BOSTON.
Published by GEO. P. REED, 17 Tremont Row.

Author's collection

Despite its awkward, even sometimes silly syntax, from the standpoint of substantive content the text is unusually sophisticated. Whether a ship be navy, privateer, merchantman, or pirate, if her flag is nailed to the mast it cannot be *struck* (lowered) to signify capitulation in a sea-fight. When a pirate thus renders his ship unable to surrender, it has to be in earnest and no mere bravado. The "powder room" is not a euphemism for the plumbing convenience, but refers to the magazine belowdecks where the gunpowder is stored. A pirate chief who claims no share in the spoils was rare, as loot not only occasioned wealth and power but tended to be a barometer of success. This particular pirate's sociopathic manifesto about his engaging in piracy as a form of vengeance, and the apparent delight he takes in violence for its own sake, coincide with the theories of some sociologists and psychologists that mistreatment in early life, or lack of recognition along the way, or lack of reward or advancement later on, are common root causes of turning to a life of crime; and violence as recreation is certainly an all-too-familiar phenomenon in our own century, no less than in the past.

To fit the melody, the repeats indicated in the first stanza also need to apply to the second and third stanzas.

1

To the mast nail our flag; it is dark as the grave,
Or the death which it bears while it sweeps o'er the wave
Let our deck clear for action, our guns be prepared,
Be the boarding-axe sharpen'd, the scimitar bared.
Set the canisters ready, and then bring to me,
For the last of my duties, the powder-room key.
It shall never be lower'd, the black flag we bear,
If the sea is denied us, we'll sweep through the air.

2

Unshared have we left our last victory's prey,
It is mine to divide it, and yours to obey.
There are shawls that might suit a sultanna's white neck
And pearls that are fair as the arms they will deck;
There are flasks which, unseal them, the air will disclose
Damieta's far summers, the home of the rose:
I claim not a portion: I ask but as mine—
'Tis to drink and our victory—one cup of red wine.

3

Some fight, 'tis for riches; some fight, 'tis for fame:
The first I despise, and the last is a name;
I fight, 'tis for vengeance: I love to see flow,
At the stroke of my sabre, the life of my foe:
I strike for the memory of long vanished years,
I only shed blood where another sheds tears;
I come as the lightning comes red from above,
O'er the race that I loathe to the battle I love.

THE PIRATE'S SONG (I)

This obscure piece was written by George W. Fraser, composed by Charles Leslie, and published in New York in 1853, after which little has been heard of it or of the principals responsible for its creation. Its simple melody is spiced up a bit by a chorus in four-part harmony (as published).

1   Come pass round the bowl and the festive board hail,
     We will drink deep tonight, for tomorrow we sail,
     What recks it tho' storms shoot across the dark sky,
     We seek for an equal game, conquer or die.

Chorus: Then swell high the Chorus, drink deep to the brave,
          Who dare be at war with both man and the wave.

2   Let them prate of their liberty, unity, all
     Who ne'er on their cheek felt the breath of a squall:
     The elves only have them in cold moony rays,
     Alone it is ours to exist in their blaze.

3   The Eagle aloft on Icarian flight,
     Feels no more at home, than we in the fight;
     He wings off in safety, and we are as free
     From a dread of our pinions being melted as he.

4.   Then hail thee! to morrow! to morrow all hail!
     And come with a breeze that will fill every sail;—
     That may waft us in sight of a prize worthy bark,
     Ere the night shade around us its mantle draws dark.

FINEEN THE ROVER

Fineen the Rover was an actual historical figure, Fínghin Ó Driscoll, a 16th-century Irishman —
or possibly two historical figures, father and son; for if everything they tell about him be true,
and he was only one man, he must have lived 125 years. He opposed the Protestant Reformation
in Ireland in the reign of Henry VIII, tangled with Portuguese merchants in 1537, was a privateer
for Archbishop Edmund of Cashel, and for a while was head of the Ó Driscoll clan (beginning in
1573). In 1587, a year before the great Spanish Armada, he was knighted by Queen Elizabeth "for
having captured eight Spanish ships,"[1] which earned him the disfavor of some Irish critics for his
complicity with England. He is also excoriated by Driscoll descendants for ill-advised wheeling-
and-dealing in the vicinity of Cork and Baltimore in the 1610s: "Fínghin Ó Driscoll, Fineen the
Rover, although famous in song and story, set in train a series of events and land deals which
were to reduce the O Driscolls to poverty and cause their leaders and many of their descendants
to emigrate...."[2] According to the song text, "He died as a brave man should die... In a fight
'gainst the foes of his country"; but the foes of *which* country, Ireland or England, is not
specified, nor is the date of his reputed demise. According to Driscoll family lore, Fineen "died
poor and alone on an island in Lough Ine" in 1629, which was a very long time indeed after
having engaged the Portuguese as an adult in 1537. Like his contemporary, Grace O'Malley, Sir
Fineen's career was only piratical from a certain point of view, and actually had more to do with
commercial chicanery, political maneuvering, and territorial control, enforced by cannon fire in
Irish coastal waters.

The lyrics are by Robert Dwyer Joyce (1830-1883), an Irish physician, poet, and songwriter,
son of Garrett Joyce, "an accomplished musician," and younger brother of Patrick Weston Joyce
(1827-1914), historian, author of *Irish Names of Places,* and pioneering anthologist of Irish songs.
Robert took a degree in medicine at Queen's University, Dublin, practiced medicine and taught
literature for a while, emigrated to Boston with his wife and family in 1866, was elected a member
of the Royal Irish Academy, and wrote "Fineen the Rover" sometime before 1873. The melody
specified for his poem is a traditional Irish air with the colorful title "You'd think, if you heard
their pipes squealing," which, unfortunately, now appears to be lost. James Healy gives a tune
he identifies as "The Groves of Blackpool" (Tune A, below); and Irish-born composer Charles
Villiers Stanford (1852-1924), a professor at the Royal College of Music in London and at
Cambridge University, composed a third, much more formal setting (Tune B).

TUNE A - "The Groves of Blackpool," from James N. Healy, *Irish Ballads and Songs of the Sea* (1967), pp. 34, 47.

---

[1] www.michaelhalm.tripod.com

[2] www.placenames.ie/capeclear/news

TUNE B - "Fineen the Rover," from sheet music anthologized by Martin Akerman, ed., *The Year Book Press Series of Unison and Part-Songs* (London, 1923), n.p.

TEXT from *Ballads, Popular Poetry, and Household Songs of Ireland, Collected and Arranged by Duncathail* (pseudonym of Ralph Varian) (Dublin, M'Glashan & Gill, 1873), pp. 130f. Also: H. Halliday Sparling, ed., *Irish Minstrelsy: Being a Selection of Songs, Lyrics, and Ballads* (London and Newcastle: Walter Scott, 1887).

An old castle towers o'er the billow
   That thunders by Cleena's green land,
And there dwelt as gallant a rover
   As ever grasped hilt by the hand.
Eight stately towers of the waters
   Lie anchored in Baltimore Bay,
And over their twenty score sailors,
   Oh, who but the Rover holds sway?

   Then, ho! for Fineen the Rover!
     Fineen O'Driscoll the free!
   Straight as the mast of his galley,
     And wild as the wave of the sea!

The Saxons of Cork and Moyallo,
   They harried his lands with their powers;
He gave them a taste of his cannon,
   And drove them like wolves from his towers.
The men of Clan London brought over
   Their strong fleet to make him a slave;
They met him by Mizen's wild highland,
   And sharks crunched their bones
     'neath the wave

Then, ho! for Fineen the Rover,
   Fineen O'Driscoll the free;
With step like the red stag of Beara,
   And voice like the bold sounding sea

Long time in that old battered castle,
   Or out on the waves with his clan,
He feasted, and ventured, and conquered,
   But ne'er struck his colours to man.
In a fight 'gainst the foes of his country
   He died as a brave man should die;
And he sleeps 'neath the waves of Cleena,
   Where the waves sing his *caoine* to the sky!

   Then, ho! for Fineen the Rover,
     Fineen O'Driscoll the free;
   With eye like the Osprey's at morning,
     And smile like the sun on the sea.

THE *VAMPIRE* (A PIRATE SONG)

Vampire is the name of a pirate schooner in this English parlor piece of 1889. The name reflects a growing British vogue for vampirism at that time, anticipating by about ten years Bram Stoker's *Dracula.* It tells of a merciless pirate who gives no quarter and is finally dispatched by a fearless Royal Navy commander. The lyrics were written pseudonymously by "Henry Martingale," the music is by Michael Watson (1840-1889), who died just around the time the sheet music was published (London: E. Ascherberg & Co.). The cover depicts a sharply-raked topsail schooner or so-called "brigantine," a skull-and-crossbones "Jolly Roger" flag, and a vampire bat in flight.

1. Creeping round a headland as the sun was brightly rising,
   Dispelling gloomy shadows of the night,
    A raking pirate schooner, under easy canvas sailing,
   Came stealing out to greet the dawning light.
   Her captain walk'd the quarterdeck where quarter ne'er was granted,
   And keenly scann'd the offing for a sail;
   His footsteps keeping measure with a song he gaily chanted,
   A ditty which reveal'd a ghastly tale:

Refrain: Dead men no secrets tell; mercy but scant we show—
   Young or old, we seize their gold; then up the plank they go.
   Jolly good luck to our flag so grim — emblem of deeds we do.
   Millions of wealth, long life, and health to the "Vampire's" crew!

2. A merchant-ship to leeward on the "Vampire's" course is steering;
   The pirate captain quick her sail espies:
   Forthwith he puts his helm up, sets ev'ry stitch of canvas,
   And falcon-like, swoops down upon his prize!
   With motley swarms of ruffians he boards the hapless trader;
   Defence, tho' stout and stubborn, proves but vain.
   A scene of death and plunder, the ship is fir'd and sinking;
   Then loud, triumphant, sounds the dread refrain. *Refrain*

3.	But England, hearing rumors of bloodshed and marauding,
	Dispatch'd a cruiser ably arm'd and mann'd,
	Commanded by a Briton, by danger nothing daunted,
	To mete out vengeance with relentless hand.
	They fell in with the schooner, and brought her soon to action:
	The combat rag'd with fury fierce and long:
	The pirates, taken captive, were hang'd beside their leader,
	Who never more will sing his gruesome song: *Refrain*

63
THE PIRATE ISLE NO MORE

This song was produced in 1889 as part of the fiftieth anniversary of Galveston, Texas, which had been one of the rough-and-tumble frontier outposts that Jean Lafitte, Lafitte's brothers, and other notorious outlaws are reputed to have selected as their bases of operation. With words by W.A. Hogan and music by H.A. Lebermann, the song is dedicated to the Semi-Centennial Board of Directors, and was performed and published by Thomas Goggan & Brother in association with a "Semi-Centennial Grand March" and other ceremonial components. The idea is that the island community, once a rowdy haven for pirates, rogues, slave-runners, and brigands, had now become a sophisticated metropolis and paragon of virtue — a "Pirate Isle no more." The cover has vignettes of Galveston in 1839 and 1889, but no trace of actual pirates. In a sense, it is much the same kind of testimonial to changing eras as the young Benjamin Franklin's "Downfall of Piracy" in 1718 [#17]. The final chorus merely repeats the first four lines of the second stanza.

Final Chorus:

1.   'Tis the semi-centennial of which we boast,
    Of dear old Galveston, the gem of the coast,
    Which once was the home of the Pirate Lafitt [sic],
    Where now Texas' proud queen of commerce does sit,
    On her Throne near the ocean boundless and blue,
    Greeting all people with a welcome that's true,
    Upward and onward for all bright years to come,
    With friendship for all and with malice for none.

2.   She will soar like the great grey eagle on high,
    The fortune of rivals will cause her no sigh,
    She will follow the paths of honor and right,
    With her well earné d glory, but just in her might.
    Bred are her sons by the wild ocean wave,
    A terror to tyrants, a friend to the law,
    Her Princes are merchants but honor'd the while,
    The hope of our State and the pride of our Isle.

3.   They bring to her people bright visions untold,
    These merchants investing their silver and gold,
    In factories grand and in buildings that reach,
    From wonderful strand to our beautiful beach.
    On the great Mexic gulf that washed her sands,
    Sail ships of all nations, of all foreign lands;
    They come to her ever with white wings of peace,
    This Island that rivals the islands of Greece.

Woodcut illustrations from Charles Ellms, *The Pirate's Own Book* (Boston, 1837).
TOP: Sea Fight – entitled "A Piratical Vessel destroying a Merchant Ship." page 359.
BELOW: Boarding – entitled "Lafitte boarding the Queen East Indiaman," page 59.

Part Five: Lyrics from the Popular Songsters

Bibliographer Irving Lowens defines a songster "as a collection of three or more secular poems intended to be sung":

> Since a songster is primarily a collection of song lyrics, under ordinary circumstances it would contain no musical notation. However, since it is a collection of poems intended to be sung, it may well contain frequent references to the names of the tunes the compiler had in mind when he chose the lyrics. More often than not, these tunes were those the average person reasonably could be expected to recognize and sing from mention of the title alone." (Lowens 1976, ix)

In addition to the various songsters continually being imported from England and Scotland, some 650 songsters were published in America prior to 1821 (Lowens, xi). Many contained no more than the requisite three-song minimum, and how many of each were printed and circulated is not recorded; in fact, more than 100 are known only by their titles, no actual specimens being extant. The ensuing few decades produced voluminous anthologies with runs in the thousands. Cheaply printed as small, vestpocket-size booklets with tiny type, the contents were calculated to appeal to the broad popular taste and the format to provide lots of lyrics at little cost. Judging from the extent to which lyrics from early 19th-century songsters were later recovered from singing tradition, it appears that these later, widely disseminated songsters were extremely influential.

Grigg's Southern and Western Songster is one of the earliest (1826) and largest (14 x 8.5 cm, 324 pages): with more than 300 songs it went through several printings. A rash of anthologies followed, with smatterings of patriotic, convivial, comic, naval, and love lyrics: *The Universal Songster* (1829), *The American Songster* (4 eds., 1830-51), *The Universal Songster and Museum of Mirth* (1835), *The Northern and Eastern Songster* (1835), and *The Popular National Songster* (1845), to name a few. The most influential and far reaching was *The Forget Me Not Songster; Containing A Choice Collection of Old Ballad Songs, as sung by our Grandmothers* (though very few of the songs were as old as the title implies). This was actually three similar, but not identical editions issued contemporaneously by different publishers in New York, Boston, and Philadelphia, circa the 1840s. The New York version gives the lyrics of some 92 songs on 254 pages in a small format (11 x 7 cm), many with a tune indicated (but most without), little of the poetry attributed, and a handful illustrated with crude woodcuts. The editors evidently assumed that the singer would either recognize the tune right away, as Lowens avers about the earlier songster texts, or could fit the lyrics to some air of appropriate meter. Temperance songsters (with so-called "cold water" songs) and other topical collections also appeared, notably several promoted as nautical — including *The American Naval and Patriotic Songster* (1831); *The Forecastle Songster* (1847 and 1850); the second, "Naval" volume of W.M. McCarty's *Songs, Odes, and Other Poems on National Subjects* (2 vols., 1842); *The American Sailor's Songster* (circa 1848); and even *The Pirate's Songster* (circa 1845). None of these has musical notation; nor are they anthologies of folk songs (even if some public-domain traditional material crept in from time to time). Typically, they gathered lyrics haphazardly from the popular commercial press, including parlor songs, music-hall songs, and, increasingly as the century wore on, blackface minstrelsy songs. Songsters with titles evoking sailors and forecastles contain songs *about* sailors and songs prescribed *for* sailors, not songs *by* sailors themselves: the lyrics were mostly written by landlubbers, who were often vocational poets or hired lyricists, emulating seafaring themes and sailor lingo, lacking authority, at best achieving only superficial credibility.

Full-fledged *songbooks* were not unknown in the popular genre. At their most rudimentary, these were merely songsters with musical notation added (sans accompaniment). The bestselling *Beadle's Dime Song Book* series debuted in 1859 in tandem with a less-extensive, parallel series called *Beadle's Dime Melodist,* which gave both the words and music of many of the same songs. But few pirate lyrics found their way into the songsters, and fewer still reappeared in these 19th-century songbooks, Beadle's or anyone else's.

BILL CUTLASS, THE PIRATE ROVER
Tune—The Roving Sailor.

This is one of seven rare, anonymous ballad texts that were published in *The Pirate's Songster* (circa 1845) and have been encountered nowhere else. The melody is traditional, from an English sailor song of 18th-century vintage that survives in several variant texts and tunes (the one here from Cecil J. Sharp). The lyrics fit the melody if the second line be adapted slightly and the verses be doubled up — that is, if stanzas 1, 3, and 5 be sung to the A part of the melody, and stanzas 2, 4, and 6 sung to the B part. To compensate the uneven number of stanzas, the first stanza can be repeated at the end.

I am a sai-lor brave and bold, long time I've ploughed the o-cean; I've
fought for king and coun-try, too, won hon — our and pro — mo — tion. I
said: My broth-er sai-lor, I bid you a-dieu, No more to the sea will I go with you;
I'll trav — el the coun — try through and through, And I'll be a ram-bling sai-lor.

1   My name's Bill Cutlass, bold and free,
    I came into the world by piracy,
    And while I can steer a craft at sea,
      I'll be a pirate rover.

2   For trade the merchant sails abroad,
    For gold he dares the ocean's flood,
    But I gain all by steel and blood,
      Like a gallant pirate rover.

3   I've roved all seas through heat and cold,
    And many prizes taken and sold,
    And when I've spent out all my gold,
      Again I'm a pirate rover.

4   There's many a maiden proud and grave,
    I've captured on the briny wave,

And on some island made her the slave
    Of Bill, the pirate rover.

5   Yet when I find poor mortals wrecked,
    I risk my life, their own to protect,
    For shipwreck lads will find respect,
      In Bill, the pirate rover.

6   I've stood in many a deck fight grim,
    Where pirates on their blood did swim,
    But ne'er could foes cut hair or a limb,
      From Bill, the pirate rover.

7   They watch for me by land and wave,
    To ship me into a rope and a grave,
    They ne'er shall grab Bill Cutlass, brave,
      The gallant pirate rover.

THE BOLD PIRATES
Tune—Come, brave the sea with me.

Parlor songs and songster pieces sometimes affect the voice of the pirate himself.   In some he is glib and unrepentant, striking an attitude rather than telling a story.   The lyrics here are from *The Buccaneer Songster* (circa 1845).   They are also printed in Luce's *Naval Songs* with the melody by Vincenzo Bellini (1801-1835), from the aria "Suoni la Triomba Intrepido" in Bellini's opera *I Purtani* (1835).

1   Still pirates bold, we'll be, boys,
     Upon the chainless sea, boys,
     We'll rove and plunder free, boys,
     Beneath our sea-blue flag.
     All dangers still we'll dare,
     Let winds be foul or fair,
     While oceans billow foam, boys,
     The waves shall be our home, boys,
     No nation will we own, boys,
     But stand to our sea-blue flag.

2   Then we'll boldly steer, boys,
     When fleets approach we'll sheer, boys,
     Should they chase—then without fear, boys,
     We'll strike our sea-blue flag.
     Though their fleets around us wheel,
     Our bullets they shall feel,
     With match and blade in hand, boys,
     True to our guns we'll stand, boys,
     And ere they shall command, boys,
     We'll sink with our sea-blue flag.

Anonymous illustration for "Pirate Songs" and "The Pirate Crew" in *The Forecastle Songster* (New York, 1850), page 223.

BOLD ROVING THIEVES
Tune—*Albion the Pride of the Sea.*

These lyrics mimic the naïveté, artificial sailor-lingo, and even the stilted colloquial contraction "d'ye see?" popularized and virtually institutionalized in songs written for the English sailor by Charles Dibdin (1745-1814), Songsmith Laureate of Nelson's Navy. But instead of being turned to patriotic purpose, as was eminently the case with Dibdin's songs, the carefree irreverence here is subversive. And while the pirates' belligerent bravado is harmonious with the Davy-Crockett-and-the-River-Pirates brand of American romantic braggadocio, the syntax is antiquated even by mid 19th-century standards. But it is certainly an English piece, likely reprinted from one of the several British broadsides, including one by Catnach. There are plenty of broadsides of "Albion, the Pride of the Sea," with words by a Dr. Houlton, but the sheet music, "as sung by Mr. Denman at Vauxhall Garden," is elusive.

You land-lubber rogues play a cowardly game,
   And skulk in false jackets—but we,
Tho' we glory in plunder, we fight for bold fame,
   The brave roving thieves of the sea.
     Tho' the land's laws may hang us,
     Their swarming fleets bang us,
     And their persons harangue us,
Still we're bold roving thieves of the sea.

No brat of a middy, or skipper high drest.
   Can give us the rope, d'ye see,
We lead the best lives for we live on the best,
   The bold roving thieves of the sea!
     No crafts can outsail us,
     No yard arm nor gallows,
     Can daunt us, nor quell us,
The bold roving thieves of the sea!

THE BUCCANEER'S SONG TO HIS LOVE

Apart from the title, this is hardly a pirate song at all, just a generic song of sailors' parting. It was printed in *The Buccaneer Songster* (circa 1845) and *American Sailor's Songster* (circa 1848), where the tune is not indicated.

1
Do you ever think of me, love?
   Do you ever think of me?
When I'm far away from thee, love,
   With my bark upon the sea.

2
My thoughts are ever turning,
   To thee, where'er I roam,
And my heart is ever yearning
   For the quiet scenes of home.

3
Then tell me, do you ever,
   When my bark is on the sea,
Give a thought to him who never
   Can cease to think of thee?

4
When sailing o'er the billow,
   Do you think I once forget
The streamlet and the willow,
   Beneath whose shades we met?

5
No! I fancy thou art near me,
   And I often breathe a sigh,
When the waves alone can hear me,
   And the winds alone reply.

6
Then tell me—do you ever,
   When my bark is on the sea,
Give a thought to him who never
   Can cease to think of thee?

68
THE BRAVE LAFITTE

The thing about Jean Lafitte (1782-1854) is that he was sometimes a pirate and sometimes not. This he had in common with Andrew Barton [#2], William Kidd [#14f], Blackbeard [#17], and a host of others; it is typical of the very best pirates. Reputed to be a native of St. Malo in France, Lafitte was actually born at Port-au-Prince, Haiti. His lair was a sinecure at Barataria, Louisiana, a kind of seagoing-freebooters' precursor of the Hole-in-the-Wall hideaways of Old West outlaws a few decades later. In the early days after the Louisiana Purchase he preyed on shipping and was feared as the scourge of the Gulf of Mexico. Forays of plundering were intermittently becalmed through periods of inactivity, variously attributed to indolence and to occasional resolutions to go straight and take up a legitimate trade. He secured a permanent place in American myth when, in January 1815, he and his band of followers rallied to the American defense of New Orleans. Wooed by both sides, with the British offering a $30,000 bounty and a full pardon, Lafitte strung them along enough to gain their confidence, learn their battle plan, and pass it to the American commander, Andrew Jackson. In the battle itself, the pirates were particularly distinguished by accurate marksmanship in unrelenting cannon fire. Lafitte was thus the Hero of the Hero of New Orleans. Though unbeknownst to the participants the battle itself occurred some weeks after a peace treaty had been signed, the Battle of New Orleans was a seminal landmark in American self-realization and helped to catapult Jackson to further exploits, including the Presidency. So, too, might have been the elevated regard in which Jean Lafitte were held today had he refrained from further piratical adventures and settled down to a quiet life of partisan politics or commercial enterprise. Instead, he moved his operation to an island in Spanish territory that is now Galveston, Texas, resuming the life of a buccaneer. His fate after 1821 is often said to be unknown; *The Pirate's Own Book* even gives the illustrated story of The Death of Lafitte. But Cordingly has it that Lafitte moved to Charleston, S.C., and, using the pseudonym Jean Lafflin, engaged in legitimate business, surviving into his seventies. The ballad ignores the larger question of Lafitte and the Problem of Good and Evil, concentrating instead on The Pirate In Love, and how, on the brink of his comeuppance, he reasserted himself forcefully and brutally. It is also notable for being one of very few to concern itself with a Female Pirate of any kind: one almost wishes the ballad were about her instead. It was printed in *The Forecastle Songster;* the tune is not specified.

1. Each young land bird, I'm sure, has heard
    Of the ocean lamb and wolf—
   For by both names he's often famed,
    This pirate of the gulf.

2. A home held, by rock and sea,
    Proof 'gainst each searching fleet;
   And, far and near, all hearts did fear
    This island king, Lafitte.

3. He roved the main, great wealth to gain,
    Won treasures rich and rare;
   'Mongst prizes bright, he took, one night,
    A treasure passing fair.

4. This treasure gay he bore away
    Unto his rock retreat;
   She soon, with pride, became the bride
    Of the island king, Lafitte.

5. Her love and smiles all care beguiles,
    And lights his cavern home;
   And, thus enrich'd, Lafitte scarce wished
    Upon the seas to run.

6. Ere months had run, a cruizer's gun
    Was heard near his retreat;
   With ships, and guards, and high rewards,
    They roused the bold Lafitte.

7. Up, up, my boys! the pirate cries;
    Let our proud bark be mann'd;
   These hunters bold shall soon behold
    My 'vengeful pirate band.

8. He clasps his bride, then hastes with pride,
    His ship's firm decks to greet;
   His bark rides out, his comrades shout,
    "Revenge, and brave Lafitte."

9. Boys, to your guns! Each pirate runs
    His port-fire to apply;
The foe draws near, their broadsides glare,
    And quick the hot balls fly!

10. Now, side by side, 'mid smoke they ride—
    Quick death the pirates meet;
With gun and sword the cruizers board,
    And rush at bold Lafitte.

11. He speaks no word, but, with his sword,
    Deals wounds and death to all;

    Their guns they raise, but, as they blaze,
        Some strange breast meets each ball.

12. He drives them from the deck, then bends
    This stranger form to greet;
'Tis she, alas! in pirate dress—
    The bride of bold Lafitte.

13. Up, comrades! turn—their fleet will burn—
    From hence they ne'er shall ride;
I'll make their blood one crimson flood,
    But I'll avenge my bride.

69
LIFE OF THE BOLD BUCCANEER
Tune—A Life on the Ocean Wave

This anonymous glee is based on the famous song of circa 1838, "A Life on the Ocean Wave," with original lyrics by the American poet Epes Sargent (1813-1880) and music by the English baritone Henry Russell (1812-1900). It appeared in the *Buccaneer Songster* and the *American Sailor's Songster* the 1840s, and when it was reprinted circa 1895 in Rinder's British anthology of *Naval Songs,* the American allusions in the second stanza remained intact.

A life on the o-cean wave, A home on the rol-ling deep, Where the scat-tered wa-ters rave, And the winds their rev-els keep. Like an ea-gle caged I pine On this dull, un-chang-ing shore; Oh! give me the flash-ing brine, The spray and the tem-pest roar!

1   The life of the bold Buccaneer
    Is ever joyous and new,
Upon the wave to steer
    With a jolly and daring crew,
O'er the deep and our narrow bark flies,
    Like a bird on the bounding air,
We smuggle or win a prize,
    And sing as our spoils we share.

The life of the bold Buccaneer
    Is ever joyous and new,
Upon the wave to steer
With a jolly and daring crew.

2   No nation in peace we own,
    But make both friend and foe,
Our daring labour crown,
    As around their coasts we go,
But then when a war breaks forth,
    Bold privateers are we,
We strike for the land of our birth,
    'Neath the starry flag of the free

Sing the life of the bold Buccaneer
    Is ever joyous and new,
Upon the wave to steer
    With a jolly and daring crew.

CHARLES GIBBS
Tune—The Rocks of Scilla

Gibbs was a notorious pirate in the Caribbean. Born in Rhode Island in 1794, he served in the Navy, failed in the grocery business in Boston, then went to sea again, "and soon found himself engaged in a mutiny, which led without much delay to a life of piracy" (Rhode Island Historical Society). He and a cohort were hanged for piracy and murder in New York in 1831. It is all narrated in moralistic detail in a book laboriously entitled, *Mutiny and Murder. Confession of Charles Gibbs, a native of Rhode Island. Who, with Thomas J. Wansley, was doomed to be hung in New York, on the 22d of April last, for the murder of the Captain and Mate of the Brig Vineyard, on her passage from New Orleans to Philadelphia, in November 1830. Gibbs confesses that within a few years he has participated in the murder of nearly 400 human beings!* (Providence, 1831).

Gibbs's brutal career of raiding and murder around Cuba should have inspired a better ballad than this. A long-winded morality polemic lacking dramatic action, it consumes nine stanzas tediously emulating traditional ballad conventions before getting to the point, reveals nothing specific about Gibbs, and ends with a formula epiphany—accomplished in more than double the customary number of verses. The tune, named in the songsters as "The Rocks of Scilla," can only be "Rocks of Scilly," which is, in any case, a perfect metrical fit for "Charles Gibbs."

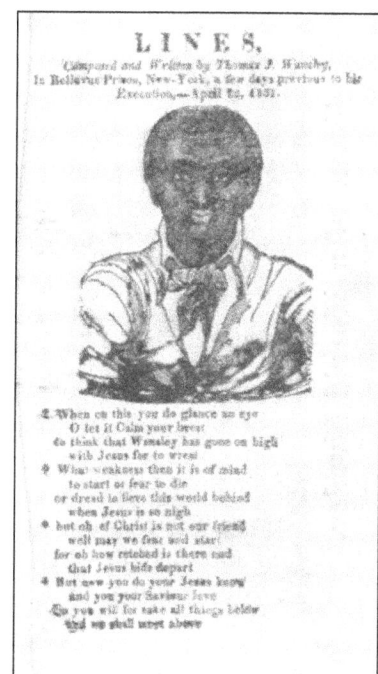

The Rhode Island Historical Society in Providence (www.rihs.org) holds important contemporaneous printed materials associated with the piratical career and execution of Charles Gibbs, including (left) the title sheet of his alleged confession, a broadside from New York (center) documenting the execution itself, and another (right) with a portrait of Thomas J. Wansley, who was convicted and executed with Gibbs, with stanzas purported to have been composed by Wansley himself while in prison, contemplating his mortality. Such confessions, warnings, and expressions of remorse by condemned prisoners were, of course, often falsified by the printers and others who, characteristically of the genre, sensationalized executions in an effort to extract a positive moral lesson from them and, in so doing, to sell books, pamphlets, and broadsides. The Rhode Island Historical Society's extensive collections can be consulted in person in Providence or online at www.rihs.org.

1   Oh, all that now stand round me,
     Take warning by my fate—
     Avoid the path of sin and death
     Before it is too late.

2   I once had tender parents,
     Who dearly loved their son;
     But I proved disobedient,
     And in folly's path did run.

3   My father oft recalled me,
     But I would not refrain,
     Till firmly Satan bound me
     In his infernal chain.

4   My father thought to change my life,
     By sending me to sea;
     But that had no effect at all,
     Though I saw brave Lawrence die.

5   In Halifax more vice I learnt
     Than here I can relate;
     And soon I took a horrid oath,
     Which sealed my dismal fate.

6   In vain my parents plead with me
     To quit the paths of sin;
     Alas! my heart was harden'd,
     And was all blank within

7   A wealthy uncle left me cash
     Which I did then abuse,
     For money I counted but as trash,
     That I might freely use.

8   At length when all my cash was gone
     I resolved to go to sea,
     And enter'd myself w/Captn Brown
     which sealed my destiny.

9   I then entered the Maria, privateer,
     Commanded by Captain Bell;
     And soon we took her from him—
     To you the truth I tell.

10   We hoisted up the Black Flag,
     And a Pirate I became;
     I then committed cruelties
     Too dreadful for to name.

11   Nor sex nor age we spared,
     But all we took were slain;
     No mercy did we ever show,
     For dead men tell no tales.

12   My bloody knife was ever ready
     For, be it understood,
     Nor God nor man I ever feared
     Upon the briny flood.

13   I after visited the land,
     And made a great display;
     For I had cash at full command,
     And that I dashed away.

14   For forty gallant vessels
     I robb'd of gold in store;
     And full four hundred souls of life:
     They welter'd in their gore.

15   No pity have I shown;
     Then who can pity me.
     Though here I die without a sigh,
     Upon the gallows tree.

16   At length when all my cash was gone
     I resolved to go to sea,
     And enter'd myself with Captn Brown
     which sealed my destiny.

17   May God have mercy on my soul!
     Is all my wretched prayer;
     His holy grace can save me yet,
     Though lost in dark despair.

18   For cursed gold my life I sold,
     And murdered without fear;
     But, at the last, I fear I've lost—
     My soul's in deep despair.

19   Now, all who see my shameful end,
     Take warning here by me,
     And don't neglect your souls in life,
     Lest you die on the gallows tree.

20   My hardened heart it will not bend,
     It still clings on to life;
     Ah! must I leave this world behind
     For one of endless strife?

21   Will furies drag my spirits home?
     Will fields torment my soul?
     All this, and more, I must endure,
     For love of cursed gold.

22   Farewell, farewell, my only child;
     May heaven in mercy spare thee
     From the shame thy father feels—
     His crimes and dark despair!

23   Farewell, my parents ever kind;
     We ne'er can meet again;
     For I must suffer for my crimes—
     Ah! where, I dare not say.

THE LOW, BLACK SCHOONER
Tune—*A Wet sheet and a flowing sea.*

These unattributed lyrics were sung to the melody of the jaunting and very popular 19th-century parlor song, "A Wet Sheet and a Flowing Sea," with words by Scottish poet Allan Cunningham (1784-1842) set to an old French military tune, "Le Petit Tambour." Cunningham's lyrics and the traditional music first appeared together in print in Cunningham's own *Songs of Scotland* (1825) and were widely reprinted in England, Scotland, and America. "The Low, Black Schooner," specific origin unknown, is one of several offshoots.

A wet sheet and a flow-ing sea, A wind that fol-lows fast, And fills the white and rust-ling sail, And

bends the gal — lant mast, And bends the gal-lant mast, my boys! While like an ea-gle free, A-

way the good ship flies and leaves Co—lum-bi-a on our lee. Oh! give me a wet sheet and a flow-ing sea,

And a wind that fol-lows fast, And fills the white and rust-ling sail, And bends the gal — lant mast.

Scrimshaw portraying a "low, black schooner" with sharp lines, heavily rigged with plenty of canvas on steeply raked masts – a general type preferred not only by many pirates, for whom speed under sail was at a premium, but also by the navies and revenue services who gave chase to the seagoing outlaws. This striking image was engraved anonymously by a whaleman on a six-inch (15 cm) plaque of sperm whale panbone (jawbone) in the mid 19th century. *New Bedford Whaling Museum.*

Come, raise the sparkling can,
   Sound the toast, each bold mess through,
Huzza, for our low, black craft, my boys,
   And her noble pirate crew.
And her noble pirate crew, bold lads,
   That rakes the broad old sea,
We make each trader pay toll,
   For pirates bold are we.

Then raise the sparkling can,
   Sound the toast each bold mess through,
Huzza, for our low, black craft, my lads,
   And her noble pirate crew.

For trade the merchantmen sail on,
   Yet spoil is their true aim,
Each man o' war cries liberty,
   Yet plunder in that name,
But battle's our delight, my lads,
   It sweetens our won store.
We're open pirates on the sea,
   And lovers on the shore,

Then raise the sparking can,
   Sound the toast each bold mess through,
Huzza, for our low, black craft, my lads,
   And her noble pirate crew.

72
THE PIRATE CREW

The Book of a Thousand Songs indicates that this is "as sung by Mr. Walton," but authorship is not ascribed and no tune is indicated. While the order of the 22 lines does not vary in the songsters, the arrangement into unequal stanzas does.

O'er the wide world of waters we roam ever free:
Sea-kings and rovers, bold pirates are we;
We own no dominion; what matter! we sail
Light-hearted and true in the loud-roaring gale.
We love the black storm as we ride o'er the billows;
The strong timbers creak, the masts shake like willows;
But, fearless in danger, we brave the mad foam—
Ever free on the deep, the wide ocean our home.

Hurrah! hurrah! hurrah!
Merry the life of the bold pirate crew;
Dauntless and daring the deeds that they do.
Hurrah! the black banner is nailed to the mast;

Death to the foe as it waves in the blast!
Crowd sail! a strange vessel is heaving in sight,
Shouts the pirate aloft; she is ours to-night.
How we dash through the foam, bearing down on the prize!
No quarter we give to the stranger who flies.
Clear the decks! Ever brave are the pirates in battle;
Our sabres flash brightly, the loud cannons rattle.
Now we board her in triumph, and bear her away;
Three cheers for the prize, as we bound o'er the spray.
Merry the life of the bold pirate crew;
Dauntless and daring the deeds that they do.

PIRATES BOLD AND BRAVE

No particular tune is specified for this piece from *The Pirate's Songster* (circa 1845), nor does the meter seem quite regular enough for it to be sung.

1

Pirates, bold and brave, are we,
Who sail on the snowy crested sea;
Our bark, without restraint or bound,
It roves the ocean circuit round.
Sometimes in lurking ambush she lies,
Then in swift pursuit o'er the waves she flies,
And we're sure to o'ertake those who attempt to flee.
For none can out strip our bark so free,
A broadside we send as we near the foe,—
We board, we plunder, then off we go,
And pursuit we dare, for none there be,
That will follow to fight us pirates free.

2

We love, oh, how we love to ride
In swift pursuit o'er the sparkling tide;
No lamp in the sky but the waning moon,
To light us to plunder so swift and soon,
If a crowded deck show a daring foe,
The range of our guns will send him below.
We live and we fight, for plunder, no more—
And 'tis seldom we visit the busy shore;
When we do, we return with a bound and zest,
As though the waves were our place of rest;
And it ever has been, and will still be to me,
And the same to all pirates bold and free.

3

We love to spend the bright red gold,
That's been by a miser's fingers toll'd,
To dispel by its flight, the curse on his guile,
That rose as he robb'd to amass the pile.
Those friends on the shore, who take part in the strife,
'Gainst the foes of the rover, we gladden for life,
'Tis with them that the fruit of our plunder we change
Trim our bark if she need it, then onward we range,
One shot as a farewell, the flag is unfurl'd,
The rover's away, and at war with the world,
The blue waves once more around us, all sorrow drown we,
And to feat, list our answer, we're pirates free.

74
THE PIRATE'S CALL
Tune—My bark is on the deep, love

Both the *Buccaneer Songster* and the *American Sailor's Songster* (circa 1845-48) identify the tune: it was evidently named for a text by the prolific hymnologist-poet Sydney Dyer that was also anthologized in various songsters, but the melody has not been located. A later printing of the "Pirate's Call" text in Rinder's *Naval Songs* provides no further enlightenment.

1 There's a prize upon the deep, boys,
    There's gold in the gathering gale,
Then to your posts quick leap, boys,
    And nimbly spread all sail.
    Awake, awake, bold pirates, &c.

2 See, see, she heavily ploughs, boys,
    With the weight of her costly freight,
Pour in upon her bow, boys,
    We'll soon make her cargo light.
    Awake, awake, &c.

3 Huzza! our broadside tells, boys,
    Her flags and her mainmast lowers,
And the wild, despairing yells, boys,
    Proclaim that victory's ours.
    Awake, awake, &c.

4 Quick sound the bugle loud, boys,
    Board! hearties bold and free,
The ocean shall be their shroud, boys,
    And their bark our prize shall be.
    Awake, awake, &c.

75
THE PIRATE'S SONG (II)

These romantic lyrics were written by the Scottish poet Allan Cunningham (1784-1842), author of the famous song "A Wet Sheet and a Flowing Sea" [see "The Low, Black Schooner," #71]. Cunningham's "Pirate's Song" was printed in various poetry anthologies and may have been printed separately in the English and Scottish press; it is also reprinted in Frank Rinder's British collection of so-called *Naval Songs* (London, circa 1895), but evidently not in any of the contemporaneous songsters, British or American. No tune has been located; in fact, there is precious little evidence that it was ever sung.

1 O Lady, come to the Indies with me,
    And reign and rule on the sunny sea;
My ship's a palace, my deck's a throne,
And all shall be thine the sun shines on.

2 A gallant ship, and a boundless sea,
A piping wind and the foe on our lee,
My pennon streaming so gay from the mast,
My cannon flashing all bright and fast.

3 The Bourbon lilies wax wan as I sail;
America's stars I strike them pale:
The glories of sea and the grandeur of land,
All shall be thine for the wave of thy hand.

4 Thy shining locks are worth Java's isle—
Can the spices of Saba buy thy smile?
Let kings rule earth by a right divine,
Thou shalt be queen of the fathomless brine.

THE ROVER'S GLEE

Tune—*Columbia's sons at sea.*

This pirate's respect for Nature (stanza 2) is his most endearing quality. Otherwise, this piece is much like the many others that trivialize the violence and destructiveness of the pirate's life. The tune has not been located.

1	2	3
True rovers bold are we,	The broad dark seas we scour,	Should chasing fleets bear near,
Our home the rock hid shore,	All nations we defy,	And showers of bullets pour,
We share our plunder merrily,	We yield us to no power;	We rovers know no fear,
And dance to the ocean's roar.	Save the angry sea and sky.	Tho' drenched with our dashing gore
We clean our balls and guns,	Yet firm as our tarry oak,	When comrades round us die.
Whet cutlass, dirk, and spear,	We rovers ne'er recoil,	And spars and masts all fall,
And when our store is gone,	'Mid ocean fire and smoke,	Defiance is our cry,
Then out for more we steer.	We gain our blood-stained spoil.	While we've a plank top crawl.
Singing, fa la, la, &c.	Singing, fa la, la, &c.	Singing, fa la, la, &c.

THE ROVER'S SERENADE

An 1834 issue of *The Metropolitan* magazine (Vol. 11, p. 132) heralds publication of this song, with words by Henry W. Challis and music by Thomas Kilner, and proclaims, "These are very pretty words, wedding to very pretty music"; but the tune itself has not been located. Even apart from its jarring syntax and inept imagery, this song is suspiciously like other, better pirate songs on the theme of The Rover Sweet-Talks a Lady, such as "The Pirate's Serenade" [#52], published in 1838; and "The Pirate's Song" [#75] by Allan Cunningham (1784-1842), merely recapitulating some of the same ideas in a more rhapsodic and less responsible vein, adding nothing new. The text here is from *The Pirate's Songster* (circa 1845).

1   Far, far to his billow,
     The red sun has gone;
  Yet the stars gem each billow
     That softly rolls on:
  The moonlight is playing,
     On blue waves so fair;
  While the sea nymph is weaving
  Green wreaths for thy hair!

3   My light bark shall dance o'er
     The silvery brine,
  Whose treasure-fill'd bosom's
     An emblem of thine;
  The waves sparkle round her,
     In many bright dyes,
  But their lustre is dim, to
     The ray of thine eyes!

2   Then awake, dearest maiden,
     Bid slumber retire,
  The night is arrayed in
     Her brightest attire;
  Come rove, and inherit,
     Love's heavenly cheer,
  My boat like a spirit,
     Is fluttering near!*

4   While the sail flutters
     And swells in the breeze,
  I'll bear thee o'er waters,
     That care never sees;
  To the rover's fair isle,
     In the heaven dyed sea,
  Where joys brightest smile,
     Shall give welcome to thee.

* Most nautical authorities would agree that boats do not "flutter"! Far better were it, "My *flag,* like a spirit, / Is fluttering near"; or, "My boat [or *ship*], like a spirit, / Is *lingering* [or *tarrying*] near."

78
THE ROVER'S SONG

In this piece the buccaneer-narrator never does get his comeuppance. Smugly satisfied that his outlaw ways provide freedom and adventure, he confesses no Victorian remorse for the life he chose. Would real pirates talk like this? The tune specified is "Bonny Boat."

1 Up, rovers, up, with sword and sail,
    True pirates, we ne'er will lag,—
  Arouse, and to the wooing gale,
    Spread out our *blood red flag.*
  A gallant bark rides on our lee,
    With gold and merchandize;
  Stand to your guns and soon she'll be,
    The gallant rover's prize.
  Then, rovers up, with sword and sail,
    The pirates ne'er will lag,
  On deck and to the wooing gale,
    Spread forth our *blood red flag.*

2 See now, within gun shot she draws,
    Blaze in upon her lee—
  She feels our light'ning, lads, huzza!
    Her mizzen swabs the sea.
  On, borders [sic], on, for victory,
    Free her decks we stride,
  Her treasures now our prize shall be,
    Her maids each rover's bride.
        Then, rovers, up, &c.

79
THE *THUNDER* CREW

This ditty in *The Buccaneer Songster* appears to be about straight letter-of-marque privateering, rather than outright piracy. It has no sea-fights or corsair bravado, and it does have the innocuous "convivial" allusions that one expects to find in songs written for or about sailors. But it falls short of the usual Yankee Lads patriotism found in songs of legitimate seagoing warfare, and it lacks the black flag (or red flag) and the We Recognize the Sovereignty of No Nation blather of the usual parlor pirate fare. It is included by reason of its equivocation, and because the phrase "of our *trade* right proud are we" implies more than simple nationalistic fervor.

1 Our iron bark's our home, you see,
    A tough old craft and true,
  And of our trade right proud are we,
    The gallant thunder crew.
  Each tar will at his station be,
    When storm or ships in view,
  He'll lend a hand and boldly stand
    By the gallant Thunder crew.

2 When all is calm—no prize in vain,
    We tilt the can about,
  And having nothing else to do,
    Dance, quarrel, sing, and route.
  But when there bears a ship in sight,
    In union we are true,
  We then shake hands an join in a fight,
    For our ship and Thunder crew.

Appendix: Related Ballads

80
AN ELEGY ON THE DEATH OF CAPTAIN WILLIAM KIDD
Who was Executed at *Execution-Dock,* on *Friday* the 23rd of this Instant *May,* 1701

This anonymous broadside of 41 lines, with an "Epitaph" of ten additional lines, is not divided into stanzas, it has no indication of a tune, and was evidently not intended to be sung. However, it appears to be an authentic contemporaneous publication of circa 1701, nowadays scarce. According to a facsimile produced at Salem, Massachusetts in 1964 by maritime historian Marion V. Brewington on his private press called "The Priceless Pearl" (Webb & Frank, 28, #10), the original was "Printed; And Sold by *A. Baldwin* in *Warwick-Lane* [London]." The original printer (and possibly also the author) was the widow Ann Baldwin, who, after her husband Richard Baldwin's death circa 1698, continued to operate the family book shop, bindery, and printing establishment at his Oxford Arms premises in Warwick Lane (Humphries & Smith, 60). The allusion in the Epitaph refers to James Whitney (1660-1694), a notorious English highwayman, who "prided himself on being 'the glass of fashion and the mould of form' and was executed at Porter's Block, near Smithfield" (Brewer, IV:237). Though he is all but forgotten today, his memory would have been fresh at the time of Kidd's execution only seven years later.

WHEN any Great and Famous Man does Die,
The World expects to have an *ELEGY*
Produc'd, to his Immortal Memory;
The End of which, we know, is to declare
What those Great Deeds and Noble Actions were
Which did compleat his Noble Character.
Well then ——
KIDD was a Man of such undaunted Spirit,
He'll face Hell-Gates, and all the Devils in it,
Were't possible to STEAL: A Golden Prize
Did so bewitch his Heart, and charm his Eyes!
When on the Seas proud Waves he boldly rid,
All strove to fly the Great and Mighty *KIDD.*
So terrible was he, where e're he came
To ROB, or PLUNDER, that his very Name
Wou'd cause a Trembling Fear and Dread in those
Who were his Friends, as well as in his Foes;
Betwixt which two, he'd no Distinction make,
But ALL THEY HAD at once he'd freely take:
First, *Sieze their Lading;* next, *their Ships destroy.*——
In short, No PIRATE cou'd the Seas annoy
More than he strove to do, while in his Pow'r;
For All that came in's way he did devour.
These Actions rais'd his Fame, and made him Great;
Still climbing high'r, he fell by his own Weight:
GOOD FORTUNE left him, and his POW'R fail'd him,
The Devil (*ready for him*) Gaol'd and Hang'd him,
To no one's *Sorrow,* rather *Joy* display;
Who weeps to see a Conquer'd BEAST OF PREY?

Thus is he carry'd off this world's wide Stage;
And where it is that he must next engage,
I cannot tell, but leave ye all to guess:
That these are my Thoughts, truly I confess.
As th' DEVIL is Mankind's Great Enemy,
And *KIDD* his *Humble Servant* chose to be
Here, while on Earth, his *Spirit* may be sent
To plague with Storms the Watry Element,
And that may Rob, since 'tis a Faculty
That may stick by him to Eternity
But be it as it will, since hence he's gone,
This EPITAPH I'll write on his Grave-stone.

EPITAPH
Reader, *Near this Tomb dont stand,*
Without some Essence in thy Hand
For here KIDD's *stinking Corps does lie,*
The Scent of which may thee infect:
He Base *did Live, and* Base *did Die,*
Therefore his Tomb and Corps reject.
Pity but he in Whitney's *Grave did lie,*
That all might Piss *on him, as they pass'd by!*
One rais'd his Fame, by Robbing *on the* SHORE,
The Other on the SEA.—*But now no more.*

THE BRIGAND'S BRIDE

This piano setting was published in an anthology of set dances entitled *The Brigand Cotillions,* along with "The Red Coats are Comin'," "Love's Ritornella," "Buy a Broom," "The Drover Boy," and "Isabella Waltz" (New York: J.L. Hewitt, circa 1832). Each piece occupies a single page, with musical settings and dance figures but without lyrics, and none of the music is attributed. The directions for "The Brigand's Bride" set-dance are: "L'ETÉ (or new Figure): Two Ladies advance and retire, two gents the same, Ladies hands across, two Ladies chassez and set opposite to their partners, then pousette to places." There is no indication whether the title refers to a seafaring brigand or a landbound highwayman, nor any clue to why the tune bears the title at all. It predates by several decades William Makepeace Thackeray's reference to an opera of that title in "Ravenswing," in his *Men's Wives* series.

THE ROBBERS OF THE GLEN

This rare song of unknown origin is styled as the first-person testimony of the chief of a band of highwaymen, who merrily extols the virtues of his Robin Hood-like career in the forest but in the end deplores the course that led to his criminal waywardness. It is appended here because it is clearly related to "The Pirate of the Isle" [#44], if not in origin then at least in syntax, sentiment, and style, and certainly also in the minds of whalemen. For, apart from a few British broadsides, "Robbers of the Glen" has been encountered only in two manuscript texts in whalemen's journals of the 1860s [Kendall Collection, New Bedford Whaling Museum]; and there, in both cases, it is paired with "The Pirate of the Isle." Its resemblance to the parlor and songster genres of professionally written pirate lyrics is unmistakable: it is a kind of landlubber's equivalent of Victorian songs about seagoing freebooters. Like "The Pirate of the Isle," "The Robbers of the Glen" seems too stable and formal to suggest a truly folkloric genesis. The tune is unknown.

1   Stand stranger stand your jewels give
    Your gold I must obtain
    T'is useless now with fate to strive
    Resistance is in vain
    Look at that band of mountaineers
    Both tried and active men
Repeat   At cares they laugh, no danger fear
       We are the robbers of the glen

2   When forth we steal at dark midnight
    Like owls that shun the day
    When the telltale moon doth shed her light
    Then we will secure our prey
    No violence save self defence
    Whilst I command my men
       No blood is shed on no pretence
       By the robbers of the glen

3   When at the festive board we meet
    I with my men all game
    They my welcome loudly greet
    My heart still clings to fame
    The ruby wine the scene inflames
    We all look merry then
       But I curse the hour that I became
       A robber of the glen

4   Through cards and dice my wealth I've lost
    I once had wealth and fame
    But now alas they are no more
    And friendship is but a name
    Yon stately castle there below
    With all its wide domain
       They once were mine; what am I now
       A robber of the glen

5   But my prospects darkened o'er
    My friend was once my pride
    He like the traitor played me false
    And then seduced my bride
    I sought him then; he would have fled
    We fought and he was slain
       And since that hour this life I've led
       A robber of the glen

6   Come fill your soul with livening glass
    Avaunt all cares begone
    No more we'll think of things that's past
    Of worldly cares be done
    Come give the song and toast the glee
    And shout my merry men
       With a loud huzza and three times three
       For the robbers of the glen

THE EXECUTION OF FIVE PIRATES
[The Flowery Land]

A latter-day broadside entitled "The Execution of Five Pirates, For Murder, which took place on Monday, February 22nd, at the Old Bailey," printed by Henry Disley (London) in immediate conjunction with the event in 1864, contains a prose narrative and song-like lyrics. While no tune is indicated and the verses may never have been sung, or even been intended to be sung, the piece as a whole typifies the sensationalism and hackneyed syntax of cheap broadsides as a medium for public suasion and the dissemination of news. The narrative names the perpetrators and journalistically exploits details of the execution, but leaves it to the clumsy lyrics to disclose such details as that it was aboard the *Flowery Land* that the crimes occurred. The editorial purpose is clearly Sin, Repentance, and Expiation, in this instance of Roman Catholic foreigners; there is also a dissident subtext of sympathy for the oppressed labor classes in general and sailors in particular. But there is little specific description of the crime itself, how many were murdered and under what circumstances, and whether the murders were actual acts of piracy in the colloquial sense, or were more in the nature of conventional mutiny. The lyrics are even equivocal about the exact number of perpetrators—five or seven—though the narrative is quite explicit that only the five named were hanged. In fact, two of the convicts were reprieved at the eleventh hour and so escaped the noose. [See illustration, page 143.]

The Execution of Five Pirates, For Murder,
which took place on Monday, February 22nd [1864], at the Old Bailey

This morning, Monday, February 22nd, 1864, will be long remembered by the inhabitants of the city of London, as one of the most remarkable in the annals of hanging, by the execution of five foreign sailors, viz: John Lyons, Francisco Bianco, Mauriccio Durranna, Marcus Watter, Miguel Lopez, alias Joseph Chances, alias The Catelan [sic], for the wilful murder of George Smith upon the high seas. The attendance of persons to witness the execution was enormous, being greater than was ever remembered by the oldest inhabitant in the City, and was much of the same class as usually attend these exhibitions, with the addition of a fair sprinkling of seafaring men. The prisoners have been very assiduously attended by the worthy Priests of the Catholic persuasion, to which creed the prisoners belong, and they had been brought to a full knowledge of the enormity of the crimes which they had committed; and to such a state of religious feeling had they been brought, that they all fully acknowledged the share each one took in the horrible crime, and recognized the justice of their punishment. The sheriffs, with their usual attendants, arrived at a very early hour at the prison, and immediately visited the various criminals in their cells. The worthy priests who had been attending the criminals since their condemnation, was [sic] in the prison the whole night, and were early in their attendance upon the unhappy criminals. After the usual formalities had been gone through of demanding the bodies of the prisoners into their custody, the executioner, with his assistants, commenced pinioning the prisoners, which operation was quickly performed, considering the number of prisoners. The arrangements having been completed, the mournful procession began to move towards the scaffold, the worthy priests praying fervently with the wretched prisoners, who appeared to have been brought to a thorough state of penitence. The prisoners ascended the scaffold in an orderly manner, and directly they appeared on the drop, the immense multitude gave a deep and loud groan, which seemed to make some of the wretched men tremble. The executioner having adjusted the fatal ropes, and drawn the caps over their eyes, left the platform, and the priests administered the last parting words of scriptural consolation to them. The signal was given, the bolts were withdrawn, and the wretched murderers were launched into eternity.

1   Is there not one spark of pity,
        For five poor unhappy men,
    Doomed, alas! in London city,
        On a tree their lives to end?
    The dreadful crime which they committed,
        On the raging, stormy sea,
    By every one must be admitted,
        They each deserved to punished be.

    Five poor unhappy sailors
        On the drop did trembling stand,
    And their lives did pay a forfeit,
        For their deeds on board the Flowery Land.

2   Sometimes at sea there's cruel usage,
        And men to frenzy oft are drove,
    They're always wrong by men in power,
        And that there's many a sailor knows.
    But those unhappy seven sailors,
        Did commit a dreadful deed,
    Killed and slaughter'd, sad to mention,
        Onboard the Flowery Land, we read.

3   Great excitement through the nation,
        This most sad affair has caused,
    Sent across the briny ocean,
        To be tried by English laws;
    Seven tried and there convicted,
        And sentenced each to hanged be,
    For the dreadful murders they committed,
        When sailing on the raging sea.

4   For two of them they did petition,
        Alas, there nothing could them save[;]
    Sad indeed was their condition,
        To lie side by side in a murderer's grave;
    Far away from friends and kindred,
        They unpitied on the drop did stand,
    Sad was the deed that they committed,
        On board the fatal Flowery Land.

5   Thousands flocked from every quarter,
        Seven unhappy men to see,
    Sailors from distant foreign nations,
        Suspended on a dreadful tree.
    The fatal signal soon was given,
        The awful drop at length did fall,
    It caused a groan—it caused a shudder,
        May God receive their guilty souls.

6   May this to sailors be a warning,
        The dreadful sight the world did see,
    In London, that fateful morning,
        The seven died on Newgate's tree.
    Was there not a tear of pity,
        While trembling they in death did stand,
    To die for crimes in London city,
        Committed on the Flowery Land.

7   Their victims they did show no mercy,
        No time for to prepare did give,
    They kill'd them in a barbarous manner,
        And though they were not fit to live,
        We pity to them on the gallows,
        Englishmen could not deny,
        Now, alas, their days are ended,
        They died on Newgate's gallows high.

Woodcut illustration from a contemporaneous London broadside entitled, *Trial and execution at the Old Bailey of seven* [sic] *seamen for murder and piracy on board the Flowery Land,* printed in 1864 by William S. Fortey, successor to James Catnach (Laws 1957, 294). Thomas Gretton remarks, "The sheet was printed and sold at the scene of the execution. Unfortunately [for the printer], two of the pirates were reprieved, and a second edition, with two of the bodies cut out, was quickly produced" (Gretton #20, p. 52).

YO HO HO AND A BOTTLE OF RUM

Robert Louis Stevenson's *Treasure Island* is the definitive literary classic of pirates and piracy. Many cherished notions are inherited directly from it, and its ambivalent, larger-than-life Captain Long John Silver stands not far behind Sherlock Holmes, Robin Hood, Ebenezer Scrooge, and Macbeth among the most familiar literary characters of all time. Thus, it is not surprising that *Treasure Island* gave rise to the most universally familiar, if not the most historically authentic pirate ditty. Stevenson's original lyrics and the song they inspired are purely literary pieces, the products of the novelist's fertile imagination and the ripples of his wake; but it would be remiss to exclude the song here on a mere technicality. Only the first four lines, styled as "Cap'n Billy Bones his song," appear in *Treasure Island*, published during 1881-83. In 1891, a Louisville journalist oddly named Young Ewing Allison (1853-1932) expanded Stevenson's brief ditty into a much longer affair of five stanzas. These he first entitled "A Piratical Ballad" and later called "Derelict," which is the title by which it was known and sung at the U.S. Naval Academy at Annapolis, in a musical setting composed for the stage by Henry Waller in 1901. According to the editor of *Bawdy Ballads and Lusty Songs,* for the rest of his life Allison continued to add to and polish his lyrics, until he had six significantly altered full-length stanzas (transcribed from the author's manuscript in J.H. Johnson, 1935, 66-69). "The Dead Man's Chest" refers neither to human anatomy nor to luggage, but to an island reef in the Caribbean where pirates are supposed to have consorted and shipping come to grief.

Fif-teen men on the Dead Man's Chest, Yo-ho-ho and a bot-tle of rum! Drink and the dev-il be done for the rest

Yo-ho-ho and a bot-tle of rum! The mate was fixed by the bo-s'n's pike, The bo-s'n brained with a mar-lin-spike,

And Cook-ey's throat was marked be-like, it had been gripped by fingers ten, and there they lay, all good dead men,

Like break o' day in a booz-ing ken, Yo-ho-ho and a bot-tle of rum!

1
Fifteen men on the Dead Man's Chest—
   Yo-ho-ho and a bottle of rum!
Drink and the devil be done for the rest—
   Yo-ho-ho and a bottle of rum!
The mate was fixed by the bos'n's pike,
The bos'n brained with a marlinspike,
And Cookey's throat was marked belike
     It had been gripped
     By fingers ten
     And there they lay
     All good dead men
Like break o' day in a boozing ken—
   Yo-ho-ho and a bottle of rum!

2
Fifteen men of a whole ship's list—
   Yo-ho-ho and a bottle of rum!
Dead and be damned and the rest gone whist!—
   Yo-ho-ho and a bottle of rum!
The skipper lay with his nob in gore
Where the scullion's axe his cheek had shore,
And the scullion he was stabbed times four,
     And there he lay
     And the soggy skies
     Dripped all day long
     In up-staring eyes,
At murk sunset and at foul surprise—
   Yo-ho-ho and a bottle of rum!

3

Fifteen men of 'em stiff and stark—
  Yo-ho-ho and a bottle of rum!
Ten of the crew had the murder mark—
  Yo-ho-ho and a bottle of rum!
'Twas a cutlass swipe, or an ounce of lead,
Or a yawing hole in a battered head,
And the scuppers glut with a rotting red.
      And there they lay—
      Aye, damn my eyes!
      All lookouts clapped
      On paradise,
All souls bound just contrariwise—
  Yo-ho-ho and a bottle of rum!

4

Fifteen men of 'em good and true—
  Yo-ho-ho and a bottle of rum!
Every man jack could ha' sailed with old Pew—
  Yo-ho-ho and a bottle of rum!
There was chest on chest of Spanish gold,
With a ton of plate in the middle hold,
And the cabins riot of stuff untold.
      And they lay there
      That had took the plum,
      With a sightless glare
      And their lips struck dumb,
While we shared all by the rule of thumb—
  Yo-ho-ho and a bottle of rum!

5

Fifteen men on the Dead Man's Chest—
  Yo-ho-ho and a bottle of rum!
Drink and the Devil had done for the rest—
  Yo-ho-ho and a bottle of rum!
We wrapped 'em all in a mains'l tight,
With twice ten turns of a hawser's bight,
And we heaved 'em over and out of sight—
      With a yo-heave-ho!
      And fare-you-well!
      And a sullen plunge
      In the sullen swell,
Ten fathoms deep on the road to hell!
  Yo-ho-ho and a bottle of rum!

Anonymous illustration from John Williamson Palmer, *Folk Songs* [sic] (New York: Charles Scribner, 1861), page 87, where it accompanies the poem "Little Brown Man" by Pierre Jean Béranger, translated from the French by William Maginn.

I'M AFLOAT, I'M AFLOAT.

I'm afloat, I'm afloat, on the fierce rolling tide,
The ocean's my home and my bark is my bride,
Up, up with my flag, let it wave o'er the sea;
I'm afloat, I'm afloat, and the Rover is free.
I fear not the monarch, I heed not the law:
I've a compass to steer by, a dagger to draw;
And ne'er as a coward or slave will I kneel,
While my guns carry shot or my belt wears a steel,
Quick, quick, trim her sail, let the sheet kiss the wind,
And I'll warrant we'll soon leave the sea-gulls behind
      Up, up with my flag, let it wave o'er the sea,
      I'm afloat, I'm afloat, and the Rover is free!
      I'm afloat, I'm afloat, and the Rover is free!

The night gathers o'er us, the thunder is heard:
What matter? our vessel skims on like a bird!
What to her is the dash of the storm-ridden main?
She has braved it before, and will brave it again:
The fire-gleaming flashes around us may fall—
They may strike, they may cleave, but they cannot
    appal.
With lightning above us, and darkness below,
Through the wild waste of waters right onward we go.
Hurrah! my brave comrades, ye may drink, ye may
    sleep;
The storm-fiend is hush'd— we're alone on the deep;
      Our flag of defiance still waves o'er the sea!
      I'm afloat, I'm afloat, and the Rover is free!
      I'm afloat, I'm afloat, and the Rover is free!

WALKER, PRINTER, DURHAM.
[11]

WHO'S DAT KNOCKING
AT DE DOOR.

Ib just come down on a little bit ob spree,
Im' berry well acquainted wid de gals I come to see,
I went to de house, but dey was all gone to bed,
And out ob de winder a colored lady said,
    Who is dat a knocking at de door?
Am dat you, Sam? No, it am Jem.
Well you aint good looking, and you can't come in,
    And dare is no use knocking at de door any more.

Who is dat knocking at de door?
Making such a noise wid his saucy jaw,
I'll call de watch, and tell dem how
Dat you come down here to kick up a row.
    Who is dat knocking at de door?
Am dat you, Sam? No, it am John,
Well you aint good looking, and you can't come in,
    And dare is no use knocking at de door any more.

Den she open de door, and she-let me in,
And I sat by de fire, and I warm my shin.
In came a watchman, two or three,
Says come along, nigger, you must come wid me.
    Who is dat knocking at de door?
Am dat you, Sam? No, it am Harry,
Well you aint good looking, and you will hab to tarry,
    And dar is no use knocking at the door any more.

They took me to de watch-house, and I stay all night,
And I neber sleep a wink until de broad day-light.
De day began to break and de chicken crew,
And some one kept a knocking at de door.
    Who is dat knocking at de door?
Am dat you, Sam? No, it am Jem.
Well your hair don't curl, and you can't come in,
    And it is no use knocking at the door.

MARY BLANE.

I once did lub a pretty gal,—I lub'd her as my life,—
She came from Lousiana, and I made her my dear wife.
At home we lib'd so happy, Oh, free from grief and pain,
But in de winter time of year I lost my Mary Blane.
Oh! fare de well, poor Mary Blane! one feeling heart
    bids you adieu,—
Oh, fare de well, my Mary Blane! we'll never meet
    again.

I went into de woods one day to hunt among de cane,
De white man come into my house, and took poor
    Mary Blane.
It grieb me bery much to tink, no hope I entertain
Of eber seeing my dear gal, my own poor Mary Blane.
      Oh, fare de well, &c.

When toiling in de cotton field, I cry and say, good bye,
Unto my broder comrade, dat, oh, soon,—oh, soon I die,
My poor wife gone,—I cannot lib amidst dis world ob
    pain,—
But lay me in de grabe to find out my poor Mary Blane.
Den fare de well, dear Mary Blane, do we are parted
    here on earth,
Oh, fare de well, dear Mary Blane, we soon shall
    meet again.

"Slip ballad" broadside printed by George Walker & Son., Durham (England), containing the lyrics to three ballads, including "I'm Afloat" ("The Rover of the Sea") (song #46). Authorship of the famous poem by Eliza Cook is not credited here, and the broadside is undated, but it was likely printed after the lyrics were set to music by Henry Russell around 1840 and perhaps after the lyrics were printed in the *Sheet Anchor,* a Christian temperance magazine for seamen in 1844. *Author's Collection,*

Sources and Notes on the Texts and Tunes

Key to abbreviations: PSI: Patricia Pate Havlice, *Popular Song Index* + numbered supplements: SI: Minnie Earl Sears, *Song Index*; SIS: Sears, *Song Index Supplement*; SIC: Desiree De Charmes and Paul F. Breed, *Songs In Collections*.

1. John Dory. Tune: canon for three voices, circa 1600, from Thomas Ravenscroft, *Deuteromelia,* 1609 (Chappell 1893, I:93). Text: Chappell 1893, I:93; Firth, 16. Ref: Chappell 1893, I:93-96; Child, V:131; Firth, 16 and 341 (cites Child; Ritson, *Ancient Songs and Ballads,* 1877, 198); L.A. Smith, 74.

2. Sir Andrew Barton. Text: composite, from Child #167B: broadsides printed in London for F. Coles, T. Vere, and W. Gilbertson, circa 1648-80; F. Coles, T. Vere, and J. Wright, circa 1655-80; W. Olney, circa 1650-1702; etc.; Hindley, *Roxburghe Ballads,* 9; and Percy's transcript of another broadside printed for J. Wright, J. Clarke, W. Thackeray, and T. Passinger, London, circa 1670-82; for which he cites (without employing italics for the proper titles) Douce Ballads, I, 18b; Pepys Ballads, I, 484, #249; Wood Ballads, 401, 55; Roxburghe Ballads, i, 2; Bagford Ballads, 643, m. 9 (61) and 643, m. 10 (77); Wood Ballads, 402, 37; Glenriddell MSS, XI, 290. Concerning the ballad's publishing history, Child cites Old Ballads, 1723, I, 159; Percy's *Reliques,* 1765, II, 177; Ritson's *Select Collection of English Songs,* 1783, I, 313; Halliwell, *Early Naval Ballads,* Percy Society, II, 4 (1841); Moore, *Pictorial Book of Ancient Ballads,* 1853, 2356; *Roxburghe,* III, 726f, "dated in the Museum catalogue 1710." Tune: "[Fair] Flower of Northumberland": [a] William Motherwell, *Minstrelsy, Ancient and Modern,* 1827, #2; [b] Gavin Greig, *Last Leaves of Traditional Ballads and Ballad Airs,* 1925, p. 9. According to Simpson, "'Come follow my love'... has apparently not survived. Traditional tunes of 'Andrew Barton' are modern" (Simpson 365, n.5); "A Warning to all Lewd Livers," evidently also lost, was a form of "Come follow my love" (589, n.6); and the tunes for "Suffolk Miracle" and "Bleeding heart" ultimately derive from "Come follow my love" (374). However, Bronson states, "The earlier copies [of the ballad text] are all in tetrameter quatrains or double quatrains. Where a direction for a tune is given, it is always, 'Come follow my Love, &c.,' which, I believe, can only be the tune of 'The Fair Flower of Northumberland' (No. 9), a song that Deloney liked well enough to include in his *Jacke of Newcastle,* c. 1597. The musical tradition for the 'Fair Flower,' so far as it is known, is late, and Scottish, but quite consistent and uniform. Its meter is 6/8, and perfectly suited to 'Barton.' But no copy of the tune as early as the seventeenth century appears to have survived" (III:133, where his further comments on "Sir Andrew Barton" are fairly extensive; see also Bronson I: 138 for several versions of "Fair Flower of Northumberland").

3. Henry Martin. Text: [a] composite, after Sharp and Bronson, as noted below; [b] William H. Keith, schooners *William Martin* of Boston and *Edith May* of Wellfleet (circa 1865-69), schooner *Cora Nash* of Boston, circa 1871; etc. [Kendall Collection, New Bedford Whaling Museum]. Tune: orthodox, after Sharp 1916, Eddy 1939, Farnesworth & Sharp 1916, etc., as noted below. Sharp and Bronson discuss in detail the relationship posited by Child between this ballad and "Sir Andrew Barton" (Child #167) and the coexistence of the two divergent forms. It is also occasionally known as "Salt Sea." Ref: SI; SIC #4631 A&B; PSI; PSIS; Rosenberg #533; Child #250; Bronson IV:24-46 (50 specimens); Cox #26; Eddy #24; Farnesworth & Sharp 1916, n.p.; Flanders, 72; Frank, *Ballads and Songs,* #5; Karpeles #22 (3 versions); Mackenzie #13; Sharp 1916 #1. See "Andrew Bardeen" [#3]

4. Andrew Bardeen. Sung by R.L. Nelms, Norman, Oklahoma (Moore & Moore, 115). For the variants named, see Bronson IV:28-4; Child V:423; Flanders & Olney, 73 and 201; Gardner & Chickering, 211(A) and 213(B); Hubbard, 32; Randolph I:177; R. Smith, 156 (the text quoted by Child). See also #1 and #2 above.

5. The *George Aloe* and the *Sweepstake*. Text: composite after Ashton 1891, 42; Child #285; Firth, 32. Tune: "The Coasts of Barbary": Baring-Gould & Sharp, 1906, #9; repr. Bronson IV:311, #15. Bronson (IV:306) describes it thus: "Quite apart from all the rest appears to stand the copy printed from an unspecified source in Baring-Gould and Sharp, *Folk Songs for Schools...* [*English Folk-Songs for Schools*]. This tune is in an authentic Æolian, with inflected seventh." Ref: Firth, 342; Rinder, 63.

6. High Barbary. Text: [a] Luce 1889, 76. [b] George W. Piper, copybook aboard the ship *Europa* of Edgartown, 1868-70 [Kendall Collection, New Bedford Whaling Museum]. [c] Horace Wood, journal aboard the bark *Andrews* of New Bedford, 1866-67 [Kendall Collection]. [d] John Masefield, *A Sailor's Garland,* 1906, 293f. Tune: *Naval Songs* (1883), 16; Luce (1889), 76; Whall (1910), n.p.; Whall (1927), 85. Transposed from G minor. Compare alternatives offered by Bronson and Colcord. Ref: SI; Child #285; Bronson III: 306-311; Laws #K-33 (erroneously attributes the ballad to Charles Dibdin); *American Sailor's Songster,* 85; Ashton 1891, 42; Baker & Miall 72; Brown Coll., 2&4, #118; *Buccaneer Songster,* n.p.; Colcord 153; Farnesworth & Sharp #10; Firth, xxi, 23, 342; Flanders 1960, III:176-187 (7 versions); Harlow, 161; Hugill, 491 (3 chantey forms); Neeser, 33; Sharp 1908, v1; Sharp 1916, #12; Shay, 91; Trident (version from Whall); Warner #142; Whall, 85.

7. Sir Walter Raleigh Sailing In the Low-Lands. Ashton 1891, 221; Child 286A (Pepys Ballads, IV, 196, #189, circa 1682-85); Euing #334 ("Sir *Walter Raleigh Sailing in the Low-lands. Shewing how the famous Ship called the* SWEET TRINITY *was taken by a false Gally, and how it was again restored by the craft of a little Sea-boy, who sunk the Gally; as the following song will declare. / To the Tune of, The Sailing in the Low-Lands... Printed for* J. CONYERS, *at the* BLACK-RAVEN *the first shop in* FETTER-LANE *next* HOLBORN [London]"). Ref: Bronson IV:312-362. See #8, "The Golden Vanity." Ref: see #8.

8. The *Sweet Trinity* [*Bold Trinity; Golden Vanity*]. Text: [a] "Sweet Trinity," journal of Edward W. Collins, ship *Condor* of New Bedford, 1829-34 [Kendall Collection]. [b] "The Cruise in the Lowlands Low," Shoemaker, 132. Tune: "The Green Willow Tree," from Flanders 1965, IV:195; collected in Vermont (compare Bronson IV:346, #80 [Hammond Coll., Cecil Sharp House, London]; Bronson IV:354, #96 [Library of Congress Archive of American Folk Song #11,435(B5)]). Ref: SI; PSI; PSIS; SIC #4617 A-H; Child #286; Rosenberg #1361 A&B; Ashton 1891, 221; Belden, 97; Broadwood, 182; Bronson IV: 312-362 (110 specimens); Brown Coll. 2&4:#47; Colcord, 154; Cox #32; Creighton 1933, #10; Davis & Tozer #15; Duncan 1905, v2; Flanders 1960 IV:188 (39 texts and fragments, 21 tunes); Flanders & Olney, 230; Fowke 1965, #4, #61; Frank 1985, #142; Gardner #83; Greenleaf #19; Harlow, 35; Hugill, 62 (3 versions); Masefield, 147-151 (3 texts); Randolph #38, I:195 (5 versions); *The Scottish Students' Song Book;* Sharp 1908, v1; Sharp 1916, #14; Sharp 1932 #41 (11 versions); Vaughan Williams 46; Warner #104. "Louisiana Lowlands": see Waite, 58; and compare Flanders 1960, IV:188-263, esp. version P.

9 and 10. Captain Ward and **Dansekar the Dutchman.** Date of first publication was 3 July 1609 (Arber, *Stationers' Register*, III, 185, b) (q. Firth, 342). Euing #327 (a) and (b) (the two ballads on the same sheet): "Printed for F. Coles, T. Vere, and William Gilbertson"; Firth, 25, 27, 342; *Roxburghe Ballads* VI:784 and VI:423.

11. Captain Ward and the *Rainbow*. Text: composite, after Ashton, Bruce, Child, Euing, Firth, and Logan. Tunes: [a] "'Twas When the Seas Were Roaring," music by George Frederick Handel (1685-1759), from *Davidson's Universal Melodist,* 1848, II: 174; transposed from G minor: the tune takes its name from a text by John Gay (1685-1732) in his musical play *The What D'ye Call It: A Tragi-Comi-Pastoral Farce* (1715); Gay also recycled it with new words in his *Beggar's Opera* (1728). [b] "Captain Ward" ("Ward the Pirate"): composite, remembered from childhood, from various sources (qq.v. below). Logan has extensive historical notes identifying in great detail the historical personages and circumstances portrayed in the ballad, including mention of the biography by Andrew Baker (1609) and a dramatization by Robert Daborn (1612), noting that "the Roxburghe ballad, reprinted by the Percy Society, has the conjectured date of 1650" (4). Ref: PSI, PSI-1, PI. Ashton 1891, 25; Barry, Eckstorm & Smyth, 248; Bell 1856, 167; Bronson IV:363; Bruce, 186; Child #287; Ebsworth's *Roxburghe Ballads,* VI, 426; Euing #108; Firth, xxiii, 30, 342; Flanders & Olney, 204; *Forecastle Songster* 1847, 201; 1850, 226; *Forget Me Not,* 41; B. Ives 1956, 38; Logan, 1; Simpson, 719f. Additionally, Child cites Buchan MSS, II, 245 and II, 417; *Douce Ballads,* III, fol. 80 b; Halliwell's *Early Naval Ballads,* 167; Kinloch MSS, I, 113 (1827); Pepys, IV, 202, N° 195; *Roxburghe,* III, 56, 416, 652, and 861. Bell's source (1856) is a broadside in the British Museum (presumably the same as cited by Child as 112. f. 44. [19]); Euing #108 was "Printed for Fr. Coles at the Sign of the Lamb in the Old-Bailey," Logan's by J. Pitts, London, circa 1821 (after a precursor of 1817).

12. Captain Every. Firth, 131ff, transcribed from a broadside in the Pepys collection. Firth ties the narrative to the record of "facts set forth at the trial of six of Every's crew in 1696" (347f). "There is an eighteenth-century version in the Madden collection (*Slipsongs* ii. 72, No. 1, 66) entitled *Bold Captain Avery.* The numerous variants in the later version are merely corruptions and not worth noting" (346).

13. Villainy Rewarded: The Pirate's Last Farewell to the World. Text: Firth, 131; from Pepys V:384. Tune: Simpson, 621. Lord William Russell was convicted of high treason. perhaps unjustly, for complicity in the Rye House plot against Charles II and James, Duke of York (later James II) in 1683. "A number of good-night ballads were written upon his death, including 'Russel's Farewell,' to the tune 'Oh, the Bonny Christ-Church Bells' (*Roxburghe Ballads* V, 324) and 'The Lord Russell's Farewell,' to the tune of 'Tender Hearts of London City' (*Roxburghe Ballads* V, 326)... [and] yet a third, 'The Lord Russels Last Farewell to the World,' 1683,... a broadside written and published by James Dean, with music on the sheet (Huntington Library; Houghton Library, Harvard University; Wood Collection, Bodleian Library; Ebsworth, *Bagford Ballads,* II:1002; *Roxburghe Ballads* V, 691)" (Simpson, 621f). See also Simpson, 48 and 700.

14. Captain Kidd. Text: "Captain Kidd": *Forecastle Songster* (New York: Richard Marsh, 1847, 209; Nafis & Cornish, 1850, 236); "Captain Robert Kidd": *Forget Me Not Songster* (New York: Richard Marsh, n.d., 28; Boston: G.W. Cottrell, n.d., 28). Tunes: [a] "Sound a Charge": per Simpson, 673; transposed from G minor. [b] "Sam Hall": from the singing of Stan Hugill, transcribed by Stuart Frank, North Stonington, Conn., May 1981; transposed from A Major. [c] "Samuel Hall": Hugill, 449 (excluded from the abridged reprint edition). [d] "Captain Kidd": H.K. Johnson, 171 (with piano accompaniment); identical to Colcord, 141 (lacking the accompaniment); transposed from G minor. [e] "What Wondrous Love Is This?": traditional "shape-note" or "Sacred Harp" singing-school arrangement, from the singing of Jeff Warner (Australian bicentennial concert tour with Mary Malloy & Stuart Frank, September 1988); corrected per T. J. Denison, et al., *Original Sacred Harp* (1911; 1936), 159 (compare Christ-Janer, et al, *American Hymns Old and New* [1980], 299). Ref: SI; SIC; PSI; Laws #K-35; Brown, 350; Colcord, 141; Eckstorm, 246; Firth, 134 (broadside circa 1701, "reprinted, for the first time, from the unique example in the collection of Lord Crawford"); Gardner, 318; B. Ives 1956, 36; H.K. Johnson, 171; Linscott, 131; Lomax & Lomax 1934, 133; Masefield, 17; Shay, 187. Concerning songs of this "distinctive stanza form" mentioned by Simpson, see Kennedy, 728. See also: George Pullen Jackson, *Another Sheaf of White Spirituals* (Univ. Florida Press, 1952); Alton C. Morris, *Folksongs of Florida* (University of Florida Press, 1950). Firth cites *State Trials,* XIV, 123 and 167; and "A Full Account of the Proceedings in relation to Capt. Kidd," in *A Collection of State Trials, published during the Reign of King William III,* III:230.

15. Bold Kidd, the Pirate. [a] Text and tune fragment collected by Helen Hartness Flanders from Professor Lucille Palmer, University of Rhode Island, 1945 (Flanders & Olney, 16). [b] Tune: widely anthologized, e.g., Owens, *Texas Folk Songs,* 72.

16. Captain Thunder. Thomas D'Urfey, *Wit and Mirth: or Pills to Purge Melancholy* (6 vols, London, 1719-20), I:282; per Edmunds, *A Williamsburg Songbook,* 56ff.

17. The Downfall of Piracy. Text: Ashton 1891, 7; Firth, 166 and 351, from *The Worcestershire Garland* (British Museum, pressmark 11621.c.4. [89]); also Masefield, 294; Rinder, 217 (in all of which it is unascribed). Tune: "The Storm," from broadside sheet music "Printed for J[ohn] Bland. N° 45. Holborn" (London, n.d., circa 1775) which attributes neither words nor music [Kendall Collection, New Bedford Whaling Museum]. There appears to be little evidence for C.S. Smith's claim that the tune "goes back at least to the beginning of George I's reign" (1714-27) or that, at least under this name, it was "so often associated with tales of the sea." Rather, it appears to date from the early part of the reign of George II (1727-60), was best known to seamen as "The Sailor's Complaint" and especially "Cease, Rude Boreas," and was first published in Walsh's *Musical Miscellany,* 1730, vol. IV (Duncan I: 257). According to Chappell, "Cease, Rude Boreas" (the poem by Stevens, formally titled "The Storm," 1754) is "the most famous" of the various texts set to permutations of it in the eighteenth century; but he prints it with a text titled "The Sailor's Complaint," identified as having come from the *Musical Miscellany*; others include: "How happy are the young lovers" ("On some rock, by seas surrounded"), which appeared in the ballad operas *Robin Hood* (1730) and *Silvia; or, The Country Burial* (1731); "Hosier's Ghost" (circa 1740), a poem by Richard Glover (1712-1785); and a companion piece entitled "Admiral Vernon's Answer to Admiral Hosier's Ghost," printed with "Hosier's Ghost" in J.O. Halliwell's *Early Naval Ballads of England* (1851) (Chappell 1893, II:165-166). Ironically on several levels, there is a ballad of circa 1656 called "The Downfall of Chancery; or, The Lawyer's Lamentation," for which the air is "Franklin Is Fled Away"; the tune was popularized as "You gallant Ladies all" in the ballad opera *The Jovial Crew,* 1731 (Simpson, 232f).

18. Will Watch. Words by Thomas Cory; music by John Davy (1765-1824). Text: "Will Watch, the bold Smuggler," ballad slip entitled A *Garland of New Songs*, Newcastle-upon-Tyne: "Printed by J. Marshall, in the Old Flesh-Market, *where may also be had, a large and curious Assortment of Songs, Ballads, Tales, Histories, &c.,"* n.d. [circa 1815-16] (other songs included are: "Jockey to the Fair"; "Come, Haste to the Wedding"; "The Maid of Bedlam"; "Jenny Nettles"). Tune: *Davidson's Universal Melodist*, 1848, II:65. Ref: SI; SIS; Hatton & Faning, 154f; *Universal Songster* [London], I:50; Whall, 39.

19. The *Flying Cloud*. Text: composite, as fixed in American revival tradition, viz: Colcord, 145; Shay, 184 (compare Grieg and both versions in Doerflinger). Tune: from the singing of Stan Hugill (one of several tunes for this ballad that were known to him); virtually identical to Colcord; differs from Shay. Ref: Belden, 128; Eckstorm, 214; Colcord, 145; Creighton 1933, 126; Creighton & Senior, 223; Doerflinger, 136f (2 very different texts with divergent tunes); Greenleaf, 349; Greig 1914, CXVIII ["William Hollander"]; Lomax 1934, 504; Mackenzie #111; Shay, 183.
\

20. The Bold *Princess Royal*. Text: [a] composite after Colcord, Creighton, Doerflinger, and Vaughan Williams (Sharp 1908, II:41). [b] *Our Island's Past, Volume III: Traditional Songs from the Cayman Islands* (George Town: Cayman Islands National Archive and Cayman Free Press, 1996), 10f. Tune: [a] R. Vaughan Williams (collector and arranger), "Folk Songs of the Eastern Counties," Sharp 1908, Vol. II, pp 40f. [b] Stan Hugill (sometime merchant sailor in square rig and steam; Aberdovey, Wales), sung at the author's home, North Stonington, Connecticut, May 1981: a variant of the same tune as Creighton 1933, 107; and Doerflinger, 143. Ref also: SI, S2; SIC; PSI; PI; Colcord, 148 ["Fair *Princess Royal*"]; Eckstorm, 256; Greenleaf, 78; E. Ives, 126; Kidson 1926, 34. [c] *Traditional Songs from the Cayman Islands*, p. 10.

21. The Bold Pirate. Text: Eckstorm & Smyth, 254. Tune: [a] E. Ives, 128. [b] Adjusted and restored after the defective tune in E. Ives, 128. Ref: Creighton & Senior, 229; *Journal of the Folk Song Society*, 27, 61-3 (1923).

22. Kelly the Pirate (I). Text: Broadside "Printed for and sold by J. Pitts, No. 14, Great Saint Andrew Street, Seven Dials, London. Printed by J. Jennings, Upper Mary-le-bone Street, London," n.d. [circa 1780-1812, per Crawford, 396]; quoted by Shoemaker, 178f. Tune: from memory in connection with "The Bold *Princess Royal*," learned at Truro, Nova Scotia in July 1969, but similar to and corrected per Creighton 1961, 151. Journal of John F. Martin, ship *Lucy Ann* of Wilmington, 1841-44 [Kendall Collection]. Ref: PSI; Rosenberg #739; Creighton 1961, 151; Greenleaf #43 (she is mistaken that her text is closer to Mackenzie's texts B and C than to A); Healy 1967 #24, #45; Mackenzie #81A; Shoemaker, 178.

23. Kelly the Pirate (II). Text: *Forecastle* 1847, 213; *Forecastle* 1850, 241; *Forget Me Not*, 75 (identical). Tune: Mackenzie #81(B), 400. PSI; Rosenberg #739; Frank 1985 #d100; Frank, *Ballads and Songs*, Appendix 5; Laws 1957, 157; Mackenzie #81 (B and C); Shoemaker, 177. See #21.

24. Bold Daniels. "Bold Daniel": MacEdward Leach, *Folk Ballads and Songs of the Lower Labrador Coast*, 57: "Sung by Peter Letto, Lance au Clair, June 1960," here with minor corrections, as indicated. Ref: Colcord, 149; Eckstorm, 257. Laws cites M.C. Dean, *The Flying Cloud and One Hundred and Fifty Other Old Time Songs and Ballads* (Virginia, Minn., 1922); Eckstorm cites Edward Thomas, *The Pocket Book of Poems and Songs for the Open Air* (New York, 1907).

25. Bold Manan the Pirate [Bold Manning]. Text: Doerflinger, 139; supplemented by Eckstorm, 259 ("Taken down in 1924 by Mrs. Heathcote M. Woolsey of Rye, New York, from the singing of Mr. Horace E. Priest of Sangerville, Maine," the implication being that this may have been one of the songs brought to America by his grandfather, "who escaped from a British man-of-war while off Boston"); and Eckstorm, 262 ("Sent in, October, 1924, by Captain Lewis Freeman Gott, of Bernard, Maine"). Tune: Doerflinger, 139 ("The singer, John Apt of Greenland, Nova Scotia, learned the ballad from a former ship's cook then working in a logging camp in New Brunswick. 'He was a big Negro,' Mr. Apt said. 'He used to sing this while he was scouring out the kettles. By Gawspel, that man could roar out a song in a wonderful voice!'").

26. Captain Coulston. Healy 1967, p. 34; Fowke 1965; singing of Ellen Cohn. See also Huntington & Herrmann, p. 113f.

27. Hicks the Pirate. Broadside by H. De Marsan, New York, 1860; John Thorn, "The Saugerties Bard," *Voices: The Journal of New York Folklore*, 31, Fall-Winter, 2005; "Execution of Hicks, the Pirate," *New York Times*, July 14, 1860, 1. Tune: "I'd mourn the hopes that leave me"—Air "The Rose Tree," in J.L. Molloy, *The Songs of Ireland* (London: Boosey & Co., 1873, p. 21. By contrast. see also O'Hea & Carey, *Gem Selection Songs of Ireland*, p. 48.

28. The *Brooklyn*. Shipboard journal of Frederick Merrill, green hand, whaling bark *Janus* of New Bedford, 1875-76; and seaman, schooner *Eothen* of New York, 1878 [Kendall Collection, New Bedford Whaling Museum]; Frank 2010, #35; Vaughan Williams & Lloyd, 1959, 90; Colcord 1938, 177.

29. Liverpool Play. Palmer 1983 (collected by Ralph Vaughan Williams).

30. The Female Smuggler. *Beadle's Dime Melodist*, 1859, p. 23 (music corrected from miscounts in measures 9 and 10; compare time signatures in Whall and Shay); Whall 1910, n.p.; Whall 1927, 27. Ref: SIC; PSI; PI; Wolf #625; *Beadle's Dime Song Book N° 9* (1862); *Beadle's Half-Dime Singer's Library N° 6* (1878); Frank 2010 #88; Shay 1948, 190. "The Dark-Eyed Sailor": SI ("variant of 'The Irish Girl'"); PSI; PSIS; JFSS; Laws #N-35; *American Songster*, 147; Ashton 1888, 245; Ashton 1891, 204; Cox #319; Creighton 1933, 29; Creighton 1961, 96, 97; Doerflinger, 300; Fowke 1965, #3; Frank 1985 #122; Frank 2010 #1; Gardner #57; Greenleaf #36; Healy 1967, #4 (tune); Huntington, 120; Karpeles #55; Mackenzie #64; Manny & Wilson #65; Palmer 1979 #108; Scarborough 267; Vaughan Williams, 104. Whalemen's MSS [Kendall Coll.]: [a] John G. Marble, R.I., circa 1846-47, in the journal of Stephen O. Hopkins, ship *Rosalie* of Warren, 1843, and bark *Perseverance* of Providence, 1849; [b] Theodore D. Bartley, ship *California* of New Bedford, 1851-54; [c] George M. Jones and Albert F. Handy, bark *Waverly* of New Bedford, 1859-63; [d] William H. Poole, ship *Minnesota* of New York, 1868-72.

31. The Smuggler's Bride. Text: Ashton 1888, 242. Tune: "The Brave Old Oak" by E.J. Loder (1813-1865), composed for a text by H. F. Chorley (1808-1872): Duncan I:306 (compare McCaskey II:103; etc.).

32. The Female Warrior (I). *The American Songster,* New York, 1830, p. 245; Baltimore, 1836, p. 245. Ref: PSI; PI; Eddy, 1435; Gardner & Chickering, 220; Kidson 1891, 99; Mackenzie, 223. See #29.

33. As We Were A-Sailing. Kidson 1893, 100. Because it mentions a ship named *Rainbow,* Kidson mistakenly associates the ballad with Captain Ward, whom Kidson erroneously characterizes as "a noted pirate in Queen Elizabeth's reign" (actually, Ward did not become a pirate until 1604, when James I had already succeeded). Ward is nowhere mentioned in the ballad and there is nothing to connect it to him except the name *Rainbow,* a fallacious association in any case. Rather, the *Rainbow* element may have been inspired by the same British naval foray to Barbary in 1637 that led to confusion in "Captain Ward and the *Rainbow*" [#11]. The name of the commander of that expedition, William *Rainborow,* combined with Ward's fame as a pirate on the North African coast a couple of decades earlier (his turf was Tunis; his zenith was 1609; he died in 1622), perhaps also influenced by a distant memory of Raleigh's *Rainbow* in the Armada era, may have led to a corruption that emerged as "Captain Ward and the *Rainbow*"—connecting the Rainborow action not only to Ward but also to Spain (via Raleigh's fame against the Armada and in the Spanish Caribbean) [see #6]. Kidson was a keen student of songs but no naval historian, so misguided notions in the ballad literature about "Captain Ward and the *Rainbow*" (traceable to Child, in this instance) could have led him astray. However, like "Captain Ward and the *Rainbow,*" the events narrated in "As We Were A-Sailing" do not coincide with the historical scenario of the 1637 expedition, in which Rainborow's squadron liberated hundreds of Englishmen that had been enslaved by the Algerine "pirates" (who had been receiving de facto Spanish support against Britain in the Western Mediterranean). The female in this ballad is thus an anomaly relevant neither to Ward nor to the Rainborow expedition. Kidson quips, "Probably some verse now lost would have explained how the damsel turned up at such an opportune moment." The verse is indeed present in "The Female Warrior" [#32 and #34]. Also compare: "The *Royal Oak*" (Vaughan Williams & Lloyd, 91); and "Captain Mansfield's Fight with the Turks at Sea" (Firth, 86: Madden Coll., Cambridge University; *Slipsongs,* i. 120, No. 260; Greig 1914, n.p.).

34. The Female Warrior (II). Doerflinger, 143. See #32 and #33.

35. The Pirate Lover. Words by James G. Percival. *Forget Me Not* (Boston ed.), 229 (4 stanzas); *New Song Book,* 13. Sheet music: G. Willig, Philadelphia, circa 1824 (Wolfe #376); G.E. Blake, Philadelphia, circa 1824 (Nº 69 in *Blake's Musical Miscellany* series; Wolfe #377)

36. The Corsair's Bride. Sheet music by J.L. Hewitt, New York circa 1830-32; lyrics ascribed to "The Lady of a Noble Duke" and the music to Leander Zerbini.

37. The Pirate's Deserted Bride. Sheet music by J.L. Hewitt, New York circa 1830-32; lyrics by Harry Stowe Van Dyke snd music by William Christian Selle (1813-1898),

38. The Rover's Bride. Sheet music by James Hewitt, New York, circa 1830-35; lyrics by Thomas Haynes Bayly and music by Alexander Lee.

39. The Rover's Home. Sheet music by Firth & Hall, New York, circa the 1830s; lyrics by Thomas Haynes Bayly and music by John Feltham Danneley.

40. The Pirate's Bark. Undated sheet music by Z.T. Purday, London; lyrics by J. Burrington and music by John W.L. Ash.

41. Come Brave with Me the Sea, Love. From the light opera *I Puritani* ["The Puritans"] by Vincenzo Bellini (1834). Sheet music: Keith's Music Publishing House, Boston, circa 1834-37; James L. Hewitt & Co., New York, 1837; Fiot, Meignen & Co., Philadelphia, 1837.

42. The Buccaneer's Bride. "BUCCANEER'S BRIDE," broadside, New York: H. De Marsan, 54 Chatham Street, n.d. [Kendall Coll.]. Sheet music "Away, away, we bound o'er the deep," words and music by Joseph Rodman Drake, arranged by T.V. Wiesenthal (Baltimore: George Willig, circa 1834). Mentioned but not quoted in William H. Keith's journal of voyages aboard Boston and Wellfleet vessels (1865-71). Ref: Dichter & Shapiro, 157; Frank 1985 #15; Huntington MS (*The Gam*) (2 texts); Wolf #216.

43. The Demon of the Sea. [a] William Histed, copybook aboard the ship *Cortes* of New Bedford, circa 1847 [New Bedford Free Public Library]; Huntington, 78. [b] Singing of James Cameron, Bloomfield Ridge, New Brunswick (Canada), collected by Edward D. Ives, *Folksongs of New Brunswick,* 151f; tune slightly revised, as noted.

44. The Pirate of the Isle. [a] Whaleman George E. Sanborn, in the shipboard journal of George M. Jones and Albert F. Handy, bark *Waverly* of New Bedford, 1859-63 [Kendall Collection]: first stanza absent. [b] Whaleman George W. Piper, copybook aboard the ship *Europa* of Edgartown, 1868-70 [Kendall Collection]. Ref: PSI; Frank 1985 #70; Harlow, 172; Huntington, 74; Luce 66; *Naval Songs,* 1883, 71. See "The Robbers of the Glen" (song #81).

45. The Wild Rover. Sheet music by Fiot, Meignan & Co., Philadelphia, n.d., circa 1835-39; words and music unascribed

46. The Rover of the Sea [I'm Afloat]. Words by Eliza Cook, music by by Henry Russell. Sheet music by George P. Reed, Boston, 1847. Text: [a] Transcribed by Charles C. Evans, in the journal of Daniel A. Chapel, cooper, ship *Benjamin Tucker* of New Bedford, 1851 [Kendall Collection], a verbatim transcription superseding Huntington's corrupt rendition of the same text (p. 80f), in which he unaccountably gives the date 1849: the manuscript is clearly dated "May 14th 1851," at which time the ship would have been in the last homeward-bound leg of a two-year whaling cruise, approaching New Bedford, where they arrived on June 1st. [b] Journal of Thomas D. Bartley, ship *California* of New Bedford, 1852; dated *"At Sea Feb 9th 1852"* [Kendall Coll.]. Virtually identical to A, except that B is more literate, with better spelling and punctuation.[c] Martha Ann Tray, Monmouth, Me.,

1846: inscribed after the fact in the whaling journal of George A. Gould, ship *Columbia* of Nantucket, 1841-46; dated *"Tuesday Feb 30th / [18]46 / Martha Ann Tray, Monmouth"* [Kendall Coll.]. Ref: SI; PSI-2; Dichter #1807; Rosenberg #4 (?); Wolf #1014; *Accordion Music*, 215; Baring-Gould 1895, I:94; Frank 1985 #69; Huntington, 80 (corrupt; no tune); Luce, 72; McCaskey, v8; *Miller's*, 202; *Naval Songs*, 26; *Sheet Anchor*, Vol. 2, N° 7; Boston, 6 Apr. 1844, p. 51; Wolf #1014.

47. The Rover of the Sea (II). Broadside by George Walker, Durham, UK.

48. The Pirate's Life for Me. Lyrics by Charles Mackay, music "Some love to roam o'er the dark sea foam" by Henry Russell; *Pirate's Songster*, 29; several editions of sheet music published at New York and Baltimore in 1836,

49. The Red Rover's Song. Sheet music by Edward Riley & Co., New York, circa 1836-42; words by Edmund Smith, music by Sigismund von Neukomm.

50. The Rover's Flag. Undated sheet music issued in London by Jefferys & Co., with words and music unascribed, arranged by Sidney Nelson; American edition by Edward Riley & Co., Philadelphia, circa 1836-42, credits the music to Montague Corri.

51. The Wrecker's Song. Sheet music published in London in 1838; words by W.H. Baker, music by William Aspull, and an introductory paragraph to set up the background.

Ballad broadside printed by Walker, Durham, England, circa 1850. Author's collection.

52. The Pirate's Serenade. Text: *American Sailor's Songster* pp. 224, 239. Tune: sheet music by Henry Prentiss, Boston, 1838 (piano setting in Eb Major); Henry Prentiss, Boston, 1839 (guitar setting in E Major by F. Blanchor); F.D. Benteen, Baltimore, circa 1838; C.H. Keith, Boston, circa 1838-42; Milleti Music, New York, circa 1838-42 [John Hay Library, Brown U.; and Mystic Seaport]. Apparently as the result of an oversight, "Pirate's Serenade" is printed twice in *The American Sailor's Songster,* with similar lyrics differently and unevenly arranged into stanzas: one begins, "Forgive my rough mood, unaccustomed to sue," which is stanza 2 in the sheet music; the other begins conventionally, "My boat's by the tower, my bark is in the bay." Unaccountably, the sheet music has only four stanzas (1, 2, 3 and 5) and some later, cheaper editions print only two. The complete text here includes the fourth stanza, which is present in the songster but absent in the sheet music; the sequence here has been reorganized to match the order and layout in the sheet music. The music was originally in Eb Major; the tune here is adapted and improved from the 1839 setting for guitar in E Major, issued by the original publishers. Two broadsides of another "Pirate's Seranade" [Library Company of Philadelphia], one printed in New York by J. Andrews and the other a reprint by R. Andrews of New Bedford (Wolf #1888; first line "Come love, come, come away"), ascribe authorship to George A.W. Langford Fahie indicate the tune "I Am Off for Baltimore" (not found).

53. The Corsair's Farewell. Sheet music by George Endicott, New York, circa 1839; words and music by George Linley.

54. Blow On! Blow On! The Pirate's Glee. *Liberty Minstrel* (1846); *Forecastle Songster* (1850), 267; sheet music by George P. Reed, Boston, 1840: words by Arthur Morrill, music by Benjamin F. Baker. See "Liberty Glee" and "March on!" in Clark, 1840.

55. The Freebooter. Sheet music by Wm. H. Oakes, Boston 1841; words unascribed, music by Jolly, arranged by Sidney Pearson.

56. Pirate's Chorus. Words and music by William Michael Balfe, from *The Enchantress,* 1845. Text transcribed by William H. Keith, whaling schooners *William Martin* of Boston and *Edith May* of Wellfleet (circa 1865-69), *Cora Nash* of Boston (circa 1871), etc. [Kendall Collection]. Ref: SI; PSI; Wolf #120, #1887. *American Sailor's Songster*, 235; *Heart Songs;* McCaskey v4. The University of Nebraska song "The Scarlet and Cream" is sung to Balfe's air (Chamberlain & Harrington, 269; Gillette & Tully, 145. Also: T.W. Allen, *Intercollegiate Song Book*, 1927; B.B. Kennedy & H.B. Kennedy, *Varsity Songs*, 1931). Not to be confused with a "Pirates' Chorus" by Alexandre Charles Lecocq, from *Giroflé-Girofla* (first line: "Ha! ha! the neatest and com-pletest" — translation of "Parmi les choses dé licates").

57. Ho! for a Rover's Life; or the Song of the Pirate. Words and music by John H. Hewitt; sheet music published by Hewitt in association with Firth & Hall, New York, 1843.

58. The *Malek Adehl*. Text: *Pirate's Songster,* 27. Tune: "Will Watch," by John Davy for lyrics by Thomas Cory see #18.

59. To the Mast Nail Our Flag: The Pirate's Song. *The Pirate's Own Book* (1837), 465; *American Sailor's Songster* (1848), 157; *Forecastle Songster* (1847), 200; *Forecastle Songster* (1850), 225; Rinder's *Naval Songs* (London, 1895), 213; sheet music by George P. Reed, Boston, 1846: lyrics by "L.E.L.," music by Horatio Dawes Hewitt.

60. The Pirate's Song (I). Sheet music by T.S. Berry, New York, 1853; lyrics by George W. Fraser, Esq., music by Charles Leslie [collection of the John Hay Library, Brown University].

61. Fineen the Rover. Lyrics by Robert Dwyer Joyce; the original music, a traditional Irish air ("You'd think, if you heard their pipes squealing"), is evidently lost; tune "The Groves of Blackpool" from Healy 1967, pp. 34, 47; tune by Charles Villiers Stanford from sheet music anthologized by Martin Akerman, ed., *The Year Book Press Series of Unison and Part-Songs* (London, 1923).

62. The *Vampire* (A Pirate Song). Sheet music by E. Ascherberg & Co., London, circa 1889; lyrics by "Henry Martingale" (an obvious pseudonym), music by Michael Watson.

63. The Pirate Isle, No More. Lyrics by W.A. Hogan, music by H.A. Lebermann, sheet music published by Thomas Goggan & Brother, Galveston, Texas, 1889.

64. Bill Cutlass, the Pirate Rover. *Pirate's Songster*, 26. Tune: "The Rambling Sailor": general, after Cecil J. Sharp, *One Hundred English Folksongs*, #43, p.98 (e.g., per Stuart Frank, LP recording *Songs of Sea & Shore*, Folkways, New York, 1978; also the singing of Louis Killen, who uses several other traditional variant texts of "Rambling Sailor" and related songs).

65. The Bold Pirates. *Pirate's Songster*, 30. Tune: "Come Brave the Sea with Me," music by Bellini, from Luce 1905, pp. 88f.

66. Bold Roving Thieves. *American Sailor's Songster*, 87; *Buccaneer Songster*, n.p.; Rinder, 207.

67. The Buccaneer's Song to His Love. *American Sailor's Songster*, 96; *Buccaneer Songster*, n.p.

68. The Brave Lafitte. *Forecastle Songster* (1850 edition), 252.

69. Life of the Bold Buccaneer. Text: *American Sailor's Songster*, 135; *Buccaneer Songser,* n.p.; Rinder, 212. Tune: "A Life on the Ocean Wave": music by Henry Russell (Ref: SI; SIC #3123; Dichter & Shapiro, 56; Fitz-Gerald, 185; *Forecastle Song ster*, 103; Frank 1985 #13; *Good Old Songs* I:38; *Heart Songs* 431; Huntington, 87 [2 texts]; H.K. Johnson,130; Luce, 68; McCaskey, v3; *Naval Songs,* 20; *Singer's Gem,* 45; Wier 1918, 260. Turner presents notes and precursors [101, 296]; *The American Songster* [227] gives a song based on "A Life on the Ocean Wave," to the same air). A parody, "The Temperance Crew" (*Forecastle Songster*, 1847, 76; 1850, 82), is sung to "The Bold Buccaneer."

70. Charles Gibbs. *Forget Me Not Songster*, 72; *Forecastle Songster* (1850), 259. Tunes: "Rocks of Scilly [Scillia]": *Book of a Thousand Songs* (1845), p. 621. Alternatives: [a] "Welcome, brother debtor" (AKA "The Joviall Cobbler" and "Come and listen to my ditty"), traditional English air published in 1730 and modified by George Alexander Stevens circa 1754 to fit his classic lyrics, "The Storm" ("Cease, rude Boreas"). [b] Other manifestations of "Sailor's Come-All-Ye" and "Jolly Sailors Bold" ballads: Colcord, 137, 138; Duncan I:51; Frank 1985, #164; Harlow, 216, 219, 231 (3 versions); Huntington, 68; Mackenzie, #95; Masefield, 182; Palmer, 1973 #29. Baring-Gould 1895 (VIII:92) documents the publishing history of a precursor, "To All You Ladies Now On Land" (1686). [c] A particular air in which the stanzas do not require coupling to accommodate the melody: I have not been able to find its proper name, but it was also used for "Jolly Sailors Bold" as well as New Bedford, Nantucket, and Martha's Vineyard folk songs of various sorts: a definitive version is "Whalemen's Wives" (Harlow, 231), some of which incorporate a few of the same phrases (such as "while I relate the same") in exactly the same relative positions in the text.

71. The Low, Black Schooner. *Pirate's Songster*, 25. Tune: "Le Petit Tambour": traditional French military tune, adapted as the air for the poem by Allan Cunningham, "A Wet Sheet and a Flowing Sea"; thereafter known by the name of the text. Ref: SI; SIC #9490; PSI; Dichter #1864; *American Sailor's Songster*, 159; Bruce, 297; *Forecastle Songster*, 40; Frank 1985 #12; Huntington, 49; H.K. Johnson, 138; Luce, 202; McCaskey v5; *Miller's*, 174; *Naval Songs*, 57; *Singer's Gem*, 6; Wier 1918, 510.

72. The Pirate Crew. *Book of a Thousand Songs* (1845); *Forecastle Songster* (1847), 198; *Forecastle Songster* (1850), 223. The arrangement of stanzas in *The Forecastle Songster* is 8, 8, 6; in *The Book of a Thousand Songs*, 6, 6, 6, 4.

73. Pirates Bold and Brave. *Pirate's Songster*, 21.

74. The Pirate's Call. *American Sailor's Songster*, 87; *Buccaneer Songster*, n.p.; Rinder, 208.

75. The Pirate's Song (II). Words by Allan Cunningham. Rinder, 209.

76. The Rover's Glee. *Pirate's Songster*, 28.

77. The Rover's Serenade. *Pirate's Songster*, 30.

78. The Rover's Song. *American Sailor's Songster*, 86; *Buccaneer Songster*, n.p. Tune: *Davidson's Universal Melodist* (London, 1848), II:355. "Bonny Boat" refers to a Scots traditional air known since the early nineteenth century for lyrics written by Joanna Baillie. In Scotland it is called by its first line, "Oh, swiftly glides the bonny boat," or by its formal title, "The Boatie Rows"; in America it is sometimes given as "The Bonny Boat" (e.g., *Book of a Thousand Songs*, 1845, 502; *Franklin Songster*, 58; see H.K. Johnson, 60). The lyrics do not fit either of the other possible tunes, the traditional Scots "Ho, My Bonnie Boatie!" or the venerable Jacobean "Skye Boat Song"; neither of these could be the same tune used for the lyrics of "Bonny Boat."

79. The Thunder Crew. *Buccaneer Songster*, n.p.

80. An Elegy on the Death of Captain Kidd. Brewington facsimile, 1964 [Kendall collection and author's collection].

81. The Brigand's Bride. Sheet music by J.L. Hewitt, New York, circa 1832

82. The Robbers of the Glen. [a] George M. Jones, bark *Waverly* of New Bedford, 1859-63. [b] George W. Piper, ship *Europa* of Edgartown, 1868-70 [both Kendall Coll.]. R e f : Frank 1985 #71; Hewins MSS. Coll., Sheffield Univ., #539A (Carnell, 21).

83. The Execution of Five Pirates. Broadside, London: H. Disley, 57 High St., St. Giles, n.d. [1864]; per *Curiosities of Street Literature*, 217.

84. Yo Ho Ho and a Bottle of Rum. Words by Young Ewin Allison (1891), based on a stanza by Robert Louis Stevenson (1850-1894) in *Treasure Island* (serialized in *Young Folks* magazine, 1881; published in book form, 1883); music by Henry Waller (1901); from the singing of Robert Kotta. Ref: PSI; Edward Jay, *The Coffee House Song Book* (New York: Oak, 1966); J.H. Johnson, 66; Trident, 42.

Bibliography[*]

Manuscripts

Collins, Edward W. (Dartmouth and Fairhaven, Mass.) Whaling journal, ship *Condor* of New Bedford, 1829-34. [Kendall].

Collins, Silas. (Dartmouth, Mass.) Whaling journal, brig *By Chance* of Dartmouth, Mass., 1825-28 [Kendall]..

Histed [Histead], William. (Pittstown, N.Y.) Copybook as shipkeeper and boatsteerer, ship *Cortes* of New Bedford, Mass., on two voyages to the Pacific Ocean, circa 1847-51 [New Bedford Free Public Library].

Jones, George M. (Milford, N.H.); Albert F. Handy (Binghamton, N.Y.); and George E. Sanborn (Lowell, Mass.). Collaborative whaling journal, bark *Waverly* of New Bedford, Mass., 1859-63 [Kendall].

Keith, William H. (Mattapoisett, Mass.) Journal of merchant and whaling voyages, schooners *William Martin* of Boston and *Edith May* of Wellfleet (circa 1865-69), schooner *Cora Nash* of Boston , circa 1871; etc. [Kendall].

Martin, John F. (Philadelphia.) Whaling journal, ship *Lucy Ann* of Wilmington, Delaware, 1840-44 [Kendall].

Piper, George Wilbur. (Concord, N.H.) Copybook as seaman, ship *Europa* of Edgartown, Mass., on a whaling voyage to the Pacific Ocean, 1868-70 [Kendall].

Wood, Horace. (New Bedford, Mass.) Whaling journal, bark *Andrews* of New Bedford, 1866-67 [Kendall].

Unpublished Secondary Materials

Elliot, Sharon. 1981. "Melville's Music [A Checklist]." Term project, Williams College Program in American Maritime Studies [author's collection].

Frank, Stuart M. 1985. *Ballads and Songs of the Whale-Hunters, 1825-1895, from Manuscripts in the Kendall Whaling Museum.* Ph.D. Thesis, Brown University.

Huntington, Gale. 1980. *The Gam: More Songs the Whalemen Sang.* MS, circa 1980 [Kendall].

Martin, Kenneth R. 1979. *John Martin's Journal.* Annotations to John Martin's MS whaling journal, ship *Lucy Ann* of Wilmington, Delaware, 1840-44 [Kendall].

Moseley, Caroline. 1981. "A Life on the Ocean Wave: Images of the Sea in Nineteenth-Century American Parlor Song." Second Annual Symposium on Traditional Music of the Sea, Mystic Seaport Museum, Mystic, Connecticut, 30 May.

Sherry, Frank. 1986. *Raiders and Rebels: The Pirate War on the World.* Uncorrected bound galleys, Hearst Marine Books, New York.

Swidersky, Richard M. 1981. "Songs of the Sirens of the Sea," Second Annual Symposium on Traditional Music of the Sea, Mystic Seaport Museum, Mystic, Connecticut, 30 May.

Swiderski, Richard M. 1982. "God's Laws They Did Forbid: Pirate Songs and Pirate Voices." Third Annual Symposium on Traditional Music of the Sea, Mystic Seaport Museum, Mystic, Connecticut, 12 June.

Books and Articles

Akerman, Martin, ed. 1923. *The Year Book Press Series of Unison and Part-Songs.* London.

American Melodies. 1841. New York: Linen & Fennell.

American Naval and Patriotic Songster (The). 1831. Baltimore: William Sewell.

American Sailor's Songster (The). Philadelphia (15 No. Sixth St), New York (74 Chatham St), and Boston (71 Court St): Fisher & Brother, n.d. [circa 1848].

American Songster (The). New York: Nafis & Cornish, n.d. [circa 1830.]; "By John Kennedy," Baltimore: John Kennedy, 1836; New York: Nafis & Cornish, n.d. [circa 1850]; [New York:] Cornish, Lamport & Co., 1851.

American Songster (The), A Collection of Songs as Sung in the Days of '76 [sic]. Philadelphia and Baltimore: Fisher & Brother, n.d. [circa 1836].

Ashton, John. 1882. *Chap Books of the Eighteenth Century.* Repr., Bronx, N.Y.: Benjamin Blom, 1966.

_____. 1891. *Real Sailor Songs.* Unpaginated. London: Leadenhall. (Repr., paginated, New York: Benjamin Blom, 1972; repr., unpaginated, ed. by A.L. Lloyd, London: Broadsheet King, n.d.)

Baker, Richard; and Anthony Miall. 1982. *Everyman's Book of Sea Songs.* London: J.M. Dent & Son.

Baring-Gould, S[abine]. 1895. *English Minstrelsie.* 8 vols. Edinburgh: T.C. & E.C. Jack, Grange Publications.

_____, et al. 1905. *Songs of the West.* London: Methuen.

_____; and Cecil J. Sharp. [1906.] *English Folk-Songs for Schools.* London: J. Curwen & Sons.

Barnhart, Clarence L., ed. 1954. *The New Century Book of Names.* 3 vols. New York: Appleton-Century-Crofts.

Barry, Phillips; Fannie H. Eckstorm; and Mary W. Smyth. 1929. *British Ballads from Maine: The Development of Popular Songs with Texts and Airs.* New Haven: Yale University Press.

Beadle's Dime Melodist. 1859. New York: Irwin P. Beadle.

Beadle's Dime Song Book. 1859-76. 34 vols. [*N° 1* through *N° 34*]. New York: Irwin P. Beadle; Boston: John J. Dyer & Co.; New York and Buffalo: Irwin R. Beadle; etc. (see Johannsen III:55-58).

Belden, H[enry] M. 1940. *Ballads and Songs Collected by the Missouri Folklore Society.* (The University of Missouri Studies, 15:1 [January 1, 1940].) Columbia: University of Missouri.

_____; and Arthur Palmer Hudson, eds. 1952-62. *Folk Ballads from North Carolina* (*Frank C. Brown Collection of North Carolina Folklore,* Newman Ivey White, general ed., Vols. 2-5.) Durham, NC: Duke University Press.

---

[*] Entries marked [Kendall] are in the Kendall Collection, New Bedford Whaling Museum.

Bell, Robert, ed. 1856. *Annotated Edition of the English Poets: Early Ballads Illustrative of History, Traditions and Customs.* London: John W. Parker & Son.

_____, ed. 1857. *Annotated Edition of the English Poets: Ancient Poems, Ballads and Songs of the Peasantry of England: Taken down from oral recitation and transcribed from private manuscripts, rare broadsides, and scarce publications.* London: John W. Parker & Son.

Book of English Songs (The). 1851. *From the Sixteenth to the Nineteenth Century.* London: National Illustrated Library.

Brewer, E. Cobham. 1892. *Character Sketches of Romance, Fiction and the Drama.* Marion Harland, ed. 4 vols. New York: Selmar Hess.

Broadwood, Lucy E. 1908. *English Traditional Songs and Carols.* London: Boosey & Co.

_____; and J.A. Fuller Maitland. 1891. *English County Songs.* London: Leadenhall.

Bronson, Bertrand Harris. 1959-72. *Traditional Tunes of the Child Ballads.* 4 vols. Princeton: Princeton University Press.

Brown Collection: see BELDEN & HUDSON.

Bruce, Charles, ed. 1874. *Poems, Songs, and Ballads of the Sea... Illustrative of Life on the Ocean Wave.* Edinburgh: William P. Nimmo.

Buck, P.C.; and Thomas Wood. [1927.] *The Oxford Song Book.* 2 vols. London: Oxford University Press.

Bumgardner, Georgia B., ed. 1971. *American Broadsides.* Barre, Mass.: Imprint Society.

Carnell, Peter, ed. 1987. *Broadside Ballads and Song-Sheets from the Hewins MSS. Collection in Sheffield University Library.* Centre for English Cultural Tradition and Language Bibliographical and Special Series N° 5. Sheffield University Library.

Cayman Islands National Archive. 1996. *Our Island's Past, Volume III: Traditional Songs from the Cayman Islands.* George Town, Grand Cayman: Cayman Islands National Archive and Cayman Free Press.

Chamberlain, David B.; and Karl P. Harrington. 1902. *Songs of All the Colleges.* New York: Hinds & Noble.

Chambers, Anne. 1979. *Granuaile: The Life and Times of Grace O'Malley.* Dublin: Wolfhound Press.

Child, Francis James. 1858. *English and Scottish Ballads.* 8 vols. Boston: Houghton, Mifflin & Co.

_____. 1882-98. *The English and Scottish Popular Ballads.* 5 vols. Boston: Houghton, Mifflin & Co. (Repr., 3 vols., New York: Cooper Square, 1962; repr., 5 vols., New York: Dover, 1965.)

Christ-Janer, Albert; Charles W. Hughes; and Carleton Sprague Smith. 1980. *American Hymns Old and New.* New York: Columbia University Press.

Clark, George W. 1846. *The Liberty Minstrel.* "Fifth ed." New York: Published by the Author.

Cohn, Ellen R. 1993. "Benjamin Franklin and Traditional Music," in J.A. Leo Lemay, ed., *Reappraising Benjamin Franklin: A Bicentennial Perspective* (Newark: University of Delaware Press; London & Toronto: Associated University Presses), 290-318.

Colcord, Joanna C. 1938. *Songs of the American Sailormen.* New York: W.W. Norton. (Expanded from *Roll and Go: Songs of American Sailormen,* Indianapolis: Bobbs-Merrill, 1924.)

Collier, John Payne, ed. 1847. *A Book of Roxburghe Ballads.* London: Longman, Brown, Green, and Longmans.

Cordingly, David. 1995. *Under the Black Flag: The Romance and Reality of Life Among the Pirates.* New York: Random House.

_____. 1996. *Pirates: Terror on the High Seas—from the Caribbean to the South China Sea.* A Worldwide Illustrated History. Atlanta: Turner Publishing.

_____; and John Falconer. 1992. *Pirates Fact and Fiction.* New York: Cross River.

Cox, John Harrington. 1925. *Folk Songs of the South.* Cambridge: Harvard University Press.

[Crawford, —.] [1898.] *Catalogue of English Broadsides 1505-1897.* Bibleotheca Lindesiana. (Repr., Bibliography and Reference Series #139, New York, Burt Franklin, 1968.)

Creighton, Helen. 1933. *Songs and Ballads from Nova Scotia.* Toronto and Vancouver: J.M. Dent & Sons.

_____. 1961. *Maritime Folk Songs.* Toronto: Ryerson.

_____. 1971. *Folksongs from Southern New Brunswick.* Publications in Folk Culture N° 1. Ottawa: National Museums.

_____; and Doreen H. Senior. 1950. *Traditional Songs from Nova Scotia.* Toronto: Ryerson.

Curiosities of Street Literature: Comprising "cocks," or "catchpennies"... street-drolleries, squibs, histories, comic tales in prose and verse... a variety of "ballads on a subject," dying speeches and confessions. 1871. London: Reeves & Turner.

Dallin, Leon; and Lynn Dalin. 1967. *The Folk Songster.* Dubuque: William C. Brown.

Damon, S. Foster. 1936. *Series of Old American Songs, Reproduced in Facsimile From Original or Early Editions in the Harris Collection of American Poetry and Plays, Brown University.* Providence: Brown University Library.

Dana, Richard Henry, Jr. [1840.] *Two Years Before the Mast.* New York: Harper Bros.

Davis, Arthur Kyle. 1929. *Traditional Ballads of Virginia.* Cambridge: Harvard University Press.

_____. 1960. *More Traditional Ballads of Virginia.* Chapel Hill: University of North Carolina Press.

Davis, Frederick J.; and Ferris Tozer. [1887.] *Sailor Songs or "Chanties."* London: Boosey.

De Charms, Desiree; and Paul F. Breed. 1966. *Songs in Collections: An Index.* Detroit: Information Service Inc.

Denson, T.J.; S.M. Denson; L.P. Odum; et al. [1911.] *Original Sacred Harp (Denson Revision).* Haleyville, Alabama: Sacred Harp Publishing Co. Repr., 1936.

Dichter, Harry. 1941. *Handbook of American Sheet Music.* "First Annual Issue." Philadelphia: Harry Dichter.

_____; and Elliott Shapiro. 1941. *Early American Sheet Music; Its Lure and Its Lore,* New York: R.R. Bowker. (Repr. as *Handbook of Early Sheet Music, 1768-1889,* New York: Dover, 1977.)

Disher, Maurice Willson. 1955. *Victorian Song from Dive to Drawing Room.* London: Phoenix House.

Doerflinger, William Main. 1972. *Songs of the Sailor and Lumberman.* New York: Macmillan. (Expanded from *Shantymen and Shantyboys: Songs of the Sailor and Lumberman,* New York: Macmillan, 1951.)

Downes, Olin; and Elie Siegmeister. 1940. *A Treasury of American Songs.* New York: Howell, Soskin (2nd ed.:Knopf, 1943).

Duncan, Edmondstoune, ed. [1905]. *The Minstrelsy of England*. 3 vols. London: Augener, n.d.

Eckstorm, Fanny; and Mary Winslow Smyth. 1927. *Minstrelsy of Maine*. Boston and New York: Houghton Mifflin Co.

Eddy, Mary O. 1939. *Ballads and Songs from Ohio*. New York: J.J. Augustin.

Edmunds, John, ed. 1964. *A Williamsburg Songbook*. New York: Holt, Rinehart & Winston; Wlliamsburg, Va.: Colonial Wlliamsburg Foundation.

[Ellms, Charles.] 1837. *The Pirate's Own Book*. Boston: Samuel N. Dickinson. (Repr., Salem: Marine Research Soc., 1924.)

Euing Collection of English Broadside Ballads in the Library of the University of Glasgow (The). 1971. Intro. by John Holloway. Glasgow: University of Glasgow Publications.

Farnesworth, Charles H.; and Cecil J. Sharp. [1916]. *Folk-Songs, Chanteys and Singing Games*. New York: H.W. Gray; London: Novello, n.d.

Firth, C.H. 1908. *Naval Songs and Ballads*. London: Navy Records Society.

Flanders, Helen Hartness. [1960.] *Ancient Ballads Traditionally Sung in New England*. 4 vols. Philadelphia: University of Pennsylvania Press, 1960-65.

Flanders, Helen Hartness; Elizabeth Flanders Ballard; George Brown; and Phillips Barry. 1939. *The New Green Mountain Songster: Traditional Folk Songs of Vermont*. New Haven: Yale University Press.

Flanders, Helen Hartness; and George Brown. 1932. *Vermont Folk-Songs and Ballads*. Brattleboro, Vt.: Stephen Day.

Flanders, Helen Hartness; and Marguerite Olney. 1953. *Ballads Migrant in New England*. New York: Farrar, Straus & Young.

Forecastle Songster (The). 1847. New York: Richard Marsh.

Forecastle Songster (The). 1850. New York: Naifs & Cornish.

*Forget Me Not Songster (The); Containing A Choice Collection of Old Ballad Songs, as sung by our Grandmothers… *. Boston: G.W. Cottrell, n.d. [circa 1840s]. [Virtually identical with the ensuing (q.v.) up to page 194, thereafter significantly different.]

Forget Me Not Songster (The); Containing A Choice Collection of Old Ballad Songs, as sung by our Grandmothers… New York: Richard Marsh (374 Pearl St), n.d. [circa 1840s]. [Notable differences with the preceding (pp 194-235) include a portion of "Rosanna" (New York ed., 225-231) instead of "The Pirate Lover" (Boston ed., 229).]

Fowke, Edith. 1965. *Traditional Singers and Songs of Ontario*. Hatboro: Folklore Associates; Don Mills: Burns & MacEachern.

_____. 1981. *Sea Songs and Ballads from Nineteenth-Century Nova Scotia*. New York and Philadelphia: Folklorica.

_____; and Richard Johnston. 1954. *Folk Songs of Canada*. Waterloo, Ontario: Waterloo Music.

Frank, Stuart M. 1996. *Oooh, You New York Girls! The Urban Pastorale in Ballads and Songs about Sailors Ashore in the Big City*. (The 1995 Vaughan Evans Memorial Lecture. Kendall Whaling Museum Monograph Series Nº 9.) Sharon, Mass.: The Kendall Whaling Museum; Perth, Western Australia: The Australian Association for Maritime History.

_____. 1998. *The Book of Pirate Songs*. Sharon, Mass.: Kendall Whaling Museum.

_____. 2010. *Jolly Sailors Bold: Ballads and Songs of the American Sailor*. East Windsor, N.J.: Camsco Music..

_____, ed. 1991. *Meditations from Steerage: The Journals of Dean C. Wright, Boatsteerer, 1841-44; and John Jones, Steward, 1852*. Kendall Whaling Museum Monograph Series Nº 7.

Franklin Songster (The). [No information. Title and half-title missing from the copy consulted. Edited by C.H.S., circa 1835.]

Friel, Redmond. 1957. *The Paterson Irish Song Book*. London: Paterson's Pubs.

Gardner, Elizabeth; and Geraldine Jencks Chickering. 1939. *Ballads and Songs of Southern Michigan*. Ann Arbor: University of Michigan Press. (Repr., Hatboro, Pa.: Folklore Associates, 1967.)

Gilkerson, William. 1991-93. *Boarders Away*. 2 vols. Lincoln, R.I.: Mowbray Publishing.

_____. 2009. *A Thousand Years of Pirates*. Toronto: Tundra Books.

Greenleaf, Elizabeth Bristol; and Grace Yarrow Mansfield. 1933. *Ballads and Songs from Newfoundland*. Cambridge: Harvard University Press.

Greig, Gavin. [1907.] *Folk-Song in Buchan*. [Buchan:] Buchan Field-Club, 1906-07.

_____. 1914. *Folk-Song of the North-East*. Peterhead (Scotland): Buchan Observer.

_____. 1925. *Last Leaves of Traditional Ballads and Ballad Airs*. Alexander Keith, ed. Aberdeen: The Buchan Club.

_____. 1963. *Folk-Song in Buchan and Folk-Song of the North-East*. Hatboro, Pa.: Folklore Associates. (Repr. of Gavin 1907 and Gavin 1914.)

Grigg's Southern and Western Songster. [1826] 1832. Philadelphia: J. Grigg. (Reissued severally to 1850.)

Gretton, Thomas. 1980. *Murder and Moralities: English Catchpenny Prints, 1800-1860*. London: Colonnade Books.

Haley, Nelson Cole. [1864.] *Whale Hunt: The Narrative of a Voyage by Nelson Cole Haley. Harpooner in the Ship Charles W. Morgan, 1849-1853*. New York: Ives Washburn, [1948] 1967.

Harlow, Frederick Pease. 1928. *The Making of a Sailor*. Salem: Marine Research Society.

_____. 1962. *Chanteying Aboard American Ships*. Barre: Barre Gazette.

Hatton, J. L.; and Eton Faning. *The Songs of England*. 3 vols. London: Boosey. n.d.

_____; and J. L. Molloy. *Songs of Ireland*. London: Boosey. n.d.

Havlice, Patricia Pate. 1975. *Popular Song Index*. Metuchen, N.J.: Scarecrow.

_____. 1978. *Popular Song Index: First Supplement*. Metuchen, N.J. and London: Scarecrow.

_____. 1984. *Popular Song Index: Second Supplement*. Metuchen, N.J. and London: Scarecrow.

Healey, James N. 1967. *Irish Ballads and Songs of the Sea*. Cork: Mercier Press.

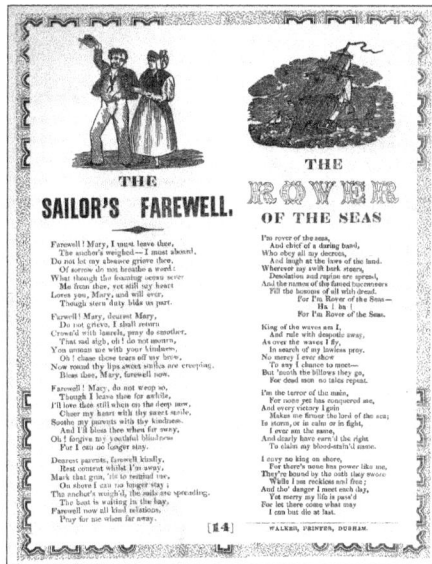

Slip-ballad broadside by Walters, Durham, England, circa 1840-50 (Author's collection)

Heart Songs Dear to the American People. 1909. Boston: Chapple; New York: World Syndicate.

Heart Throbs. 1905-1911. 2 vols. New York: World Syndicate.

Hindley, Charles, ed. 1873-76. *The Roxburghe Ballads.* 4 vols. London: Reeves & Turner.

Hugill, Stan. 1961. *Shanties from the Seven Seas.* London: Routledge & Kegan Paul; New York: E.P. Dutton. (Repr. 1969; abridged 1980; abridgement repr. by Mystic Seaport Museum, 1994, with into. by Stuart M. Frank.)

_____. 1969. *Shanties and Sailors' Songs.* London: Herbert Jenkins; New York: Praeger.

_____. 1977. *Songs of the Sea.* New York: McGraw-Hill.

Humphries, Charles; and William C. Smith. 1954. *Music Publishing in the British Isles from the earliest times to the middle of the nineteenth century: A Dictionary of engravers, printers, publishers and music sellers... .* London: Cassell & Co., Ltd.

Huntington, Gale. 1962. *Songs the Whalemen Sang.* Barre: Barre Gazette [Barre Press]. (Repr., New York: Dover, 1970.)

_____. 1966. *Folksongs of Martha's Vineyard.* (Northeast Folklore, Vol. III.) Orono: Northeast Folklore Society.

_____; and Lani Herrmann, eds. 1990. *Sam Henry's Songs of the People.* University of Georgia Press,

Ives, Burl. 1953. *Burl Ives Song Book.* New York: Ballantine.

_____. 1962. *Song in America: Our Musical Heritage.* New York: Duell, Sloan and Pearce.

Ives, Edward D. 1989. *Folksongs of New Brunswick.* Fredericton, N.B.: Goose Lane Editions.

Jack's Kit: or, Saturday Night in the Forecastle. Being a Choice Collection of Naval Songs, Nautical Jokes, Dog Watch Yarns, and Galley Witticisms. "By An Old Salt." New York: G. & S. Bunce, n.d. [circa 1840].

Jackson, George Pullen. 1952. *Another Sheaf of White Spirituals.* Gainesville: University of Florida Press.

Jay, Edward. 1966. *The Coffee House Songbook.* New York: Oak.

Johannsen, Albert. 1962. *The House of Beadle and Adams.* 3 vols. Norman: University of Oklahoma Press.

Johnson, Clifton, ed. 1908. *Songs Every One Should Know.* New York: American Book Co.

Johnson, Helen Kendrick. 1881. *Our Familiar Songs and Those Who Made Them.* New York: Henry Holt & Co. (Repr. 1889; 1909, as part of the series, *Popular Culture in America 1800-1925,* New York: Arno, 1974.)

Johnson, John Henry. 1935. *Bawdy Ballads and Lusty Lyrics.* Indianapolis: Maxwell Drake.

Karpeles, Maud. 1970. *Folk Songs from Newfoundland.* Hamden, Ct.: Archon.

Kennedy, Peter. 1975. *Folksongs of Britain and Ireland.* New York: Schirmer.

Kidson, Frank. [1890.] *British Music Publishers, Printers, and Engravers: London, Provincial, Scottish, and Irish. From Queen Elizabeth's Reign to George the Fourth's.* [London, 1890.] (Repr., New York: Benjamin Blom, 1967.)

_____. 1891. *Traditional Tunes.* Oxford: Tophouse & Son.

_____. 1893. "Supplement to Chappell's *Traditional Tunes,*" in William Chappell, *Old English Popular Music,* ed. H. Ellis Woodbridge, London, 1890 (repr., New York: Jack Brussel, 1961), separately paginated.

_____; and Alfred Moffatt. 1926. *A Garland of English Folk-Song.* London: Ascherberg, Hopwood and Crew.

Laws, G. Malcolm. 1957. *American Balladry from British Broadsides.* (Publications of the American Folklore Society Bibliographical and Special Series, Vol. VIII.) Philadelphia: American Folklore Society.

_____. 1964. *Native American Balladry.* (Publications of the American Folklore Society Bibliographical Series, Vol. I, "Revised Edition.") Philadelphia: American Folklore Society.

Leach, MacEdward. *Folk Ballads and Songs of the Lower Labrador Coast.* Ottawa: National Museum of Canada. 1965.

Linscott, Eloise Hubbard. 1939. *Folk Songs of Old New England.* New York: Macmillan. (Repr., Hamden: Shoe String, 1962.)

Logan, W.H. 1869. *Peddlar's Pack of Ballads and Songs.* Edinburgh: William Paterson.

Lomax, Alan. 1960. *Folk Songs of North America.* Garden City: Doubleday.

Lomax, John A.; and Alan Lomax. 1934. *American Ballads and Folk Songs.* (New York: Macmillan. (Repr. 1946, 1968.)

_____; and Alan Lomax. 1947. *Folk Song U.S.A.* New York: Duell, Sloan & Pearce.

Lowance, Mason, Jr.; and Georgia B. Bumgardner. 1976. *Massachusetts Broadsides of the Revolution.* Amherst: University of Massachusetts Press.

Lowens, Irving. 1976. *A Bibliography of Songsters Printed in America Before 1821.* Worcester: American Antiquarian Society,

Lozier, Horace Gillette; and Richard Walton Tully. 1902. *Songs of the Western Colleges.* New York: Hinds & Noble.

Luce, Rear Admiral S[tephen] B. 1889. *Naval Songs.* New York: W.A. Pond. (Repr. 1902, 1905.)

McCarty, William, ed. 1842. *Songs, Odes, and Other Poems on National Subjects. Part Second—Naval.* Philadelphia: William McCarty.

McCaskey, J. P., ed. 1881-91. *Franklin Square Song Collection.* 8 vols. New York: Harper.

Mackenzie, W. Roy. 1928. *Ballads and Sea Songs from Nova Scotia.* Cambridge: Harvard University Press. (Repr., Hatboro, Pa.: Folklore Associates, 1963.)

MacMahon, Desmond, ed. 1938. *The New National and Folk Song Book... being a collection of well-known national and folk songs arranged for use in schools.* 2 vols London: Thomas Nelson.

Masefield, John, ed. 1906. *A Sailor's Garland.* New York: Macmillan.

Mayhew, Henry. [1851.] *London Street-Folk.* (Volume 1 of Henry Mayhew, *London Labour and the London Poor,* 4 vols., London: Charles Griffin & Co., 1851-64.)

Miller's New British Songster... 1853. Edinburgh: J.M. Miller.

Minstrel Songs Old and New. 1882. Boston: Oliver Ditson & Co.

Molloy, J.L 1873. *The Songs of Ireland.* London: Boosey & Co.,

Molnar, John W., ed. 1972. *Songs from the Williamsburg Theatre.* Williamsburg, Va.: Colonial Williamsburg Foundation.

Moore, Ethel; and Chauncey O. Moore. 1964. *Ballads and Folk Songs of the Southwest.* Norman: University of Oklahoma.

Morris, Alton C. 1950. *Folksongs of Florida.* Gainesville: University of Florida Press.

Motherwell, William. 1827. *Minstrelsy: Ancient and Modern, with an historical introduction and notes.* Glasgow: John Wylie.

Munch, Peter A. 1970. *The Song Tradition of Tristan da Cunha.* Bloomington: Indiana University.

Naval Songs. 1883. New York: Wm. Firth & Co.

Neeser, Robert W., ed. 1938. *American Naval Songs & Ballads.* New Haven: Yale University Press.

New American Singer's Own Book (The). 1841. Philadelphia: M. Kelly.

New Song Book (The), Containing a Choice Collection of the Most Popular Songs, Glees, Choruses, Extravaganzas, &c.... 1847 and 1851. Hartford: S. Andrus & Son.

Niles, John Jacob. 1961. *The Ballad Book.* New York: Bramhall.

O'Hea J.J.; and John Carey. *Gem Selection Songs of Ireland.* Dublin: Valentine & Sons, n.d. [circa 1900].

Our Island's Past, Volume III: Traditional Songs from the Cayman Islands. 1996. George Town, Grand Cayman: Cayman Islands National Archive and Cayman Free Press.

Palmer, Roy, ed. 1973. *The Valiant Sailor.* Cambridge: Cambridge University Press.

_____, ed. 1983. *Folk Songs Collected by Ralph Vaughan Williams.* London: J.M. Dent.

_____, ed. 1986. *The Oxford Book of Sea Songs.* Oxford and New York: Oxford University Press.

The Popular National Songster... 1845. Philadelphia: John B. Perry.

Quiller-Couch, Arthur, ed. 1910. *The Oxford Book of Ballads.* Oxford University Press. (Repr. 1927, 1946).

Randolph, Vance. 1946-50. *Ozark Folk Songs.* 4 vols. Columbia, Mo.: State Historical Society of Missouri

Rediker, Marcus. 1987. *Between the Devil and the Deep Blue Sea: Merchant Seamen, Pirates, and the Anglo-American Maritime World, 1700-1750.* New York: Cambridge University Press.

Smith, Reed. [1928.] *South Carolina Ballads.* Freeport, N.Y.: Books for Libraries Press.

Rinder, Frank. *Naval Songs, and Other Songs and Ballads of Sea Life.* London: Walter Scott, Ltd., n.d. [circa 1895].

Ritchie, Jean. 1965. *Folk Songs of the Southern Appalachians.* New York: Oak.

Roberts, Leonard. 1979. *In the Pine: Selected Kentucky Folksongs.* 2nd ed. Pikeville, Ky.: Pikeville College Press.

Rosenberg, Bruce A. 1969. *The Folksongs of Virginia: A Checklist of the WPA Holdings, Alderman Library, University of Virginia.* Charlottesville: University Press of Virginia.

Schnapper, Edith B. 1957. *The British Union-Catalogue of Early Music printed before the year 1801: A Record of the holdings of over one hundred libraries throughout the British Isles.* 2 vols. London: Butterworths Scientific Publications.

[Scott, Sir Walter.] 1810. *Minstrelsy of the Scottish Border.* 3 vols. Edinburgh: James Ballantyne / A. Constable & Co.; London: Longman, Hurst, Rees & Orme.

Scottish Students' Song Book Committee. 1897. *The Scottish Students' Song Book.* A.G. Abbie, et al., eds. London and Glasgow: Bayley & Ferguson.

Sears, Minnie Earl, ed. [1926, 1934.] *Song Index: An Index To More Than 12000 Songs In 177 Song Collections Comprising 262 Volumes.* (Repr, Hamden, Ct.: Shoe String, 1966.)

Sharp, Cecil J. 1908-12. *Folk Songs of England.* 5 vols. London: Novello.

_____. 1914. *English Folk Chanteys.* London: Simpkin, Marshall / Schott.

_____. 1916. *One Hundred English Folksongs.* Boston: Oliver Ditson.

_____. 1920. *English Folk Songs.* 2 vols. Boston: Oliver Ditson.

_____. 1932. *English Folk-Songs from the Southern Appalachians.* Ed. Maud Karpeles. 2 vols. London: Oxford UP.

Shay, Frank. 1927. *My Pious Friends and Drunken Companions.* New York: Macaulay.

_____. 1928. *More Pious Friends and Drunken Companions.* New York: Macaulay.

_____. 1928. *Drawn from the Wood.* New York: Macaulay.

_____. 1948. *American Sea Songs and Chanteys from the Days of Iron Men and Wooden Ships.* New York: W.W. Norton. (Expanded from *Iron Men and Wooden Ships,* New York: Doubleday, Page, 1924.)

Shoemaker, Henry W. 1931. *Mountain Minstrelsy of Pennsylvania.* Philadelphia: Newman F. Magirr; Altoona: Times Tribune.

Simpson, Claude M. 1966. *The British Broadside Ballad and Its Music.* New Brunswick, N.J.: Rutgers University Press.

Smith, Carleton Sprague. 1980. "Broadsides and Their Music in Colonial America," in *Music in Colonial Massachusetts 1630-1820; I: Music in Public Places* (Conference proceedings, Colonial Society of Massachusetts, Boston, May 1973), 170-176.

Smith, Laura Alexandrine. 1888. *Music of the Waters.* London: Kegan Paul, Trench. (Repr., Detroit: Singing Tree, 1969.)

Songster's Companion (The). 1815. Brattleboro, Vt.: Printed for the Book-Sellers.

Sonneck, Oscar George Theodore; and William Treat Upton. 1945. *A Bibliography of Early Secular American Music [18th Century].* Washington: Library of Congress. (Repr., New York: De Capo, 1964.)

Stanley, Jo. 1995. *Bold In Her Breeches: Women Pirates Across the Ages.* Hammersmith and San Francisco: Harper Collins.

Stone, Christopher. 1906. *Sea Songs and Ballads.* Oxford: Clarendon.

Thorn, John. 2005. "The Saugerties Bard," *Voices: The Journal of New York Folklore,* 31, Fall-Winter.

Trident Society. 1939. *The Book of Navy Songs.* Garden City: Doubleday, Page & Co.; Annapolis: U.S. Naval Institute. [1926].

Universal Songster (The). 1829. New York: Solomon King.

Universal Songster and Museum of Mirth (The). 1835. Boston: Charles Gaylord.

Universal Songster; or Museum of Mirth (The). 3 vols. London: Geo. Routledge & Sons, n.d. [circa 1825-29].

Vaughan Williams, Ralph; and A.L. Lloyd. 1959. *The Penguin Book of English Folk Songs.* London: Penguin Group.

Waite, Henry Russell. [1868]. *Carmina Collegensa.* Boston: Oliver Ditson & Co., 1876.

Warner, Anne. 1984. *Traditional American Folk Songs from the Anne & Frank Warner Collection.* [Ed. Jeff Warner.] Syracuse, N.Y.: Syracuse University Press.

Webb, Robert L.; and Stuart M. Frank. 1982. *M.V. Brewington: A Bibliography & Catalogue of the Brewington Press.* Sharon: The Kendall Whaling Museum.

Whall, W.B. [1910] 1927. *Sea Songs and Shanties.* Glasgow: Brown, Son & Ferguson.

Wheeler, Mary. 1937. *Kentucky Mountain Folk-Songs.* Boston: Boston Music.

Wolf, Edwin, 2nd. 1963. *American Song Sheets, Slip Ballads, and Poetical Broadsides, 1850-1870: A Catalogue of the Library Company of Philadelphia.* Philadelphia: The Library Company of Philadelphia.

Index of Titles and First Lines

Index of Lyricists and Composers

Stuart Frank is Senior Curator at the New Bedford Whaling Museum, Founder/Director of the Scrimshaw Forensics Laboratory®, and Executive Director Emeritus of the Kendall Whaling Museum. A native of New York City, he was educated at Wesleyan, Yale, the Munson Institute of American Maritime Studies, and at Brown, where his Ph.D. dissertation was *Ballads and Songs of the Whale-Hunters*. He founded the sea music program and the annual Sea Music Festival and Symposium at Mystic Seaport, has been Artist-in-Residence and Scholar-in-Residence at the Virginia Museum of Fine Arts, President of the Council of American Maritime Museums, a board member of the International Congress of Maritime Museums, an American Friends of Canada Fellow, an Australian Bicentennial Foundation Fellow, an elected Fellow of the Massachusetts Historical Society, and a Visiting Fellow at museums on four continents, and has taught at Brown, MIT, the Williams College Program in Maritime Studies, the Munson Institute, and the Sea Education Association in Woods Hole, Mass. He served on the Secretary of the Interior's Advisory Panel on Maritime Preservation and has received awards from the North American Society for Oceanic History and the National Maritime Alliance. In addition to several books, he is the author of 15 monographs and more than 50 scholarly and popular articles on maritime art, music, history, literature, and culture. With his wife, Mary Malloy, he has lectured about and performed historic sea music, cowboy songs, and other occupational music in concerts across the USA and in Canada, Europe, Japan, and Australia.

www.ingramcontent.com/pod-product-compliance
Lightning Source LLC
Chambersburg PA
CBHW080506110426
42742CB00017B/3016